An Edible Journey

Exploring the islands' fine food, farms and vineyards

An Edible Journey

Exploring the islands' fine food, farms and vineyards

ELIZABETH LEVINSON

TouchWood Editions
VICTORIA • VANCOUVER • CALGARY

TouchWood Editions
#108 – 17665 66A Avenue
Surrey, BC V3S 2A7
www.touchwoodeditions.com

TouchWood Editions
PO Box 468
Custer, WA
98240-0468

Library and Archives Canada Cataloguing in Publication
Levinson, Elizabeth, 1958–
An edible journey: exploring the Islands' fine food, farms and vineyards /
Elizabeth Levinson. — 3rd ed.

Includes index.
ISBN 978-1-894898-90-4

1. Natural foods — British Columbia — Vancouver Island. 2. Natural foods — British Columbia — Gulf Islands. 3. Natural food restaurants — British Columbia — Vancouver Island — Guidebooks. 4. Natural food restaurants — British Columbia — Gulf Islands — Guidebooks. 5. Vancouver Island (B.C.) — Guidebooks. 6. Gulf Islands (B.C.) — Guidebooks. 7. Cookery (Natural foods). I. Title.

TX369.L47 2009   641.3′02′097112   C2009-900984-6

Library of Congress Control Number: 2009920169

Edited by Marlyn Horsdal
Front cover painting by Grant Leier
Interior design by Gabriele Chaykowski, www.straitcom.com
Maps by Katherine Melnyk
Author photo by Clive Levinson

Canada Council   Conseil des Arts
for the Arts   du Canada

BRITISH COLUMBIA
ARTS COUNCIL
Supported by the Province of British Columbia

TouchWood Editions acknowledges the financial support for its publishing program from the Government of Canada through the Book Publishing Industry Development Program (BPIDP), Canada Council for the Arts, and the province of British Columbia through the British Columbia Arts Council and the Book Publishing Tax Credit.

Mixed Sources
Cert no. SW-COC-001271
© 1996 FSC
FSC

The interior of this book was printed on 100% post-consumer recycled paper, processed chlorine free and printed with vegetable-based inks.

1 2 3 4 5 12 11 10 09

PRINTED IN CANADA

Nicholas, this one's for you.

ACKNOWLEDGMENTS

Thank you to Pat Touchie, Ruth Linka and Emily Shorthouse of TouchWood Editions for encouraging and supporting part three of the *Journey*; to my editor, Marlyn Horsdal, for her intelligent, good-natured advice; to Sinclair Philip and Michael Ableman, for their generous forewords; to Grant Leier, for so vividly reflecting the flavour of my journey in his painting on the cover; to my father, Sam Macey, for reading the manuscript; to my mother, June Macey, for setting a lifelong example of eating locally and seasonally; and to my husband, Clive Levinson, for taking the new photos and driving the great distances.

More thanks to Deirdre Campbell and Andrea Wickham-Foxwell of Tartan PR; to Tom Ryan of Tourism BC; to Frances Sidhe and Daniel Beiles; to Thomas Render, Cynthia Cooper, Leyland Cecco, Lizzie Brown, Nicholas Brown and others who cheerfully accompanied me on parts of this incredible edible journey. Never-ending thanks to the farmers, chefs and food producers who took the time to share their delicious stories.

Heartfelt thanks to my sister and business partner, Caroline Macey-Brown, for so graciously enabling this project to proceed just as we also launched another shop, and to our incredible staff at Café Mela and Mela's Tearoom, for so tolerantly putting up with the inevitable interruptions and mood swings of an author on deadline.

CAVEAT

The selection of "best food experiences" was made by the author. It was not intended to be exhaustive; rather, the choices were made to introduce readers to a wide variety of organic farmers, artisan food producers and restaurants on Vancouver Island and the Gulf Islands. No financial support was solicited or accepted from any person or business included herein. Every attempt has been made to ensure the accuracy of all data presented. The author and publisher assume no legal responsibility for the completeness or accuracy of the contents of this book.

CONTENTS

Forewords xvi
Introduction xix

SOUTH ISLAND AND THE GULF ISLANDS

VICTORIA
Brasserie L'École 3
Café Brio 5
Choux Choux Charcuterie 8
Fol Epi 9
FoodRoots Co-op Pocket Markets and Sustainable Feasts 12
Habit Coffee and Culture 14
Hernande'z on Yates and Hernande'z on Bay 16
Mirjana 17
Moss Street Market 18
Ottavio's Italian Bakery and Delicatessen 19
Planet Organic 22
Plenty Epicurean Pantry 23
Red Fish, Blue Fish and One Fish, Two Fish 25
Share Organics 27
Stage 29
Travel with Taste Tours 31
Zambri's 33

SAANICH/BRENTWOOD BAY
Dragonfly Hill Vineyard 36
Fruit Trees & More 38
Marley Farm Winery 40
Mount Newton Cottage 43
SeaGrille at Brentwood Bay Lodge 43
Victoria Spirits 46

METCHOSIN

The Broken Paddle 49
Happy Valley Lavender and Herb Farm 51
Metchosin Farmers' Market 52

SOOKE

Cooper's Cove Guesthouse and Angelo's Cooking School 53
Little Vienna Bakery 55
Markus' Wharfside Restaurant 57
Outer Coast Seaweeds 59
Ragley Farm 60
Sooke Harbour House 61
Tugwell Creek Honey Farm 67

SALTSPRING ISLAND

Bright Farm 69
Foxglove Farm Retreat and The Centre for Art, Ecology and Agriculture . 71
Hastings House 73
House Piccolo 77
Jana's Bake Shop 79
Market-in-the-Park 80
Monsoon Coast Exotic World Spices 81
Moonstruck Organic Cheese 83
Morningside Organic Bakery and Café 85
Salt Spring Flour Mill 86
Salt Spring Island Bread Company 88
Saltspring Island Cheese Company 90
Saltspring Island Garlic Festival 91
Salt Spring Vineyards 92
Soya Nova Tofu 94
Wave Hill Farm 95

PENDER ISLANDS

Aurora at Poets Cove Resort 97
Iona Farm 99

Jane's Herb Garden 100
Morning Bay Vineyard and Estate Winery 101
Pender Island Bakery Café 103
Pistou Grill 104

SATURNA ISLAND
Haggis Farm Bakery 106
Saturna General Store and Café 107
Saturna Herbs 109
Saturna Island Vineyards 110

MAYNE ISLAND
Deacon Vale Farm 111
Mayne Island Farmers' Market 113
Oceanwood Country Inn 113

GALIANO ISLAND
Daystar Market and Market Café 116
Donna Marben 118
Max & Moritz 120

MID-ISLAND

SHAWNIGAN LAKE
Amusé 123
Elford Farm Bakery 124
Steeples 125

MAPLE BAY
Grapevine on the Bay 127

GLENORA/DUNCAN
Alderlea Vineyards 129
Black Coffee and Other Delights 131

The Community Farm Store and Corfield's Coffee Shop 132
Deerholme Farm and Cottage 134
Fairburn Farm and Culinary Retreat 136
Feast of Fields 138
Godfrey-Brownell Vineyards 139
Providence Farm Community Lunches 141
Vigneti Zanatta 142

COBBLE HILL/COWICHAN BAY
The Asparagus Farm 144
Blue Grouse Vineyards 145
Broken Briar Fallow Deer Farm 147
Cowichan Bay Farm 148
Drum Roaster Coffee 150
Glenterra Vineyards and Thistles Café 152
Hilary's Cheese Company 154
Merridale Ciderworks 156
Saskatoon Berry Farm 158
True Grain Bread 159
Venturi Schulze Vineyards 162

CEDAR/YELLOW POINT
Cedar Farmers' Market 165
The Crow and Gate Pub 165
Mahle House Restaurant 166
Yellow Point Cranberries 168

LADYSMITH
Hazelwood Herb Farm 169
Kiwi Cove Lodge 171
Page Point Inn 172

NANAIMO
Carrot on the Run and 24 Carrot Catering 175
Island Natural Markets 177

McLean's Specialty Foods 177
Mon Petit Choux 179
The Wesley Street Café 180

GABRIOLA ISLAND
Gabriola Agricultural Association Farmers' Market 182
Gabriola Gourmet Garlic 183
Heavenly Flowers and the Good Earth Market Garden 185

LANTZVILLE/NANOOSE BAY
Black Dog Café 187
Harvest Bounty Festival 188
Nanoose Edibles 189

PARKSVILLE/QUALICUM BEACH/COOMBS
Creekmore's Coffee and Espresso Bar 191
The Final Approach 193
Fore & Aft Foods 194
La Boulange Organic Breads 194
Little Qualicum Cheeseworks 196
Qualicum Beach Farmers' Market 197
RainBarrel Farm 199

DENMAN ISLAND
Denman Island Chocolate 200
Denman Island Farmers' Market 201
East Cider Orchard 202
Jacquie's Ices 203
Windy Marsh Farm 203

HORNBY ISLAND
Hornby Island Co-op 205
Hornby Island Farmers' Market 205
Savoie Farm 206

NORTH ISLAND

CUMBERLAND
Cumberland Village Bakery 211
The Great Escape 212
Hazelmere Farms 214
Seeds Natural Food Market 215

COURTENAY
Atlas Café and Bar 216
CakeBread Artisan Bakery 218
Edible Island Whole Foods Market 219
Hot Chocolates 220
Locals 222
Natural Pastures Cheese Company 224
Tita's Mexican Restaurant 227

COMOX
Benino 229
Portuguese Joe's Fish Market 230
Thyme on the Ocean 232

CORTES ISLAND
Cortes Café 233
Cortes Island Farmers' Market 234
Hollyhock 235
Reef Point Farm 237

CAMPBELL RIVER
Anglers Dining Room at The Dolphins Resort 239
Cheddar & Co. Specialty Foods 241
Haig-Brown House 243

TOFINO

Chocolate Tofino 247

Festival of Oysters and the Sea 249

The Goat Lady 250

Hungry Bear Naturals 252

Long Beach Lodge 252

Oyster Jim 255

Raincoast Café 257

Shelter Restaurant 259

600 Degrees Bakery 261

SoBo 263

The Pointe Restaurant at The Wickaninnish Inn 266

Driftwood Lounge 270

Wildside Grill 271

Photo Credits 275

Contacts 276

About the Author 288

FOREWORDS

As a farmer and lover of land and good food, I always dreamed that there was some place that embodied the right combination of climate, soils and attitudes to establish an agrarian renaissance. California once held that promise for me, with its ideal growing climate, deep alluvial soils and history of progressive thinkers. But after 30 years of farming there, watching populations surge and rich farmland give way to real estate development, I decided to look elsewhere.

While I resigned myself to the fact that apples and pears would have to replace avocados and citrus, Vancouver Island and the Gulf Islands have many of the elements for the revival I have been seeking. Far from ideal, with much of the food still being imported from the mainland, and full-time farmers only a fraction of the population, this region does have a committed group of growers, chefs and activists working hard to create a shift in how fresh food is being valued, produced, prepared and consumed. I have always believed that real change will only take place when media, whether books or articles or film, replace the harangue—the constant drumbeat of all that is wrong—with positive and hopeful models, and focus on placing those models firmly into people's minds.

Elizabeth's book does just that. It introduces us to those individuals who are forging a new way and provides us with an intimate view into their lives, their land, their kitchens and the food that they so lovingly bring to our tables. It is a celebration of the best culinary experiences that the islands have to offer, without the stuffiness and exclusivity that is too often associated with such works.

This book also accomplishes something else very important to me. It recognizes and honours farmers as highly skilled artisans and craftsmen, and places them at the heart and the centre of a movement that is restoring food as the gathering point for our families and our communities.

Michael Ableman, Foxglove Farm Retreat, Saltspring Island
author of Fields of Plenty, From the Good Earth *and* On Good Land

If healthy, ethical and pleasurable dining is your focus, Elizabeth Levinson will help make your food purchases and restaurant choices easy and fun. For the first edition of this book, Elizabeth received the highly coveted Cuisine Canada Gold Medal Award for Canadian Food and Culture; it will provide you with a delicious introduction to the foods of our region and also with insights into the worthy people behind this wonderful food. *An Edible Journey* is an excellent guide to one of the world's promising, emerging culinary regions—Vancouver Island and the Gulf Islands.

The world needs to discover regions such as ours to understand the promise of bringing pleasure and health back into our daily lives. The planet is riddled with increasingly unsafe, unhealthy and unsatisfying food choices and is polluted with globalist food litter that is destroying our health, our environment and the lives of many of the workers who provide us with this so-called food. Through this book, Elizabeth nourishes us all with delicious, satisfying and soul-enriching alternatives. She is an active Slow Food member and offers us what the International Slow Food Movement promotes: eco-gastronomic pleasure. She is clearly an authority on the best places to unearth ingredients, where to buy the best regional wines and where to dine on our remote island reaches. Her recommendations are always underscored by an altruistic and generous desire to share ethically produced and natural foods with her readers and friends. Elizabeth has become an important advocate for the natural- and organic-food movement and is familiar with all of our best markets, food suppliers and restaurants, from the most elegant temples of gastronomy to cafés steeped in counterculture.

If we frequent the restaurants, markets and suppliers recommended in this book, we support a community of local producers as well as the preservation of agricultural land. Eating local foods will bring more good foods to our area. Through the descriptions of the restaurants in this book and her introductions to their local suppliers, Elizabeth gives us a chance to reconnect with the foods we eat and familiarize ourselves with the stewards of our land and sea.

Over the last few years, *Travel + Leisure* magazine has portrayed Vancouver Island as one of the best tourist destinations in the world. As this book attests, our restaurants, foods and wines have improved tremendously over the past 25 years and Elizabeth's book will lead you to the doorstep of many of our culinary treasures.

Sinclair Philip, Sooke Harbour House, Sooke
Canadian Representative to the International Slow Food Council

INTRODUCTION

The pursuit of good, clean food has become a keen interest (some say an obsession) for me. Even before the food scares—salmonella, E. coli, BSE, listeria, Avian flu, et al.— I always wanted to know where my food came from and how fresh it was. More recent scares—deaths from spinach grown and peanut butter produced in the United States (and found on the shelves in Canada), and a major recall of ground beef from a prominent British Columbia grocery chain—have only reinforced my personal decision to know as much as possible about the food available to us.

The 100 Mile Diet, which advocates eating only food produced within a hundred miles of one's home, and the locavore movement generally have raised awareness of the virtues of eating locally. When we eat what's grown near us, we are consuming fresher, more nutritious food; we are also supporting the local economy and we are more engaged with the story of our food. Once I began connecting with local growers and food producers, I discovered an exciting community of people who felt the same way I did. These people aren't just consumers like me; they are putting their livelihoods on the line with food made devotedly, simply and in small batches, to ensure quality and freshness.

The increased availability of fresh, local fruit and vegetables, humanely reared meat and lovingly crafted cheeses, breads and specialty foods fulfills my twin desires to eat well and support businesses in my community and region. And the stories behind the food only heighten my appreciation for its producers. My inherent need to "share" has prompted me to write it all down.

From a charcuterie in Victoria to an organic chocolate factory on Denman Island, from a citrus farm on the Saanich Peninsula to a meadery in Sooke, from a balsamic vinegary in the Cowichan Valley to a nutritional-greens farm in Nanoose Bay and a chèvre-maker high in the hills near Ucluelet come the unmistakable signs of hope. Good food does exist on Vancouver Island and the Gulf Islands. One just has to know where to find it.

Determined to unearth the best food experiences and then pass them along, I packed up the car in Victoria and headed north. Taking my notebook, and only my appetite and curiosity to recommend me, I went in search of the growers, the small, artisanal food producers, the innovative chefs and the grocers who are making a difference and offering an alternative. When I returned home, I couldn't write fast enough to tell you about it.

This is a book about the doors that opened, the food that I ate and, most importantly, the passionate people I met—the independents—who are putting fresh, local, seasonal eating back in the centre of our plates. That this is now the third edition of the *Journey* is a testament to the increased interest of ordinary people like me who want to know—and have a right to know—what fuels them.

Enjoy your edible journeys!

Elizabeth Levinson, Victoria

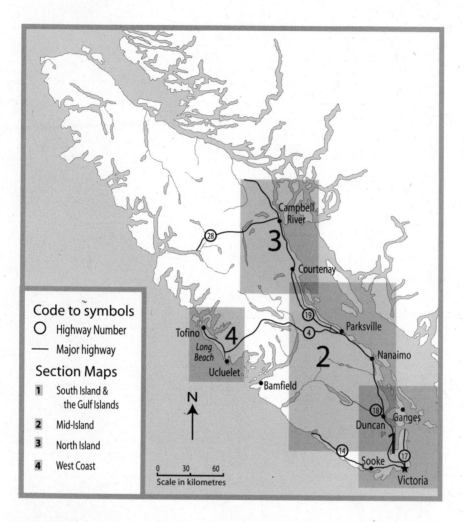

Code to symbols
○ Highway Number
— Major highway

Section Maps
1 South Island & the Gulf Islands
2 Mid-Island
3 North Island
4 West Coast

N
↑

0   30   60
Scale in kilometres

Travel + Leisure magazine has rated Vancouver Island "the best island destination in the continental United States and Canada" two years in a row. Its natural beauty and outdoor activities offer the ideal backdrop to gastronomic journeys. This book is divided into four geographic areas, but the possibilities for combining them or mapping one's own trail are endless.

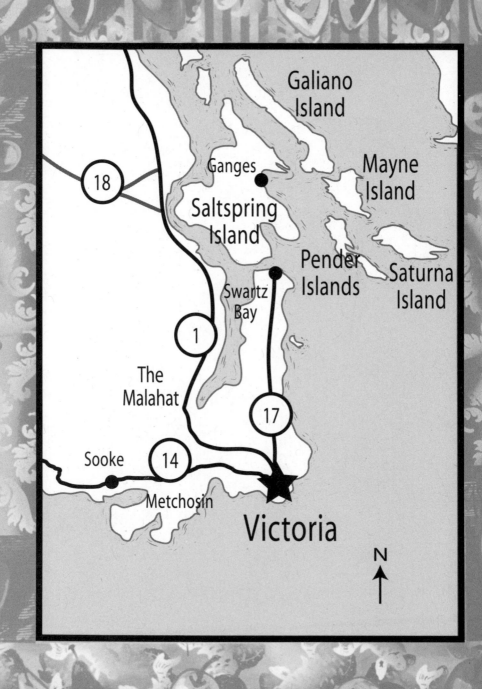

Galiano Island

Mayne Island

Ganges

18

Saltspring Island

Pender Islands

Saturna Island

Swartz Bay

1

17

The Malahat

Sooke

14

Metchosin

Victoria

N

VICTORIA

 *Brasserie L'École*

Sean Brennan is contemplating a future herb-and-vegetable garden in the perfect little enclave behind Brasserie L'École. He knows how well suited the hideaway is, because he had a garden there in a previous incarnation: the brasserie moved in where The Met Bistro used to be, and Sean did a stint in its kitchen. "Over there," he shows me, "were the tomatoes, and all along the wall here, thyme and arugula." His plan is to restore the garden, both for its bounty and as a backdrop for alfresco dining. It has such appeal, tucked in behind this historic building in Victoria's Chinatown, that I encourage him, and look forward to booking a table in summer.

I've come to the back door because I want to see behind the scenes of what has quickly become, and then, more importantly, has stayed, the hottest table in town. In 2002, Brasserie L'École was named the third-best new restaurant in Canada by *enRoute* magazine. The magazine's reviewer, Amy Rosen, was looking for restaurants that "had to blow your mind." Says Marc Morrison, Sean's partner and the restaurant's congenial host and sommelier, "The rating came out on a Thursday, and after that, every night has been a Saturday night." Sean calls it a "happy craziness" that has been further bolstered each successive year with glowing reviews from *Travel + Leisure*, *The New York Times* and *Wine Access Magazine*, to name but a few.

> *"A meal without wine is like a day without sunshine."*
>
> — on the chalkboard at Brasserie L'École

How do they handle the popularity? As far as I can see, like pros. Both have impressive restaurant backgrounds (Sean cooked at Vancouver's Raintree and Victoria's Vin Santo, among others, before making his mark in Café Brio's kitchen in Victoria; Marc is a bike racer turned sommelier who also worked at Vin Santo and Café Brio). Front and back of house are well choreographed, and the wait staff is first class. There's a warm conviviality in the restaurant, and table-hopping is often part of the scene. It's not unusual to go on a Saturday night and have everyone in the place know each other. Even a special cheese and dessert-wine tasting I attended mid-week turned into one of the year's best parties.

Top: *Sommelier and co-owner Marc Morrison enjoys a rare relaxed moment at Brasserie L'École.*

Bottom: *Chef and co-owner Sean Brennan strikes a pose in the kitchen at Brasserie L'École.*

Like any mind-blowing restaurant, it all starts in the kitchen. Today, Sean has just received a delivery from Josephine Hill of Sooke's Ragley Farm: large buckets of mesclun—surprisingly prolific for the middle of January—hearty mustard greens and arugula. Earlier, oysters arrived from Cortes Island—large, meaty Steller Bay oysters and the small, sweet Kusshi variety—and Finest At Sea Ocean Products dropped off sides of high-end sablefish that were, as the company's name suggests, processed at sea

("to retain the natural oils," Sean tells me). I welcome a tour of the walk-in fridge, one of the most immaculate I've ever seen (the word is local health inspectors show trainees around the place so they can see what restaurant kitchens should look like).

There are inviting stacks of cheese, an increasingly popular course here. Sean buys his cheese from Andrew Moyer at Ottavio's Italian Bakery and Delicatessen every Friday. Andrew often calls excitedly during the week to tell him about "something you have to try." The brasserie serves pasteurized and unpasteurized cheeses from France, Quebec and Saltspring Island. Sean is keen that people order their cheese course before the meal to ensure proper serving temperature. It's all about making sure patrons have the best possible culinary experience.

While Sean begins to prepare a pistou broth with soisson beans for the lamb shank, I ask him about the evening's menu. It is, as always, small and select, with the emphasis on fresh, local ingredients cooked to order. What could be finer? There are half a dozen starters, from soupe à l'oignon gratinée to Sean's famous duck-leg confit with braised red cabbage. One of my favourites is the endive salad with mustard wine dressing, apple slices and freshly picked hazelnuts. Mains include the hugely popular steak frites, mountain trout with bacon, chard, dried tomato and mushroom-potato hash and albacore tuna with onion marmalade and Jerusalem artichokes. It's always a stellar night when my husband finds braised buffalo or ostrich on the menu.

As a past president of the Island Chefs Collaborative, which promotes local food, Sean says if he can't get something that's been produced locally, he seriously considers the "food miles" attached to using other products. He's concerned about depletion of wild fish stocks and clearly does his bit by supporting local growers and food producers. As he says himself, "I am very comfortable with what I do." Sean says they want to be known for having "a very good, well-rounded restaurant, with the focus on the food, service, wine and ambiance." I say he can stop wanting; he and Marc have all that and more. Still, Sean tells me he "will like the place even more in a few years. It will look better when it's worn in a bit."

Café Brio

The last supper I ate for this *Journey* was rustled up by Café Brio's unflappable chef, Laurie Munn, one February afternoon as glimmers of spring sunshine filtered through the restaurant's wrought-iron gates outside the window. I took it as a good omen that a puréed Jerusalem artichoke soup, finished with an artist's brushstroke of hazelnut brown butter and served with a crispy

Enter Café Brio with an appetite.

bread-crumb tuile, was placed before me. Its earthy, unctuous goodness reminded me that our unusually harsh winter was waning and the delicate tuile was, to me, a sign of light and new life ahead.

The pheasant breast, poached in butter, served with a delightful fritter made of the bird's leg meat, carrots, celery and a little cheese, and a side of sautéed apples, pears and herbs atop apple and onion purée, reminded me how sublime yet *real* Laurie's cooking can be. And this, of course, speaks to the philosophy of Café Brio (*brio* means lively or spirited): this is a restaurant that has always favoured local suppliers and shown creativity and respect for ingredients in its kitchen.

To set the scene in the evenings here, one is greeted warmly at the door with a "Hi, you two" from owner and bon vivant Greg Hays, a man whose food-industry experience spans the Herald Street Caffe and The Marina restaurant. Greg and his partner in life and business, Silvia Marcolini, have hit on a concept that combines her Italian heritage with the couple's commitment to featuring quality regional ingredients— and the rest, as I've said before, is a notable chapter in Victoria's culinary history.

The dining room, with its deep Tuscan yellow and rust walls laden with paintings by local artists, its surprisingly wide choice of seating—from private booths to see-and-be-seen tables for 12 in the centre of the room to relaxed dining on the patio—and its friendly, central bar, is immediately inviting. Being family run, the restaurant exudes a comfortable sense of dining in someone's home, and though centrally located, it has an appealing hideaway quality.

When Laurie was offered the position of chef two years ago, he was essentially coming home to a restaurant he knew well and an extended family with whom he'd worked before; starting in 2000, he was Brio's sous-chef for a couple of years under Jeff Keenliside (now of The Marina restaurant). In the interim, Laurie worked in Vancouver at the highly rated Bis Moreno and C restaurants, but he and his wife wanted to "get out of the city." He describes his appointment at Café Brio as "a happy fit," where he enjoys "showing the diversity of what the island has to offer."

Laurie is grateful for "the freedom that I have here to do things to the highest quality." That includes making everything from scratch, including butchering whole animals (pigs from Qualicum Beach's Sloping Hill Farm, sides of beef from Cowichan Bay's Quist Farm and lambs from Metchosin's Perry Bay Farm) and making pasta with a Torchio. The latter is a beautiful stainless steel machine brought in from Italy, which Laurie uses for rigatoni, spaghetti and tagliatelli. Other pasta is entirely hand-formed—like the agnolotti, which, the day I visited, was being stuffed with grilled sausage and ricotta.

Organic fruit and vegetables play a major role in the kitchen, and Laurie buys them from Gavin's Greens in Saanich ("whatever he has, we'll take— salad, herbs and braising greens") and from the Saanich Organics co-op. He and his wife stop by Ottavio's Italian Bakery and Delicatessen every Saturday morning for breakfast and "to select cheeses for the week from Andrew [Moyer]" (see Ottavio's). Having lived in France for a while during his competitive cycling days, Laurie tells me he is partial to Comté and l'Edel de Cleron cheeses, so they can often be found on the menu at Café Brio.

One of the best offerings at Café Brio came about after the Raging Grannies dined in the restaurant. They'd requested that their meal be served "family style," which Laurie says "went really well." So he introduced the con- cept of the Brio Family Meal, wherein a selection of five or six dishes—chosen by the chef but customized according to food preferences—are served family style for the entire table to share. The family meals have been incredibly well received; they have all the taste and quality of a tasting menu but none of the pretentiousness.

Because I visited Café Brio before service, I entered and left by the back door, so I couldn't help nosing around and noticing the quiet efficiency in its kitchen. It's no wonder that what emanates from this happy culinary haven of Laurie, pastry chef Kalyn Sarkany (she of the fabulous chocolate truffles, angel food cake and baked toffee pudding fame) and the other members of the brigade is food that sings just as quietly but assuredly on the plates in the dining room. Café Brio is becoming a legend.

Choux Choux Charcuterie

I'm tucked into one of two window booths in the tiny red-and-golden Choux Choux Charcuterie on a particularly grey and rainy day. On my plate the sun is shining in the form of the deli's excellent duck confit atop a warm lentil salad with Parksville's Artisan Edibles summer berry compote. This is one of the best bets for an authentic plat du jour and the lively atmosphere only adds to my enjoyment. That it's a small place means I often feel part of the conversations at the counter between owners Luke Young and Paige Symonds and their customers—and I've been known to interject but, naturally, only for journalistic reasons.

Today, Café Brio co-owner Greg Hays pops in, checks out what I'm eating ("What's today's *plat*?") and asks Paige for "that cheese *Saveur* says is the best for grilled-cheese sandwiches." Paige, who has spent time working on a chèvre-producing farm in France and is the expert behind the shop's stellar cheese selection, tells him the magazine was recommending Comté, which she doesn't have. So she advises him to buy Abondance, which is very similar: "It's a good melting cheese with a nice fruity-nutty flavour." Greg goes away happy with the cheese and some sausages to grill.

Both chefs, Luke and Paige met when they worked at Raincity Grill in Vancouver about five years ago. They travelled around France on work visas, cooking as they went, then returned to Vancouver where Luke

Sandwich board outside Choux Choux Charcuterie.

"went off-line and worked as a butcher." Paige returned to France to work on the goat farm, and then they "did some thinking about putting our interests together and starting something in Victoria," which is where Paige grew up.

The result is Choux Choux, Victoria's first really fabulous charcuterie and it's on every foodie's list for sausages, pâtés and terrines. The meat is sourced locally, with non-medicated, vegetarian-fed hogs supplied by Sloping Hill Farm in Qualicum Beach. Says Luke, "We use everything, from the head to the toes: head cheese, bones for stock and trotters for jelly for pâtés." On Friday afternoons, customers queue for freshly butchered tenderloins, chops and spare ribs.

In addition to the eye-popping lineup of salami, soppressata, prosciutto *cotto*, *saucisson sec* and *Mettwurst*, there are fresh and unique pâtés—like my favourite, chicken liver mousse with green peppercorns, or the more exotic pheasant and walnut terrine, and rabbit rillettes and pork and duck rillettes. Wild boar or caribou pâtés can be custom ordered and there are vegetarian options like the roasted vegetable terrine. The shop is well stocked with accompaniments such as cornichons, olives and dried fruits and Fol Epi's incomparable baguettes.

You'll find the shelves lined with all manner of preserves and condiments, and this should be your stop for very special Christmas goodies like goose confit, glazed chestnuts and *boudin blanc*, the traditional French holiday pork or chicken sausage made with cream, eggs and truffles.

 *Fol Epi*

How could four empty brown paper bags fill me with so much anticipation? That's easy! They were four of some 40,000 bags just delivered to an almost-open Fol Epi organic bakery at Dockside Green. When I read their labels, I started salivating for the day they'll hold freshly baked loaves.

The Jeune Hiver Rye will be made of whole rye flour, water, wild yeast culture, whole wheat flour and salt (the name is an endearing play on words as this bread was created for Fol Epi owner Cliff Leir's wife, Jennifer, when she was pregnant and "couldn't bear the smell of wheat"). A traditional wheat

Fol Epi's Cliff Leir, at five o'clock in the morning!

flour baguette will fit snugly into the long brown bag, and there will also be a *blé entier*, made, as the name implies, entirely of wheat flour—well, almost entirely, as there will be a little rye flour thrown in for good measure. The fourth kind will be *pain de campagne*—the "country loaf" that will be the everyday staff of life for our breadbaskets.

But wait! How could I possibly have this information even before the doors have opened on Harbour Road? Well, that can be attributed to the skulking around done by food writers in the dark of night when there is still snow on the ground and one's breath can be sharply seen against the backdrop of sustainable architecture that is Dockside Green. There, tucked into a corner as the road turns back toward the Inner Harbour, I lock eyes on Fol Epi.

Even though the bakery is not yet open for business, I ruthlessly knock on the window and tear Cliff away from some last-minute bricklaying for "just a couple of questions." An hour later, after he's made me a very good cup of Caffè Fantastico coffee—served in a Mason jar—I start to form a picture of what his "dream bakery" is going to look, feel and smell like. From what I can already see, the place has a rustic charm in an area that, though built for environmental sustainability, still has an industrial appearance.

The juxtaposition of building materials is appealing. A concrete floor and exposed piping overhead give way to counters and a refrigerated pastry case built of structural wooden beams reclaimed from the old Princess Mary Restaurant; the fir flooring in the working part of the bakery is also from the old restaurant. The bread display area is a monumental fashioning of brick and stonework that Cliff tells me was difficult to build but which looks stunning.

At the rear of the shop is the mother of all wood-fired ovens. Cliff had built it in his nearby temporary location at The Princess Mary, so it had to be moved to the bakery's new site. "When the crane operator tried to set it into place," he tells me, "I had to take my diamond drill and cut an eighth of an inch off either side so that it would fit." It is an indirectly fired brick oven, which means the baker has full control over the temperature. "Instead of having to fire it up and then let it cool to the required temperature, I can release more heat into the oven to suit our baking requirements."

To a layperson like me, that translates into starting the oven at 225°F first thing in the morning in order to bake the delicate croissants and *pains au chocolat*, then increasing the temperature to 250°F for the whole wheat baguettes, and then adding more heat for heartier bread baking as the day progresses.

Cliff modestly describes his vision for the bakery's output, "We just want to make a few things and do them really well." Those of us familiar with his bread and pastry know the art, science and love that he will bring to every Danish pastry, every loaf. Cliff and Fran Lynott will mainly be creating the artisan breads, while Mark Aitken will focus on the pastries.

Mark is a classically trained baker who, in addition to croissants, *pains au chocolat*, *Schnecken*, Danishes, madeleines, crisp chocolate wafers and *Kugelhupfs*, will be making *cannelés*! These, in my book, are the best of French inventions, and I hear that he has ordered special copper moulds from Paris "to ensure the right level of carmelization."

Cliff's bread is so good because he understands the science behind his craft. He aims to "achieve a balance between the flavour of the grain and the fermented taste of the wild yeast," which, he tells me, "is ultimately all about temperature and time." In this dream bakery, he will have the benefit of climate-controlled fridges that can proof and retard the dough, allowing overnight fermentation of flavour and development of texture. The bottom line is that Cliff and his bakers will get a better night's sleep, and he is looking forward to having dough "to the point I want it at" when he begins work at 5:30 a.m. each morning.

Quality organic ingredients will be the other factor in his success, starting with Red Fife wheat, the heritage grain grown for Fol Epi by Mark Loiselle and his family in Saskatchewan. Cliff has just received five tonnes of the grain in one of his two eight-tonne-capacity silos located behind the bakery. Being able to mill the flour as needed ensures a unique freshness for the baking, and customers will be able to see the stone mill sifting out the bran and leaving behind the creamy-coloured, soft and "slightly sweet" wheat flour from which he'll make magic.

Cliff has always taken the Slow Food approach: "Whatever is available in season, we will use in our sweet and savoury baking." So you can expect to find Cowichan Bay chicken, buffalo mozzarella from Natural Pastures and ham from Choux Choux on Fol Epi's pizza; smoked lox from FAS on its open-faced sandwiches; and organic sour cherries and mulberries from a newly certified organic grower in Saanich baked into morning pastries. One day, Cliff hopes to be milling organic Vancouver Island-grown wheat, "I've set up the infrastructure to receive it when farmers start to grow it."

"The possibilities," he says with a gleam in his eye as he waves me goodbye, "are endless."

(And the possibilities have already extended to coffee. Victoria's well-regarded Caffè Fantastico has opened a shop adjacent to Cliff's bakery. The combination of great java and excellent organic pastries will make every morning a whole lot more special.)

FoodRoots Co-op Pocket Markets and Sustainable Feasts

I think pocket markets are the best thing to have hit the streets in Victoria's urban core. Organized by FoodRoots, a co-operative that gathers and then distributes local produce and foods produced in the region, these markets are bringing Vancouver Island sustainability one step closer to reality.

Pocket markets comprise just one or two tables but many local farms and food producers are represented. The benefit to consumers is that they are able to shop from many different farm-gates in one stop and, because the markets are set up in residential areas, most can walk to do their shopping. The benefit to farmers is that they get to stay on their farms and do what they do best, instead of taking time away from growing and harvesting to sell their products.

These markets are held all over town, from the Student Union Building at the University of Victoria to the Cornerstone Café in Fernwood to the Cedar Hill Recreation Centre. When my sister and I opened Café Mela at The Belvedere in the Humboldt Valley, we realized that the only thing missing in that steel-and-concrete, high-density residential area was access to fresh fruit and vegetables.

We called Lee Fuge, the dynamo who operates FoodRoots (along with Susan Tychie of Share Organics and Brian Hughes of Kildara Farm in Deep Cove) and, within weeks, she'd arranged a Friday afternoon pocket market right in front of our café. It's turned into a great retail and social success, and when the market takes a hiatus from October to March, we have lots of long faces coming into our café asking, "Where's *our* market?"

Also organized by FoodRoots, sustainable feasts are another brilliant addition to the Victoria food scene. These monthly buffet-style suppers showcase our local bounty in a delicious meal that's cooked by volunteers. While the dinners have traditionally been held at the Fairfield Community Centre, FoodRoots is currently reaching out to other locations. This year, very convivial dinners have already taken place in a University of Victoria cafeteria and at Abkhazi Gardens.

Dishing up dinner at tables all over town helps FoodRoots get the word out about the quality and availability of the area's local produce and its pro-ducers, and about their food co-operative. At each feast, there is always a farmer or food producer on hand to talk about his or her specialty, whether it's cranberries or mushrooms, cheese or wine. And I'd say the best part of the meal is that one sits festival-style at tables of 12 people, so making new friends is also part of the sustenance.

Habit Coffee and Culture

Habit attracts hipsters, young and old. As owner Shane Devereaux says, "We seem to have created a social hub of hip, interesting people."

One hipster is my 87-year-old father who, with me in tow, quietly but determinedly marches toward a particular seat at the back of the place every Sunday morning. From this spot, he can watch the action as it unfolds and enjoy a French-press coffee and a muffin. I'd be disappointed if he didn't turn to me every Sunday and ask why the French press takes so long to make, in the same way that he'd miss hearing the barista's answer: it's timed to achieve perfection. As we nibble a banana-walnut muffin and solve the world's problems, we always stop to appreciate the relaxed ambiance, the good-start-to-the-day feeling we get from our fellow java hounds and from Shane and his excellent staff.

This is a coffee shop that was destined for greatness from the start. Shane, a Saskatoon native, travelled the world for five years—Asia, Australia, Europe and the Caribbean—before settling down in Victoria. He worked as the bar manager at Canoe for four years as part of the management team that took the place from its former Canoe Club self to its current state. Shane says he "learned a lot about re-branding through that process. I figured if I knew what it took to run a multi-million-dollar brew pub, I could run a coffee shop."

But it was while running a backpackers' hostel in Perth, Australia, that Shane first had the vision of opening his own coffee shop. "The Aussies just seem to do everything better related to food," he tells me (and I must say I agree where coffee is concerned, having experienced the best and most consistent coffee while visiting Australia—from fancy cafés in Noosa to truck stops in Newcastle). Shane was hooked and when he returned to Victoria, he began planning his own shop, which included spending time with roasters and baristas at places like Portland's Stumptown.

Although he had his eye on three locations, it was 552 Pandora Avenue that he most wanted. It became available quite by chance and "all of a sudden, it was go time." With his father helping him, Shane spent some 120 hours chipping drywall off a wall that he knew was solid brick underneath, and meticulously converted what was "an ugly

Barista Zack Simon and owner Shane Devereaux take coffee seriously at Habit Coffee and Culture.

space into a beautiful room." He likes that the location is "on the fringe of downtown" and that it caters to locals first and foremost.

I've been a fan from the beginning, whether it's for a mocha made with chocolate milk or a double Americano. The baristas—like former Caffè Fantastico man Zack Simon—really know how to work their bar (in Habit's case, a stunning shiny red and stainless steel La Marzocco three-group espresso machine). The coffee, roasted by Hines Public Market Coffee in Vancouver, is superb: hand-picked, direct-trade organic beans from Ethiopia, Kenya and Uganda.

Shane spent five weeks training the growers at the plantations he buys beans from—"getting them to taste their coffee and improve its quality, giving them a model to improve their livelihoods." His enthusiasm for the "new wave of quality cafés in the Pacific Northwest" and his intense, hands-on interest in where and how his coffee is grown, roasted and prepared in the shop has resulted in a well-deserved local following. And all I can say is, this is a good Habit to have.

Hernande'z on Yates and Hernande'z on Bay

As Tamara Hernandez puts it, "We've messed with the hours and the locations; what we've never messed with is the food." And that is why I am choosing not to "mess" with my first impressions of Hernande'z, the little restaurant with five generous hearts behind it. Since I first met them, the Hernandez family has migrated from the original Hernande'z restaurant on Yates Street, and from Toro, its street-food kiosk in a parkade, and has now relocated Hernande'z in two new locations: one downtown, the other in the family's own Fernwood neighbourhood.

Both offer the same *ganas*—the passion, the appetite—for food and community and for life itself. The *ganas* is manifest in the cool glass of *Agua de Flores* (literally, water of flowers) made by Tamara and in the heaping portion of rice, black beans, salsa, sour cream and organic greens atop the sandal-shaped *huarache* made of corn; it pulses from the stereo or from the strings of Jerson Hernandez's own guitar; and it radiates from the portrait of the Virgin of Guadalupe on the wall and from the colourful, whimsical *loteria* cards (Mexican bingo cards featuring diverse images, from *La Sirena* to *El Corazon*) that decorate the tabletops and can be used by patrons to flag down Tamara to check on their food orders. But mostly the *ganas* comes from Tamara and Jerson, whose intelligent philosophies and commentaries are key ingredients in the success of their restaurants.

When I dine alone at either Hernande'z, I am greeted with a warm hug from Jerson and—before eating—a good conversation, such as the one I had with him about how "efficiency is killing community and inefficiency brings us together." I leave with a full belly and ideas to digest. And so, for me and many other devotees of the Hernandez family, it matters not if their restaurants are keeping regular hours or even where they are located; what's important is that their hearts are in the right place. Ultimately, they will feed their customers in the same way they feed their family and they will make you feel part of their warm and generous home—wherever it happens to be.

 *Mirjana*

For me, the sun rises and sets on Victoria's tiniest restaurant, Mirjana. Located in Chinatown's Dragon Alley, it's right in the city, yet away from the madding crowds; the menu demands nothing of me, i.e., you get what you get; the food is fresh, made daily and expertly prepared; and its dynamic owner lacks every pretense known in the restaurant business.

Mirjana is a hunter-gatherer after my own heart. She tells me that "walking and talking" enable her to familiarize herself with her surroundings, to seek out the best ingredients for her cooking and the freshest blooms for the single, elegant floral arrangement in her restaurant. "The more I walk and talk," she says, "the better gatherer I become." And being located in the heart of Chinatown gives her an endless supply of exotic fruits and vegetables to incorporate into her cooking.

The entryway to Dragon Alley in Chinatown leads to Victoria's smallest restaurant, Mirjana.

On Valentine's Day, I dined with friends on roasted beet and yam cannelloni in a sauce of ginger, orange, Brie and cream, decorated with pomegranate seeds and red grapes; braised lamb shank finished with quince, shallots, fresh herbs and chocolate (the secret ingredient is out, Mirjana!) served on polenta; and a true artist's rendering of chocolate pâté with a flourish of cream and a glimmer of gold leaf. At the end of that exquisite meal, Mirjana joined us to drink her strong, black stove-top coffee and talk of many things.

Mirjana is an interesting woman: proud mother of two international human-rights lawyers (Deborah-Miji works for the UN in Split, Croatia, and Elizabeth works in London); political activist (having lived through war and lost family to war, she often shares her views on the chalkboard); and famous cook (her Saltspring Island restaurant, Pomodoro, was widely praised in reviews from *Vancouver Magazine* to *Vanity Fair*). Her progression, from "starving artist" in London to restaurant owner in Victoria, has been filled with great experiences. When she was in London, friends suggested she become a personal chef in order to make ends meet. That turned into "a real upstairs, downstairs position" when Mirjana became the cook for a large household and was sent off to get her Cordon Bleu diploma in Marylebone Lane. "I was the only student who arrived on foot," she tells me. "Everyone else pulled up in Bentleys."

With her certification in hand, Mirjana came to Canada. Here, she decided to take a break from cooking and became a gatherer of another sort. She worked with food, fashion and interior design, doing styling for the advertising business. Three years later, Mirjana opened the 100-seat Pomodoro, which she operated for four years.

Her new eponymous venture finally feels like the right fit for Mirjana. A lifelong proponent of fresh, organic food, she always chooses quality over quantity. Her mother told her, "You're not rich enough to buy cheap things," and she carries that adage with her as she gathers superior ingredients for her cooking. Though her roots are in Mediterranean cuisine, Mirjana's style is decidedly fresh and innovative. She tells me, "Food, politics and life are all one thing," and I'm telling you that heady combination sings on the plates at Mirjana.

Moss Street Market

This year, Victoria's flagship organic farmers' market will celebrate 18 years of success. Started by a small group of dedicated organic growers, including Mary Alice Johnson of Sooke's ALM Organic Farm, the market offers produce from

Fresh food and good conversation at the legendary Moss Street Market.

Umi Nami Farm, Eisenhawer Organic Produce, Rebecca Jehn's Organic Garden, as well as from noted growers Tina Fraser, R.J. Fisher and Robin Tunnicliffe.

Once the bell rings at 10 o'clock (every Saturday, May through October) you can shop for top produce, cheese, flowers, preserves, sausages and delicious, freshly made bite-sized doughnuts. And watch the papers for the annual Christmas Market, held inside the Fairfield Community Centre, which always puts one in the holiday spirit.

Ottavio's Italian Bakery and Delicatessen

I'm not the only hapless hostess who has gone knocking on the door of Ottavio's to find out how to put a cheese tray together, nor the only day tripper seeking some morsels to pack in the picnic hamper. However, what surprised me was how un-intimidating it was, how inspiringly and humorously things were explained, and particularly how much fun I had with Ottavio's owners, Monica Pozzolo and Andrew Moyer.

They certainly have come by their business honestly. Monica's grandparents operated a family bakery in Turin in 1921. When her mother, Ubalda, married her father, Michele Pozzolo, they immigrated to Canada and opened the Italian Bakery, which is now run by Monica's brother, Alberto, and his wife, Janet Cochrane. Andrew was a soccer buddy of Alberto's. He and Monica opened Ottavio's in 1997, and so the legend continues.

While Ottavio's has many gastronomic offerings, from breads and baked goods to the city's finest range of olive oils, home-made lasagna, soups and pasta, Andrew and Monica have developed a stellar reputation as purveyors of quality cheese.

If you love cheese, it is a treat to spend time in the company of these passionate cheese merchants, to hear them wax poetic about a raw-milk Saint-Nectaire they found on a recent journey through the Loire Valley, and to share Andrew's excitement as he demonstrates his new double-handled cheese knife from E. Dehillerin, the famed cooks' supply shop in Paris. They describe an impromptu feast they had of cheese, half a chicken, some good bread and a bottle of wine from an incredible *fromagerie* at the side of the road. Ah, the glorious journeys one can have en route to great meals.

Co-owners Monica Pozzolo and Andrew Moyer proudly display their croissants at Ottavio's Italian Bakery and Delicatessen.

Monica and Andrew carry over 200 cheeses in their sunny Oak Bay *gastronomia*, with at least 150 in stock at any one time. They range from soft to hard types, made from cow's milk to sheep's milk, from French, Italian and Spanish origins to cheeses from Quebec, Ontario, and a good showing from Saltspring Island. In short, they have the makings of many delectable cheese courses for both the uninitiated and the educated palate.

For a basic cheese course, Andrew suggests I choose three or four cheeses; any more, he warns, and "your taste buds might get lost." He says the key is to let texture and flavour guide my selection. As he speaks, he sets out on a thick piece of grey slate the following beauties: Vieille Mimolette, an aged, unpasteurized hard cheese made from cow's milk, with a deep orange colour, smooth but firm texture and mild taste; Blossom's Blue, an organic, pasteurized, cow's milk blue cheese from Saltspring Island's Moonstruck Organic Cheese, which is both sweet and has a bite similar to Stilton; Saint Albray, a soft, pasteurized cow's milk Brie-like cheese that's made at the foot of the Pyrenées; and finally, Valençay, which he describes as "the stinky cheese that's not as scary as it looks." Legend has it this ash-crusted, unpasteurized, goat's milk cheese, with its meltingly smooth white interior, was first served to Napoleon when he returned to France from heavy losses in Egypt. The cheese looked too much like a pyramid for the general's liking, so he lopped off its top. (By the way, the ash is a tasteless charcoal-dust coating that's simply used to protect the cheese during aging; historically, it kept the bugs off!)

The cheese tray that Andrew has composed seemingly without effort sits before me as an evocative balance of texture, taste and colour. Of course, there's nothing effortless about the years he and Monica have spent researching, tasting and reading about cheese. Their depth of knowledge is a great resource, not only to customers in the shop, but also to the many local chefs who buy Ottavio's cheese for their restaurants, which include Brasserie L'École, Zambri's, Matisse, Café Brio, Fire & Water, Feys + Hobbs Catered Arts, Vista 18 and Temple, to name a few.

Back to the tray in front of me: there is soft cheese, hard cheese, blue cheese and the proverbial stinky or pungent cheese for more adventurous guests. The variations and permutations for a cheese course are, of course, endless. You can focus on a country or a region, or serve all cow's milk or all sheep's milk cheeses. Monica says her family's cheese course always includes one or two goat's milk or sheep's milk cheeses for those who are lactose intolerant.

The choice of accompaniments is equally infinite. Andrew suggests steering clear of acidic condiments like olives at the end of a meal. He and Monica agree that texture plays a big role in successful accompaniments so they recommend roasted or caramelized hazelnuts or almonds, seasonal berries, dates or figs, a drizzle of honey, a piece of quince paste or panforte (that divine concoction of figs, dates, raisins and toasted nuts), and sweet or savoury biscotti (the latter is particularly good with creamy chèvre). Monica loves cheese with rusks

Andrew Moyer advises choosing just three or four cheeses "so your taste buds don't get lost."

or plain baguette. Neither she nor Andrew favours flavoured cheeses or fancy breads, preferring to let the cheese quality speak for itself.

Presentation is also important and can be fun. Monica suggests that this is the time to show off that special plate, piece of slate, cutting board or small straw mat (she found hers in Chinatown). Choose a vibrantly coloured surface, as most cheeses are light in colour, but you can decorate a plainer surface with grape or chestnut leaves or edible flowers before arranging the cheese.

Planet Organic Market

My mother and I shop at the Planet Organic grocery store every Tuesday morning—and may it always be so. We love that when we walk in the door, the floor gleams, the 100 per cent organic produce looks and feels like it has just been picked and the staff responds to our food queries with genuine interest and knowledge. We appreciate that the store supports many local growers and producers. We enjoy the homey atmosphere combined with good service and efficiency.

When I meet the owner, Diane Shaskin, I can see why Planet Organic is in a galaxy all its own. Above all, she is passionate about food. She and her husband, Mark Craft, are experienced grocers. Diane is committed to—no, *adamant* about—stocking only organic produce; she listens to her customers.

In the early 1990s, Diane was a producer for CBC Television in Edmonton; Mark built energy-efficient homes. But Diane knew she wanted to be involved with food, so, when a natural foods store came up for sale, the couple bought it. At that time, they had no experience with food or retail, but they welcomed the learning curve. Within a year, they had transformed the business. Terra Natural Food Market, with its distinctive Italian country-grocer look and feel, took off running.

Says Diane, "Initially, we offered organic and some conventional foods, but quickly found that organics outsold conventional even when the price was higher." She made the decision early on to focus on organics. A Slow Food proponent, she "doesn't like the idea of doing what's convenient." Even though "only 15 per cent of the population shops at health food stores," she is fully committed to her market.

Diane and Mark ran Terra for seven years before looking at expansion options. With help from Darren Krissie, they went public. In the style of US company Wild Oats—which owned Vancouver's Capers before being bought out by Whole Foods—Planet Organic's owners are looking to "consolidate the health food industry" in Canada. The company now owns 10 Planet Organic stores, in BC, Alberta, Ontario and Nova Scotia; Sangsters, a chain of natural health stores across Canada; Mrs. Green's Natural Markets (12 locations in New York and Conneticut); and Trophic Canada, a vitamin manufacturer based in Penticton. While the structure is corporate, the real mission, says Diane, is "to provide the highest quality organic and natural foods while emphasizing customer service, employee satisfaction and community involvement."

It's evident to me that supporting local food producers is the foundation of their business. In the Victoria store, I often run into growers I know dropping off their wares, and I was shopping for produce one day while *EAT* magazine's Gary Hynes merrily snapped photos; Planet Organic veggies had just made the magazine's "50 Great Things to Eat" list.

Plenty Epicurean Pantry

There is one pantry that is forever engraved in my memory. My Auntie Cis, whom we visited at her home in Loughborough, England, every year until she died, had a classic pantry where she stored all manner of "put up" veggies and fruits from my uncle's garden. It was always terribly cold in there in winter, which ensured that whatever my aunt asked me to fetch would be procured instantly so that I could return to the warmth of her kitchen. Still, the pantry gave me a homey feeling of sufficiency. One didn't need to shop; one could always concoct a meal from what was in the pantry.

Today, I can relive that pantry philosophically and physically at Plenty Epicurean Pantry, Trevor Walker and Erica Sangster's shop on Victoria's famous Antique Row, which literally brims over with local edibles. Truly, if

one cannot take an edible journey of Vancouver Island, one can still find and taste many of its food products courtesy of Plenty's shelves. And it's worth noting note that those shelves are almost edible—they're made of pressed wheat.

In fact, it's an effort not to want to try everything at once, for there are so many unique and tasty things to buy. To appreciate fully the care that has been taken in selecting goods for the store, shop assistant Linda Jane Schmid (ask to see her whimsical honey bee acrylics) suggests I peruse the contents of the antique apothecary's cabinet. The many little drawers that once housed "choice pressed herbs," as the original sign reads, are today packed with, well, choice herbs and spices from Organic Fair. Across from the spice section is a case of beautiful cheeses, many from Vanouver Island cheese pro-

Shop assistant and artist Linda Jane Schmid proffers saffron from the apothecary's cabinet at Plenty Epicurean Pantry.

ducers, such as Hilary's and Natural Pastures. Gort's Aged Gouda from Salmon Arm is another popular organic cheese available here.

There are fabulous handmade truffles from Patty Doyle's Pearl Chocolates in Duncan, and her irresistible caramels covered with dark chocolate and grey sea salt. Bread is a big seller here because you can custom order loaves from Bloom Breads on Saltspring Island and True Grain Bread in Cowichan Bay. Another section of the store has rows and rows of Powell River's Mountain Ash chutneys, salsas, pickles, relishes and pickled beets. There is wonderful chocolate from Organic Fair; Sea Cider organic cream honey from Sea Cider

Farm and Ciderhouse on the Saanich Peninsula (my mother's favourite—and she knows her cream honeys!); the best oatcakes to go with all that cheese from Victoria's Bonnie Bea; the amazing Pomegranate Mustard, Orange Chipotle Mustard and Chocolate Wine Sauce from Dana Zaruba's Hot Chick Spice Company in Cobble Hill; hazelnuts (plain, spiced and candied) from Bud Butler's farm in Saanichton; and so much more to be discovered by the peripatetic foodie.

I was pleased to see Saltspring Gelato in the cooler. One of the varieties, Fruit Tree Apple Pie, is made in conjunction with Victoria's admirable LifeCycles' Fruit Tree Project, where fruit that would otherwise be left to rot on the trees of private gardens is harvested by volunteers and put to good use. Much of it is donated directly to organizations that serve the needy but Feys + Hobbs Catered Arts, Level Ground and Spinnakers are just some of the partners who have developed some of that fruit into other interesting products over the years.

Plenty is a well-thought-out and terrifically well-stocked pantry, which also has beautiful cookware and an excellent selection of cookbooks. Visiting this urban pantry is like taking an edible journey of Vancouver Island under one roof!

Red Fish, Blue Fish and One Fish, Two Fish

It is a myth that a foodie is by definition in some kind of exalted snack bracket, eating only in five-star restaurants and quaffing 1983 Château Margaux. Indeed, my experience is that real foodies gravitate to excellence wherever it is found, which is why I was blissfully happy to find Red Fish, Blue Fish on a hot summer's day.

Architecturally, it is nothing more than a cargo container sitting on the dock in the Inner Harbour, but it has been cleverly fashioned into a basic 2.5- by 6-metre cooking facility. There are some rough-hewn high bar tables to sit at and a help-yourself shelf of condiments, cutlery and the like. But what gems one finds on exploring a little deeper!

Partner Simon Sobolewski takes an order at Red Fish, Blue Fish.

There are four partners—chef Kunal Ghose; business manager (and actor on the side) Simon Sobolewski; fisher Steve Johansen and designer Barbara Houston—and they have a very tasty, sustainable thing going on in that cargo container. They're serving fresh, line-caught local fish that's approved by Ocean Wise (a Vancouver Aquarium conservation program that helps restaurants and their customers make environmentally friendly seafood choices), and they're getting a lot of other things right on the sustainability ledger.

Compostable or recyclable are the buzzwords here, from the bamboo cutlery and the recycled newspapers used to wrap the food (picking up my packet takes me back to buying fish from the corner "chippy" in England) to the green roof on their establishment, which sprouts thick, fleshy-leaved sedums that help to cool the inner cooking sanctum.

Only the name is Dr. Seuss, so it's a relief to find that green eggs and ham never made it onto the menu. Really, order anything here and you'll love it. The fish used for fish and chips is moist within its crispy tempura batter. The coleslaw is alive with flavour. The chips, made with Kennebec potatoes, are "hand cut and twice fried" to crispy perfection. Instead of the typical English mushy peas, you can go the healthy and delicious mushy-edamame route. And real foodies can go one step further: this place is known for its tempura-battered pickles with tartar sauce for dipping (I admit to not having gone there yet).

For me, the highlight is the fish wrap known as a "tacone." It's a big, soft tortilla stuffed with fish (barbecued wild salmon, seared albacore tuna or barbecued Fanny Bay oysters), sweet-smoked chili-adobo sauce, pea shoots and lemon-pickled onions. A tacone, along with a little tub of mushy edamame and a cup of their very good chai, made with soy milk, has been known to sustain me through many a writing deadline.

Of course, the best experience is to eat your food right there on the dock, looking at the fishboats and, in summer, the luxury yachts moored in the harbour. There's always a good mix of people doing just that, mostly locals but also tourists who've taken a lucky turn in their wanderings, and the cosiness of the seating provided means conversations are easily struck up between diners.

One Fish, Two Fish is the partners' latest venture. It's a small, open cart located on the ground floor of historic Market Square (between lower Pandora and Johnson streets), where there is always a big simmering pot of their popular Pacific Rim Chowder, loaded with sweet garlicky whitefish confit, corn and the zingy flavourings of chipotle and coconut, on offer. Often there are concerts or other events in the square (such as the 50 tuba players who perform together every December), which can make for a memorable street-food lunch experience.

Share Organics

Susan Tychie dropped by my house herself with a hamper brimming with fruit and veg. Normally, her produce is delivered by one of her five helpers on Tuesday or Wednesday by bicycle or a car booked through the fuel-efficient Victoria Car Share Co-op.

Susan had just returned from a "once-in-a-lifetime holiday" with her children in Spain, yet her jet lag was not noticeable, particularly when she started to tell me about the produce she'd brought. The winter months are, not surprisingly, her busiest. The farmers' markets have closed up and gardens are less productive, so she gets a lot of calls on grey days from folks like me seeking some inspiration in the kitchen.

Susan supports farmers who use organic growing methods and maintains a "local first" policy, importing from the mainland or California only when she has to. Today she's brought me white

Kennebec potatoes, McIntosh apples, oranges, lemons, kiwis, Bosc pears, a big bunch of bananas, hearty Lacinato kale, beets, onions, romaine lettuce and a bag of oyster mushrooms.

I follow her suggestions of sautéeing the onions until caramelized, then laying the kale over top to wilt and finally drizzling the combination with a little balsamic vinegar; sautéeing the oyster mushrooms and mashing the potatoes with a whole head of roasted garlic. Finally, I grill some sole, cut up the fruit for an easy dessert and, presto, a healthy dinner is on the table.

It's always fun to create meals from brown-box delivery programs. I'm a big fan of Susan's Share Organics because the produce is fresh and mainly local,

Sandwich board for Sooke's dynamic ALM Organic Farm.

she offers a good range of add-on products (from Cowichan Bay Farm chicken to Silk Road teas and Nature's Path cereals) and her heart is in the right place.

A former employee of Victoria's Nature's Fare health food store, she began her own business as a food co-operative serving a handful of families. It evolved from there into a weekly box program for 140 singles and families throughout Victoria. Susan says she caters mainly to young families and university students.

Share Organics' produce comes from well-regarded local organic growers, such as Mary Alice Johnson of Sooke's ALM Farm, Heather and Lemont of Saanichton's Northbrook Farm, Brian Hughes of Deep Cove's Kildarra Farm and Violet Leclair of Metchosin's Bentback Farms. Susan says she enjoys "connecting with the farmers." She loves it when the veggies arrive at her own door to be sorted into the boxes and tells me, "Often I'll get lettuce bouquets so beautiful you could walk down the aisle with them!" The romaine she's brought me is just such a bouquet.

With her commitment to "be as green as possible and sell as reasonably as possible," Susan is making a big impact on the health of many local families. Check out her website's virtual farm tours, which instantly connect customers with the farmers who grow their food.

 *Stage*

You might not agree, but when a chef offers to give you a tour of his back of house, that's a good sign in my book because it shows confidence. So when George Szasz of Stage invited me "downstairs" just before service (i.e., when the cooks are in full flight and one has to be alert to keep from banging into someone carrying a hot pot of duck confit), I followed him with interest.

Bread was being mixed in the Hobart (the restaurant makes some of its bread and the rest comes from Cliff Leir (see Fol Epi), and there were vast trays of gnocchi and squash prepped for a new menu item: squash gnocchi with sage and Marcona almond brown butter. How divine will that be? There were also sausage machines at the ready to make the fresh sausages and terrines for which Stage is known.

George tells me that charcuterie is in his blood as both his Hungarian father and grandfather worked for the Pick Salami Factory in Szeged, Hungary— "the largest in the world at that time." After immigrating to Canada, his parents ran Szasz Deli in Vancouver. Recently, the family discovered George's grandfather's own recipes for cured sausage, with their priceless ratios of meat to fat to seasoning to sodium nitrate. George has had them translated from Hungarian and is working to replicate sausages with names like Spinata Romano—"a take on Genoa sausage but with more heat to it."

"Even before I could afford a commercial sausage-stuffing machine, I was working with a domestic one and a piping bag," says George. I'm impressed to see that everything is made from scratch here: farmer's sausage, salami, duck prosciutto, terrines, lamb merguez sausage and chicken-liver parfait (the latter two being firm favourites of mine—and I'm certain the rest would be as well if I ate pork!).

The walk-in fridge is a match for the one at the Brasserie L'École, and though the back of house here is small (including the partially open kitchen and dishwashing area upstairs), it is clearly an immaculate, efficient set-up. From it great things happen, and George is quick to praise his staff for that, "I have such good people here. I try to give back as much as I can, and it's an incredible feeling to watch them grow and glow."

I meet Jamie Major (formerly of the Noodle Box, Paprika and Pescatore's) and Alison Beitz (ex-Brasserie L'École) who are partners in the kitchen and also in real life. There is a calm synchronicity in the kitchen here: Jamie is busy checking a pot of trimmed lamb-shoulder sausage that's simmering in seasoned duck fat and Alison is portioning rockfish just in from Albion Fisheries, but they graciously take time to chat and answer my questions.

"It comes down to pride in what you do and how you do it."

— George Szasz

George had a whole lamb brought in the day before "to keep everyone's butchery skills fresh," and he tells me that generally everything arrives whole—fishes, pigs, et al. "It comes down to pride in what you do and how you do it," he says. "It wouldn't be fair not to [do it this way]—to my upbringing, to the profession, to the customers."

The charcuterie, though a major feature here, is really only one part of a small plates menu that includes a stellar cheese program, vegetarian plates such as the popular grilled Halloumi cheese with local tomatoes and herb vinaigrette, fish dishes like the crispy fried local octopus and lemon, and meat and poultry stars like the duck confit with caramelized caraway cabbage and wine syrup and chicken curry with grilled pappadum and house chutney.

And, of course, centre stage at Stage is the wine bar, which is made from a piece of the old Mayfair bowling lanes. The bar is brilliantly run in the evenings by Steven Quigley, an affable Irishman who has good service down to an art form. The pithy wine menu is chosen to match the restaurant's small plates by sommelier Marlisa Beadle and George's wife and front-of-house doyenne, Linda Szasz (formerly of Bishop's in Vancouver). "They both have excellent palates," says George.

I have always liked the fact that everything posted on the chalkboards is open for drinking by the glass in three-ounce or five-ounce quantities, which really makes it possible to create one's own wine flight paired to the dishes you're trying—and I trust Steven's advice with those pairings.

Stage, of course, is a new venture for George and Linda. They ran the very successful Paprika bistro in Oak Bay's Estevan Village for 10 years, and they have now handed it over to chef Anna Hunt, who trained under George and who is also the daughter of Brian Murray (see Victoria Spirits).

Fernwood's Neighbourhood Residential Group "kept bugging us about the vacant space in the heart of the village, so Linda and I finally had a couple of drinks and decided to go for it," laughs George. Their concept for a small-plates wine bar has turned out to be a great move, because more and more people are looking for a chic, high-quality food and wine experience without having to break the bank.

George and Linda, and their two daughters, live just down the street from Stage, so they can walk to work. And "having such a great team there" means they are able to plan a family holiday to Europe this year. George says he's excited to go away for a time—"to get back deep into the food again"—and says we can expect some fabulous new small-plate creations when he returns.

Travel with Taste Tours

When Kathy McAree was in her teens, she once asked her grandmother, "How do I know how to make all these things?" Her grandmother replied, "When you were younger, you watched your mother in the kitchen like a hawk." Kathy's grandparents owned a restaurant in her native Winnipeg, giving her early exposure to the foodie life.

Owner Kathy McAree checks for clarity during a Travel with Taste tour.

Kathy was working as an account representative for Kellogg Canada when she decided to take a break and do some travelling. Her wanderings took her to Ecuador, Australia, New Zealand, Las Vegas and Vail, but it was a hands-on cooking vacation on the Amalfi Coast that ended up changing her career. She knew then and there that she wanted to offer her own culinary tours.

A keen gastronome, Kathy is now sharing her love of good food and wine with Vancouver Island locals and tourists through her Travel with Taste Tours. These tours range from a seven-hour wine tasting in the Cowichan Valley to day-long "behind the scenes" culinary tours on Saltspring Island to week-long itineraries that include private meetings with chefs, cooking classes, mushroom foraging, six-course meals in Relais & Châteaux dining rooms, hands-on cooking classes and visits to interesting farms, cheesemaking operations and bakeries. (Relais & Châteaux is an association of luxurious, privately owned hotels and restaurants in 51 countries around the world.) Says Kathy, "I want my clients to leave thinking Vancouver Island is an amazing place for culinary delights."

It's not difficult to be impressed on one of Kathy's intimate tours. Taking groups of 4 to 44 participants at a time, she does all the driving and organizing. Her clients can literally sit back and enjoy themselves, without having to worry about how many glasses of wine they sample, or where their next meal is coming from. Working closely with many of Vancouver Island's fine food producers and purveyors such as Hilary's Cheese Company, Spinnakers,

Brasserie L'École, Marley Farm Winery, Salt Spring Vineyards, Hastings House and Sooke Harbour House—to name only a few—Kathy has created the kinds of indulgent itineraries that foodies from across the planet are lining up to sample.

In recent years, Kathy has introduced Saturday walking tours for foodies in downtown Victoria. She'll take you to hidden gems, including a legendary bakery and historic chocolatier, and there are exclusive tastings at a tea merchant and wine shop. Kathy and a gaggle of foodies (her tours attract both visitors and locals) can often be seen having "way too much fun" on the streets of Victoria.

Zambri's

It's four o'clock and Zambri's restaurant is between sets. Lunch has concluded and dinner is on the horizon. The owners, siblings Peter and Jo Zambri, and their staff have a short intermission, but nobody's sipping champagne. Instead, the restaurant is fully cleaned, dinner is prepped, candles are set out on the tables and flowers and fruits are arranged. Before the curtain goes up, Peter pours two glasses of Friuli-Venezia Giulia wine, hands me one and invites me into the kitchen.

It is always an honour to be taken behind the scenes. As I follow Peter, his phone rings. Without missing a step, he banters a little with chef Edward Tuson of Sooke Harbour House while he leads me to a section devoted to the evening's antipasti. In immaculate stainless steel containers are roasted red peppers; mushrooms marinated in olive oil, balsamic vinegar, carrots and basil; marinated Kalamata olives; red Italian onions roasted cut-side down in balsamic vinegar, olive oil, salt and pepper; and celery sticks with Gorgonzola and mascarpone. They will be added to house-made meats and wonderful cheeses from Ottavio's to comprise the antipasti platters for which Zambri's is known.

The previous Sunday, Peter took delivery of a 200-pound pig from Andrei Fedorov of Mon Plaisir Farm in Sooke. He'd spent the day preparing pancetta from the belly, *coppa* from the neck,

 even *fromage de tête*. A highly regarded chef who is also a talented butcher, Peter takes pride in using every part of the animal. He bemoans the absence of traditional salami-making here, and is determined to keep making his own and challenging himself to "always learn."

Peter's been cooking all his life. He effectively started his professional career as a teenager when, with his buddy Rob, he operated a catering business out of his mother's basement in Toronto. It's a career that has taken him from cooking stints in Italy, to Toronto's Windsor Arms Hotel, Vancouver's Wedgewood Hotel, Chateau Whistler and Sooke Harbour House (it was Peter who hired Edward Tuson, and the two are good friends). At Sooke Harbour House, Peter was the chef, but he also gardened and developed the inn's highly efficient organic composting system. When the concept for Zambri's restaurant came together in 2000, it was the culmination of Peter and Jo's lifelong commitment to serving good food, simply prepared.

Peter is a great supporter of local organic vegetable producers, including Mary Alice Johnson of ALM Farm, Dave Wiebe of Cowichan Valley Organic Farm, Michael Ableman of Foxglove Farm and Candace Thompson of

Co-owners and siblings Jo and Peter Zambri on the line at Zambri's, voted best casual restaurant in 2005 by Vancouver *magazine*.

Eagle Paws Organics. He tells me he particularly loves the summertime, when he can buy everything locally. Several island vineyards are represented on the select wine list: Blue Grouse, Alderlea and Venturi Schulze. I'm impressed that Peter sees the restaurant as a place not only to feed people, but also to educate them about the benefits of local, seasonal and, as much as possible, organic cooking. This is a man whose food ethic I have always admired. Though many will not know this, he cooks a free lunch on Saturdays for Moss Street Market vendors from their leftover produce.

The night before I visited Peter in his kitchen, I attended a general meeting and special dinner for Vancouver Island's Slow Food convivium, which was held at Zambri's. The dinner began with lasagna made with local organic winter broccoli, was followed by Cowichan Bay Farm chicken involtini with Saltspring Island Cheese Company's truffled goat's milk cheese *fonduta* and finished with Poplar Grove blue-cheese semifreddo with an Alderlea Hearth (port) glaze and an Italian anise cookie. The convivium's membership includes some of the most gifted island chefs, and it is a mark of Peter's own ability and his complete lack of pretension that he not only pleases the palates of so auspicious a group, but also has fun with it. Says Peter, "I love to cook, especially for people who are happy and enjoying themselves." With his cooking, what's not to enjoy?

"I love to cook, especially for people who are happy and enjoying themselves."

—Peter Zambri

SAANICH /
BRENTWOOD BAY

Dragonfly Hill Vineyard

In addition to its two acres of Ortega, Schönburger and Pinot Auxerrois grapes, Dragonfly Hill farm grows blackcurrants and various nuts. "The squirrels go crazy for the nuts, but then they can't remember where they buried them," laughs owner and vintner Carol Wallace, "so we have lots of little unexpected nut trees popping up in the spring."

The nuts aren't being marketed yet, while Carol "concentrates on my winemaking," but every so often, local chefs will persuade her to leave a bag of walnuts or hazelnuts on her back step for them. And then there are the kiwis that Carol incorporates into her bumbleberry dessert wine, which have also been requested by chefs. She is always obliging.

When Carol acquired the historic 13.5-acre farm in 1993 (it was an apple orchard a hundred years ago, then a strawberry farm), "everyone gave me advice about what I should be planting." Carol was determined to grow "something that was neither prickly nor back-breaking." Her stepfather, who grows grapes in southern Ontario, told her, "You can grow grapes here," and she agreed.

So she set to work researching the prospect of a vineyard and "read the entire Duncan Project report," a government-sponsored effort to determine which grapes would really grow well in these parts. Taking her direction from "what ripened when," she settled on Ortega and Pinot Auxerrois, which ripen at about the same time, and launched the first commercial vineyard in Saanich.

"The Schönburger was a mistake that's worked out well," she tells me. When the cuttings arrived for the other varietals, 12 turned out to be Schönburger, but "they're great backyard grapes because you can eat them and make a jug of wine." (That is, if there are any left. Carol has a daughter who "sneaks out to the vineyard and loves eating big bowls of them.") Over the years, Carol has propagated thousands of Schönburger vines for other vineyards all over the island.

Carol is happiest when she's working in the vineyard. She has planted her vines "from the height of my waist, and [I] keep them no taller than the height of my outstretched arm, and the rows are wide enough to accommodate my big John Deere tractor." She follows sustainable growing practices, using no herbicides or pesticides. Instead, she sprays a foliar feed of "goodies like kelp extract, Epsom salt, sulphur and zinc to keep the vines happy. If they're stressed, they become susceptible to mildew." She puts a minimal amount of manure from her sheep at the base of the vines and covers it with straw ("We never need to weed!").

Effervescent owner and vintner Carol Wallace in her stockroom at Dragonfly Hill Vineyard.

Dragonfly Hill also produces a Merlot/Cabernet blend using grapes from Oliver's Stonequail Vineyard and a Chardonnay using grapes from Oliver's Osprey Vineyard. The red came about as a result of her federal government colleagues, on hearing she was going to start a vineyard, asking, "What's your red?" Many simply expected that, because it was a popular quaff, she'd also make a Chardonnay and she obliged. And then there are her estate-grown wines, of which Carol is justly proud.

The bumbleberry dessert wine—"a mix of Saanich Peninsula berries and other fruits such as my kiwis, apples, rhubarb and figs"— is a nod to "Gwen's fabulous bumbleberry pie [that would be Gwen who ran the Viteway restaurant on West Saanich Road several decades ago]." It was first released in the fall of 2008, and, let's be frank, it got me sweetly through many long nights of writing this edition of *An Edible Journey*.

Carol's other pride and joy has yet to be grown and bottled, but I can see her heart is in La Belle (Dutch for dragonfly), the early-ripening red Valentine Blattner cross that she has been developing with Salt Spring Vineyards' winemaker Paul Troop. "We have 200 plants out there ready to put in the ground," she tells me wistfully when I visit her in January when the vineyard is under a foot of snow.

Carol's friend and neighbour, former Orcas Island organic farmer Ianine Taylor, joins us for a cup of tea. Ianine is working with Carol to market the wines and they hope to have a tasting room up and running next season. The two are keen advocates for "locals supporting locals" and often merge the produce from their gardens with seafood from Brentwood Bay to create "fantastic five-mile-diet feasts."

Fruit Trees & More

I began 2009 eating tangelo marmalade on toast, noteworthy not only because it was delicious but because it was made by Bob Duncan and his family from tangelos he'd grown on the Saanich Peninsula. I'm not talking about fruit from a plant long ago smuggled into the area from California or Israel or some other prized citrus-growing region, but a tangelo vine that was grown from a seedling grafted onto a trifoliate orange root stock by a local hobby horticulturalist. Yes, the climate is changing and some exotic fruits are being grown successfully in our midst!

When Duncan invited me to tour his .75-acre plot in Saanich on the last day of December, there were still six inches of snow on the ground, but—amazingly to me—there was fruit on some of the vines. Having heard that this retired entomologist was successfully growing *lemons* in what can hardly be considered a Mediterranean climate was sufficient to pique my interest. What I didn't expect, however, were the limes, mandarins, mandalos (a cross between mandarin and grapefruit), grapefruits, navel oranges, pomegranates, kumquats, loquats, kiwis, olives and figs. And I was not at all prepared for the bananas!

In the exotic fruit salad that is Bob and Verna Duncan's garden, we began to consider the figs. Bob chose the Desert King variety because "it produces a large *breba* crop," the early harvest that usually comes in August. Bob tells me, "When we have an exceptionally warm summer, then we also get a later main crop. If the current warming trends continue, maybe we'll always get a [fruit-bearing] main crop." But this year the summer was not warm enough so there are undersized, underripe figs from the main crop left clinging to bare winter branches.

On his house's western wall is a "Kalamata-type" olive tree, which Bob grew from a seedling. I tell him about the olive trees recently planted by Dave Godfrey in Glenora, and ask if there's a chance we'll see olive oil in this region some day. He feels olives are "still in the experimental phase," but he's in touch with several people who are moving the dream of an olive-growing industry forward.

Next to the olive tree is an apricot tree and there are also several apricot trees under cover in the garden. Apricots are Bob's favourite fruit, but he says there's a reason why "it's traditionally an Osoyoos crop—the plants need to be kept dry." His trees produce some 1,000 apricots each, proving that ideal conditions can be created this far from the Okanagan desert.

The cold frame's doors are open for my visit. I've seen the famous *orangerie* in Paris, but not even that compares with the rustic charm of Bob's tiny, hand-built, unheated cold frame with its eye-popping oranges, grapefruit and kumquat trees. Heat is introduced only if the interior temperature drops below freezing, but otherwise a simple irrigation system is the only intervention.

Bob tells me that the fruit has to be protected from freezing because "the citrus tree is completely unlike fruits we Northerners are accustomed to in that they carry their fruit through the winter. And the fruit holds onto the tree up to a year after it ripens. So, instead of storing it in the fridge, we store it on the tree, and it actually gets sweeter the longer it hangs there."

As we tramp around under the 20-year-old kiwi vines (five female and one male vine ensure "an incredible production of some 1,000 fruits including a yellow-fleshed variety"), I ask Bob about his speaking engagements. He is in demand to address garden clubs, agricultural societies and research stations across the globe; he had recently returned from New Zealand and was about to depart for Israel. His farm is also a big hit during the annual North Saanich Flavour Trail in August. Because "there is no history of any of this [the citrus plants] growing here, this place gets people's attention, that's for sure."

Bob has some 200 varieties of apples and pears planted "according to different systems," which means he can demonstrate to people who buy his propagated fruit trees "the different training systems that make it possible to achieve high-quality, high-yield crops from small spaces." I make a mental note to install a lemon tree on my balcony.

While Bob and Verna aim to "grow as great a diversity of temperate, Mediterranean and sub-tropical fruits as the local climatic conditions can sustain without extraordinary inputs of energy to heat them," lemons and limes may become their stock in trade. And how welcome that would be to a populace used to buying these citrus fruits only after they've travelled great distances from California or Mexico.

So when we finally arrive at the lemons, I feel I am looking at a crop that could one day (certainly if global warming continues) be considered indigenous. Against a south-facing wall at the back of the garden is a lemon tree with fruit at all stages of development.

Bob has a Remay cover that he can hang over the tree if it freezes and there is a small string of Christmas lights, "not for decoration, but to provide just enough heat to prevent the fruit from freezing." A Plexiglas overhang "ensures the plants are 10 per cent warmer when the sun shines." And that's all the special treatment these fruits receive. Unlike sweet citrus fruits, the more acidic lemons and limes don't require high temperatures to grow.

Lemons have always been absent from the kitchen at Sooke Harbour House, precisely because they—and so many other foods that we take for granted because they can be shipped to us—are not indigenous to this area. But that may change some day because I have it on good authority that the inn's gardeners have paid a visit to the Duncans.

Who would have guessed that we would be able to grow lemons in Lotus Land? Or, as Bob Duncan puts it, "There is a bit of a silver lining to climate change."

Marley Farm Winery

For me, there is always something magical about driving out to the Saanich Peninsula, and I have many fond memories of accompanying painter Cynthia Cooper on her early-morning forays to photograph sleepy country scenes "when the light is filtering." This morning, I'm alone and enjoying the "mists and mellow fruitfulness" of late autumn. I have an appointment with Beverly Marley, doyenne of a hugely fun and colourful boutique winery that she runs from her 47-acre homestead in the Mount Newton Valley.

As I pull in, a worker is quietly pruning the vines, preparing them for their long winter slumber. Beverly's pet pigeons flutter about. A bevy of ducks waddles past. It's a bucolic scene and a well-deserved one. In 1975, Beverly and her former husband travelled a great distance from political unrest in Jamaica to start their new life in Canada, a country they chose for its freedom and safety. One day, they attended a meeting of the Vancouver Island Grape Growers Association about family wineries and, right then and there, they decided to plant grapes.

It helped that Beverly had always loved to make fruit wines and dandelion wine. They planted five acres of Ortega, Pinot Grigio and Pinot Noir grapes in 2000 and by 2003, with help from consulting Okanagan winemaker Eric von Krosigk, were bottling their own grapes. Eric found a higher mineral content in the soil here than in the Okanagan—a distinctive element of this region's *terroir*.

Marley Farm Winery uses no chemicals. They spray rigorously with an organic kelp solution and make their own compost to continually improve the soil. Their sheep "mow" and fertilize the fields. As Beverly puts it, they aren't trying to be "holier than thou"; they just want to do things the way they believe is right. "We farm with a conscience. When my grandchildren take over, this land is going to be even better than when we found it."

She leads me into the tasting room and gift shop, which are run by her daughter-in-law, Danielle. As reggae music sets the tone, the promise of "a kaleidoscope of flavours and bouquets" is gloriously fulfilled. On pour today is the clean and fresh Pinot Grigio; as well as Novine White, the estate-grown blend of Pinot Grigio and Ortega; Kiwi, with its sweet aromas of apricot, lemon zest, apple and kiwi and smooth, full finish; and Blackberry Gold, the harvest-style wine that I serve as port after dinner. Beverly makes wine from local kiwis, rhubarb, quinces, pears, gooseberries and many other fruits. She smiles and tells me, "Every time you come here, you'll get a taste sensation you've never had in your life."

Yet there are more sensations than just great wines here because vinegars have always fascinated Beverly. Thanks to an early experiment with grapes that

produced "awful wine but fabulous vinegar," she is now making lively blueberry, bumbleberry, kiwi and peach vinegars. She tells me they're actually harder to make than wine.

Depending on the day you visit, you may also get to participate in one of the Marleys' much-anticipated community events: the Kiwi Squeeze gets everyone in on the fruit-squeezing process; at Ewe Hoo, sheep-shearing, wool-spinning and felt-making are demonstrated; and Summer Frolic features an exciting horse-driving competition, a sport that is a great passion of Beverly's. She says she gets a lot of pleasure from "people who have tasted the great wines of the world, then try something like my kiwi wine and love it," but she also loves sharing the farm life with children through these community events.

In the early fall, I attended Grape Notes at Marley Farm, an exuberant annual event featuring good eats and dancing that raises funds for the local hospital. On another evening in summertime, on long communal tables in their courtyard, Beverly presented a sumptuous Jamaican feast to friends and suppliers. The estate wines flowed and the steel drums played reggae long into the night. It was a great celebration of local, seasonal food and wine and an impressive benchmark of generosity.

When the Marleys started the winery, they named it Carriage Hill Estate Winery, but were later persuaded by *National Post* wine writer Michael Vaughan to change it to reflect their roots and to honour Beverly's former cousin-in-law, the legendary reggae mon Bob Marley. And nothing rings truer here at Marley Farm Winery than the words he sang, "Let's get together and feel all right."

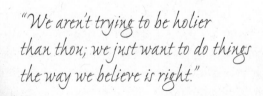

"We aren't trying to be holier than thou; we just want to do things the way we believe is right."

— Beverly Marley

Mount Newton Cottage

Mount Newton Cottage is simply the most charming place to stay during one's Saanich/Brentwood Bay peregrinations. A self-contained suite for two people on the top floor of a heritage home with views of Tod Inlet, it is the perfect respite at the end of a day spent trawling the farmgates and sampling the wines and spirits of this bucolic region.

Mount Newton Cottage is owned by David Crone and Jenny Cameron, personal chef, cooking instructor and co-author (with her mother, Noël Richardson of nearby Ravenhill Herb Farm) of *Herbal Celebrations* (Whitecap Books, 2000). Jenny brings to the styling of the bed and breakfast suite and her "made to order" breakfasts a lifetime immersed in farming and cooking. She is a graduate of Dubrulle culinary school who did "an informal apprenticeship" at the renowned Deep Cove Chalet in North Saanich. She has travelled extensively in Europe, which gave her "a passion for a variety of cultures and foods," but she most credits "life at my parents' farm, which nurtured my love of the fresh, local herbs that play a major role in my cooking."

Jenny and David—whose acting skills I heartily enjoyed in the magical *A Midsummer Night's Dream* that was performed at Ravenhill Farm one summer—are congenial and relaxed hosts. In fact, as you lay your head down on the comfy bed, listening to nothing more than the nature that surrounds you, you may indeed be induced into having your own midsummer night's dream.

SeaGrille at Brentwood Bay Lodge

Entering the foyer, one is instantly captivated by the soaring West Coast architecture that demands that nature be let inside. Large windows draw the eyes across the room to the charming bay (which I'm later told is the deepest fjord in British Columbia) with its fishboats and pleasure boats. Even in the guest rooms, the sense of being surrounded by the lushness of the outdoors is ever-present. Though the rooms are luxurious, I found myself regularly looking outside, so as not to miss any wildlife or any shimmer of light on the bay.

The background of superb luxury in the rooms, the world-class spa and kayaks at the ready for relaxation and recreation is, to me, really just a foil for the dining experience ahead. While one can dine pretty well in the lodge's pub and on its casual summertime deck, it is the newly named SeaGrille dining room that beckons foodies.

Edible journeys—indeed, my own edible arrivals—don't always coincide with traditional dinner hours, but I was readily accommodated for dinner at 3:00 p.m. so that I could do another interview in Victoria at 6:00 p.m. I'd already experienced the pub food in summer: mimosas and chicken wraps on the deck made me feel as though I was on vacation.

The dining room, just after a particularly busy winter holiday season, is calm and elegant, and I welcome the chance to spend time with executive chef Peter Whatmough and sommelier Benjamin Howard. Peter says the two "make a really good team," and that becomes evident throughout the service, although their backgrounds couldn't be more different.

Peter knew he was interested in cooking at age 14 when he was working as a dishwasher in Oakville, Ontario, and would "watch the chefs on the line, and liked what I saw." That was back in the days when you could transfer directly from high school to George Brown College's culinary program. At age 16, Peter was on his way.

He apprenticed at the Four Seasons Inn on the Park in Toronto, then worked mainly as a "fix-it guy," designing and redesigning kitchens for some top Calgary and Victoria eateries. He worked on contract, most recently helping to establish the kitchens of Catch and Wildwood in Calgary. Finally, he moved his family to Victoria, where he "was able to take a couple of years off" before bringing his hefty 25 years of French and Italian fine-dining experience to SeaGrille in August 2008.

Benjamin was a performer with Cirque du Soleil, although that amazing feat is getting slightly ahead of his story. He was born in Kelowna, where, as he was growing up, "the Okanagan wine industry started to get its legs." He "[fell] in love with wine" working as a server at Belvedere in Calgary, Emerald

Lake Lodge in Field, British Columbia, and Hastings House on Saltspring Island, and is very excited to be working at SeaGrille, where "we're right in the nucleus of the Vancouver Island wine scene, and we have such a beautiful dining room in which to enjoy it."

Like any Vancouver Island restaurant worth its salt, SeaGrille is paying attention to the importance of sourcing local foodstuffs. Peter works with several local growers through Saanich Organics; brings duck and chicken in from Cowichan Bay; mussels (and lamb when it's available) from Saltspring Island; oysters from several bays along Vancouver Island's coastline (and sometimes an octopus!); and he relies on James from Marconi Mushrooms who "can get anything locally but also things like fresh white truffles from Alba, Italy." He hasn't found a local supplier of venison "as good as Brag Creek in Alberta," and when I have the chance to taste the grass-fed specimen, I have to admit it's some of the best I've eaten.

I thoroughly enjoy SeaGrille's monthly tasting menu. At $55, it is well priced and I'm intrigued to find that, while the first four courses are prescribed, diners can select from any dessert item. That's about enough choice for me when my main purpose is to relax and appreciate the art and science of the kitchen.

Organic garden greens with Golden Delicious apple slices, Stilton and pecans and a pear-pancetta vinaigrette are matched with a fruity Wild Goose Blanc de Noirs, a wine that Benjamin describes accurately as "having more character than the average BC blush." A soup of roasted pumpkin warmed with nutmeg, cinnamon and cloves, and served with generous Gruyère shavings, a drizzle of white truffle oil and fresh thyme is served in a bowl the size of a pudding basin, cleverly designed to slant toward the diner and give its contents great presence. The wine pairing, Lake Breeze's Pinot Blanc, has a fresh acidity that perfectly complements the soup and rich cheese.

The pan-seared sablefish that follows on a bed of lentils, with portobello mushrooms, chanterelles, shiitakes and roasted root vegetables presented both whole and puréed, is divine. The local Averill Creek Pinot Noir is, as Benjamin puts it, "all about the dirt." It goes well with the oily fish, the puréed beets and the overall earthiness of the dish. And I'm delighted to hear the word "dirt" used with refreshing lack of pretense (I'm afraid I'm getting a bit cynical about everything coming from this or that *terroir*).

Another great wine match by Benjamin is from nearby Chalet Estate Winery. Served with the venison course, it's a Cabernet/Merlot blend that definitely has "enough structure to stand up to the gamey meat."

Those with more resistance might have concluded this perfectly cooked and presented meal with a light sorbet, but I was inspired to try one of Peter's signature desserts: the Phyllo Dream. Again an oversized bowl arrived, this time with an elegant swirl of spun sugar and a baked phyllo pouch containing banana, hazelnuts and white chocolate. A little Elephant Island Framboise was drizzled around the edges, and a pleasingly tart Cape gooseberry finished the dish. Almost! A glass of Quail's Gate Late Harvest Optima, with its lovely apricot and peach nose and finish, made this dessert experience one to savour and remember.

Victoria Spirits

According to me but more significantly according to Jim Murray, author of *Jim Murray's Whisky Bible 2008*, Victoria Gin is "the best gin in the world." Who knew it would be made by an affable doctor and his microbiologist son in a bucolic vineyard in Saanich? And who knew that this perfectly balanced botanical elixir would have so stirring an effect that the pair is now racing to keep pace with demand?

I meet Dr. Brian Murray (no relation to the aforementioned author) at the Victoria Spirits distillery after he's finished his rounds at the local youth correctional facility (he also works as a general practitioner in town), and he leads me into the operation's nerve centre. The shiny copper-and-stainless-steel Müller still, which he had sent from Germany last July, appears to be an alchemist's dream machine. It looks very impressive, but how does it work?

It turns out that part is even more impressive, although I think it's also important to recognize that the recipe and the distillers are just as intrinsic to creating a perfect, unique gin. I start to understand the process when I relate it to making an espresso on my Cimbali: it's definitely part quality product, part experienced barista and part immaculately clean and fully functioning machine.

Owner Brian Murray and the stunning Müller still used to make Victoria Gin.

The gin process begins when a brew of ethanol, "our fabulous well water" and mostly certified organic botanicals—including lovelies like star anise, lemon peel, coriander, angelica, rose petals and, of course, juniper berries—is poured into a vast stainless pot that operates like a double-boiler (it's wood-fired from beneath).

Brian explains to me that, since the boiling point for alcohol is lower than for water, the alcohol boils off into the "hat," a big round contraption on top of the still. Inside, the alcohol condenses and it's ultimately pushed through a pipe into another condenser. The operator can control the rate at which the alcohol condenses before it is recycled through the process until it reaches 80°C. At that point, the liquid shoots over to the cooling column.

It's now 88 per cent alcohol and ready to be collected in a stainless steel bucket, then blended, according to the distiller's taste, with gin that has been stored from previous distillations. The 2,500-litre storage tank in one corner of the distillery is one large jug o' juice! The whole process takes about 2.5 hours, and Brian tells me that he and his son, Peter Hunt, can produce 450 bottles "in a long, 10-hour day."

Brian launched Victoria Gin in the Fairmont Empress Hotel's Bengal Lounge in the spring of 2008 and was very pleased with the response. Almost immediately 75 British Columbia liquor stores ordered the spirit, followed by Alberta stores. "We began to produce whole pallets of bottles very quickly," Brian tells me. And it looks as though that will only increase after a huge launch on Victoria Day, 2009, in Toronto. Though he's tickled by the popularity of the spirit, Brian says, "We had a pretty good idea that it would do well."

Brian's son Peter, who now has "a substantial history making our gin and has become passionate about it," is moving from Vancouver to concentrate on the distillery. The family has another foodie root in the Victoria community. Daughter Anna Hunt has recently taken over the kitchen at Paprika in Oak Bay's Estevan Village, and she's been known to concoct delicacies like venison crusted with the same botanicals used for Victoria Gin.

And speaking of those botanicals, 11 are used in Victoria Gin but one is a "secret ingredient" that I couldn't guess and, determined though I was, I couldn't get Brian to reveal it. This is what he does say, with a knowing smile, "If you think about the flavours, you can pretty well pick out any of the botanicals." Sure, maybe 10 of them. Let me know if you can guess the elusive one!

"If you think about the flavours, you can pretty well pick out any of the botanicals."

—Dr. Brian Murray

METCHOSIN

 *The Broken Paddle*

I was delighted some three years ago when a small coffee shop opened within walking distance of the Metchosin Farmers' Market. From May through October, my Sunday mornings were suddenly complete: I could stop in for a nice coffee or a house-brewed chai latte and a freshly baked scone before heading to the market.

Today, I've come out mid-week and out-of-season to chat with owner Shannon Meeker, a tree-planter-turned-chef who loves her café so much that "when the time comes, they'll have to bury me out back." She had been cooking for people with special diets in the health care field, including a stint teaching cooking for the Canadian Diabetes Association. When there were labour cuts in that industry, and she lost her staff, she started to think about doing something on her own.

Broken Paddle owner Shannon Meeker and some of her fresh baking.

"I wanted to put together a place where I could be creative and focus on small-batch, low-sugar baking," Shannon tells me, "and I wanted to be outside of the city and create somewhere for me and my daughter to work together." Her 15-year-old daughter, Brigit, helps in the café, but often Shannon is on her own, baking, making great coffees and dishing out local banter with her neighbours in "this very welcoming community." Even before she opened the door, Shannon was confident that "if the community wanted it, they would come," and she was right.

Her lovely date squares, scones, muffins and cookies are well received, as are her Broken Eggers, a baked egg on an English muffin with cheese, ham and green onion. She tells me that the café's signature breakfast was invented one morning when "a young man came in and asked for eggs. I told him if he had a couple of minutes, I'd whip something up for him." He loved it, and the Broken Egger became a fixture on the menu.

I've always worried that there was a sad story behind the broken paddle in the name of Shannon's café, but it's quite the opposite. She's a canoeist who simply liked the name and had a couple of paddles on hand to use in the shop's decor. In fact, Shannon credits paddling with "saving me. Before I started the shop, I quit smoking and got happy." She loves the country life and spends her time off riding her horse or paddling her canoe.

And we all know how I spend my time off: sipping coffee at cosy little spots like Shannon's Broken Paddle, with its own happy culture of local art and local people.

"I wanted to be outside of the city and create somewhere for me and my daughter to work together."

— Shannon Meeker

Owner Lynda Dowling crouches in her field of lavender at Happy Valley Lavender and Herb Farm.

Happy Valley
Lavender and Herb Farm

Lynda Dowling always knew she would farm on Happy Valley Road: her property originally belonged to her grandmother and she used to spend summers there. When Lynda was very young, her grandmother had told her, "There will be a piece of land here for you."

Lynda, her husband, Michael, and their children moved onto the property in 1986 and turned it into a little corner of Provence. On one acre, there are five sections with 800 to 1,000 *Lavandula angustifolia* plants each. The overall effect is purple-luscious, and I love the little eccentricities scattered about: the canopy bed in the middle of one block, the mannequin dressed in lavender finery. Lynda says the farm is so much work that they like to have a little fun decorating the gardens. Behind the lavender are lovely ornamental beds and greenhouses.

All the lavender is organically grown. As Lynda says, "We eat it, so there is no other way to grow it." And now you know where many local chefs buy their lavender. In lavender season, the Dowlings open the place for visitors to enjoy the harvest in many ways: there are tours, as well as lavender sachets, lavender lemonade and lavender shortbread, lavender soaps and lavender plants and seeds for sale. Lynda composes a new lavender recipe every year to encourage her customers to cook with the ancient plant.

How did she choose lavender in the first place? "I didn't," she tells me. "It chose me." Lynda used to regularly visit an elderly lady to pick lavender until one January the lady arrived on Lynda's doorstep with a huge plant. She had decided to move to a smaller home and wanted Lynda to have her lavender. From that plant, Lynda took 500 cuttings and started her first garden.

Metchosin Farmers' Market

The Metchosin market is a favourite of mine because it is so naturally presented. It's held on Sundays, outdoors, just behind the fire hall, and never fails to impart that lovely sense of being in the country. The pace is slow, the vendors are friendly and the produce always looks and tastes like it was picked only minutes before you arrived.

You'll find organic farmer extraordinaire Dieter Eisenhawer with his tiny, perfect fingerling potatoes, arugula, beans and tomatoes; Yoshiko Unno and Tsutomu Suganami of Umi Nami Farm with their exquisite Oriental vegetables; Gini and Peter Walsh of Swallow Hill Farm with apples, Asian pears, blueberries and rhubarb; and Bernie and Marti Martin-Wood of Two Wings Farm with the most amazing salad mix, heirloom tomatoes and organic seeds.

There are 15 to 20 stalls at every market. Call ahead for the date of the Harvest Festival in the fall, when local musicians, clowns and a pit-roasted lamb dinner add to the fun.

Cooper's Cove Guesthouse and Angelo's Cooking School

I'd driven by the immaculate little blue house perched above Sooke Basin many times before a knowledgeable voice on the other end of the phone line said, "You really should check out the cooking classes at Cooper's Cove." I was delighted to find former Culinary Team Canada chef Angelo Prosperi-Porta offering afternoon cooking classes followed by kitchen suppers and lovely sea-view rooms for the night. Angelo, "a Canadian born with a Roman heart," and Ina Haegemann, his German-born partner, have created a unique culinary experience that has been featured on *Oprah* but is still something of a secret locally.

In the comfortable and well-equipped kitchen, I join other guests for a cooking class that features many local, seasonal and organic ingredients. Angelo proffers a large bowl of seaweeds harvested that morning by Diane Bernard, owner of Sooke's Outer Coast Seaweeds. We sample sea lettuce, sugar kelp, alaria, dulse and, my favourite, feather boa—"all very healthy and full of minerals," says our host. Using the seaweeds, cornmeal and wheat flour, we make bread moulded into fanciful seaweed shapes.

Angelo simmers white wine and dices cucumber for a sorbet and tells us what excites him about cooking: "It's not just the act of eating. When I cook the dishes I grew up with, it keeps my heritage and family memories alive." He grows most of his own produce and is proud that his fruit trees are descendants of his father's trees, that he brought the *minucia* in his garden from Italy.

We all get involved making seaweed pesto to be served with seared albacore tuna, then learn how to concoct a surprisingly simple fresh fruit terrine. Angelo leaves the kitchen at one point to "go fishing," and returns with a stunning

Chef Angelo Prosperi-Porta makes dinner at Angelo's Cooking School.

sockeye salmon. He gives us tips on buying fresh fish: the eyes should be clear, the gills bright red and the whole fish firm to the touch. He demonstrates scaling and filleting, then makes a tasty crust for the fillets using flax, sunflower, poppy, pumpkin and sesame seeds. We later enjoy the salmon with a chervil lemon butter sauce, accompanied by sautéed spaghetti squash, radishes and green beans with garlic and mint.

After the lesson, we soak in the hot tub before returning to the kitchen to feast on our earlier efforts. Ina had laid the centre island with white china and flowers from her garden, Angelo poured a dry Riesling, and the Buena Vista Social Club set the tone on the stereo. We ate and drank, laughed a lot and had some fantastic new recipes to take home the next day.

Angelo's classes may be booked as part of a two- or three-night getaway at Cooper's Cove Guesthouse. For those more inclined to eat than cook, his sublime meals are available for breakfast and dinner. This is a spot to unwind, to learn about food from someone who really has reverence for his ingredients and a true mastery of his craft, and to eat remarkably well. Angelo shares some of his culinary secrets in his beautiful independently published cookbook, *Flavours of Cooper's Cove*.

Little Vienna Bakery

Andreas and Michelle Ruttkiewiczs' Little Vienna Bakery has slipped into Sooke like a hand into a well-fitting glove, which is ironic, really, as one doesn't think of this as a town craving strudel or Sachertorte. In fact, they hadn't planned on settling in this small community, but Michelle tells me, "There are some 40 bakeries in Victoria. We saw interesting changes in Sooke and decided to take the plunge." And I am always standing in a long line of jovial locals when I drive out to satisfy my cravings for pastries as fine as those I found years ago in Vienna's Café Demel. Michelle tells me they are "amazed at the number of people who thank us every day for being here."

I love to take my time perusing the pastry display case, where mille-feuilles, raspberry linzer tortes and slices of Nusstorte, Mozart torte and poppy-seed torte compete for my attention. Inevitably, I pick a slice of apple strudel because it takes me back to my European heritage, and because I know of no better rendition of this sweet pastry. Even my father, whose roots into the pastry shops of Germany and Austria go deeper than my own, is smitten with Michelle's strudel. And, of course, there is more to Little Vienna Bakery than pastries.

Its cheery premises are located just past Sooke's only traffic light. The decor is an eclectic mix of big gilt mirrors, local artwork (major shows are often hung here by the Sooke Arts Council) and cosy tables. A piano against one wall often inspires impromptu concerts by local pianists, and book readings

by local authors are on the menu in winter. In summer, it's a pleasure to kick back on the outside deck with a local beer like Phillips India Pale Ale and a hearty sausage served with Bavarian mustard.

I sit down to chat with Michelle against the bustle and merriment of Christmas shoppers and diners. She tells me she is thrilled with the reception her bakery has received and is particularly pleased that they are now employing 11 locals. Staff members range from students to retirees and "they feel like an extension of our family." Miles Nickerson, who makes me a good, strong macchiato at the front counter, is also a noted guitarist and often plays during special events. Two sisters who help in the kitchen are students at the local high school. Michelle is teaching her staff what she knows, from her pastry training at Frau Friedel's *Konditorei* in Vienna to the memories of the café society that she and Andreas grew up with on Saint-Denis Street in Montreal.

Michelle tells me she sees Little Vienna as "a gathering place where I hope people can be very much at home." That sense of hominess is the Ruttkiewiczs' aim. They are recreating both pastry shop and *Heuriger*, the Austrian family restaurants where patrons go to sample new wines, especially young Rieslings, and to enjoy live music and simple food like roasted chicken, rösti, potato salads, dumplings and savoury strudels. Michelle says she will soon introduce the famous Emperor's Pancake with plum compote to delight her customers in winter.

Michelle and Andreas—who tell me their bible is *Men are from Mars, Women are from Venus*—seem to have found the right recipe for working together to create something that Sooke never knew it needed but now can't live without.

"We are amazed at the number of people who thank us every day for being here."

—Michelle Ruttkiewiczs

Markus' Wharfside Restaurant

At the end of Maple Avenue, just before you hit the water, stop at the small blue cottage on the left. Markus and Tatum Wieland have opened one of those friendly little restaurants with great food that one reads about in *Saveur* and then always hopes to stumble across. I'd heard that Sooke Harbour House and many of the area's bed and breakfast establishments were sending guests there, so I felt the restaurant came well recommended.

I arrive solo without a reservation and find myself warmly greeted and shown to a window seat with a spectacular view of Whiffen Spit and the Olympic Mountains. The decor is simple but elegant, with white tablecloths and colourful art on the walls. My server is knowledgeable about the menu, and I soon selected a vegetable risotto to start, followed by sautéed prawns with a garlic, white wine and herb butter sauce. A glass of Gewürztraminer came to mind, and a generous glass was soon set before me to enjoy, along with some Siciliano bread from the neighbouring Little Vienna Bakery and that lovely view.

Markus' Wharfside Restaurant was the vision of Markus and his father when they visited Sooke and came upon the cottage a year ago. A crowd of workmen moved in to transform something that had been neglected into something charming. Says Tatum, "It was such a beehive of activity in here for months that I didn't actually see the vision until the tables were set!" In addition to giving their customers the benefit of her International Sommelier Guild sommelier experience, Tatum keeps the books, while her husband runs the kitchen. It's a successful division of labour that has garnered them a loyal local following.

Markus was born in Mexico to German parents and raised with an appreciation of "cooking from the region." He prefers to use local ingredients as much as possible and is "not too much into fusion." Markus' food is what it is, and that's a good thing. A supporter of the Slow Food philosophy of eating regionally, he draws on Silver Cloud Organics, Ragley Farm and Sonneleiten

Farms for fresh produce; on local fishers and Cooper's Cove clams; and on farmer, and food photographer, Andrei Federov for ducks and turkeys. As well, the restaurant is actively putting many island ciders (including Merridale Cidery and Sea Cider Ciderhouse products) and wines on the menu.

Markus has a world of experience, having apprenticed at Seehotel Silber in Konstanz, Germany, and cheffed in Switzerland, Italy and France before opening his own place, the Alabaster Restaurant, in Vancouver's Yaletown. He then catered in Vancouver and did some private cheffing in Mexico before a short stint at Sooke Harbour House drew his attention to Sooke and the idea of opening a small restaurant there.

Tatum says she is enjoying being a restaurateur and working with her husband. The two met in the Okanagan where they were both show jumping horses. Now that they are settled in Sooke, they have bought a horse and are getting back into the ring in their spare time. I end my meal with the *grande dame* of all desserts (permanent note to self: we only live once!), a trio that includes tiramisu, Belgian chocolate mousse and, my favourite, pannacotta with caramel sauce, and a good coffee. Tatum says she likes that "every night we make people happy." As one of those happy people, I take the slow road back to Victoria and plan my next visit.

In the last couple of years, Markus and Tatum have built their own house adjacent to the restaurant ("so that we don't have any commute," says Tatum), and they're enjoying growing lots of their own produce in a newly installed greenhouse. Their restaurant has also become a member of the prestigious La Chaîne des Rôtisseurs, but, most importantly, says Tatum, "Our life is really great: every day we see a great view, eat good food and feed happy people!"

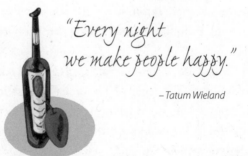

"Every night we make people happy."

– Tatum Wieland

Outer Coast Seaweeds (a.k.a., The Seaweed Lady)

In some ways, Diane Bernard has progressed naturally to her nickname: The Seaweed Lady. She was born to Acadians and lived half her life in the Maritimes. She has a strong background in coastal communities and a passion for the ocean, so, as she says, "I came by my new profession honestly."

That new profession—gatherer and purveyor of West Coast seaweed under the Outer Coast Seaweeds banner—has local chefs and gastronomes buzzing. At the 2002 Feast of Fields, Diane teamed up with chef Edward Tuson of Sooke Harbour House to serve a raw seaweed salad to the 600 participants. It was a huge hit. In the lineup was Lisa Ahier, then chef at Long Beach Lodge in Tofino, who encouraged Diane to "walk into restaurant kitchens with your bucket and show chefs what they can do with seaweed."

Diane credits Lisa, and her friends Sinclair and Frédérique Philip of Sooke Harbour House for mentoring her in her new venture. Sinclair encouraged her to begin working with chefs, so she spent a season taking them out to see the seaweeds and introducing them to their "good, healthy, distinctive yet subtle" properties. At first, she found it was the "progressive, more avant garde" chefs who took an interest, but now she is inundated with enquiries. Once people see and taste the possibilities, they're hooked.

The nutritional value of seaweed is extremely high. As Diane points out, seaweed has no root system: it attaches itself by its stipe to a rock, a log or to other seaweed. Which means "the nutrients

The Seaweed Lady, Diane Bernard, gathers seaweed near Port Renfrew.

taken in directly from the ocean" are all available to the eater. Seaweeds are "nutritionally dynamic. They're high fibre, low fat and have no cholesterol."

Diane collects her seaweeds west of Sooke, often hiking out great distances along the Juan de Fuca Strait where "no industry or big ships" interfere with the environment. She harvests eight to 10 different types. Her personal favourite is Alaria, or winged kelp, a versatile variety with a very rich, sweet-pea taste and rhubarb smell. Her family goes through about a pound of seaweed a week and, as she says, "I've got teenagers!" I'm reminded of the tofu-eating teens on Saltspring Island (see Soya Nova Tofu), and start to have hope for the next generation.

In addition to her online wholesale business, Diane is now supplying the retail market through various markets and brown-box programs in Victoria.

Ragley Farm

Josephine Hill left her job as a systems manager with a wholesale food company in Victoria to become a working farmer on 30 acres in East Sooke. Her husband, Rob, was a key grip in the Vancouver film industry and now works on the farm and on his cars. They've never looked back.

Saturdays (and Sundays in season), Josephine opens up part of her barn to sell the fruits of her labour. Customers can take a wicker basket, then fill it with tomatoes, collard greens, chard, baby radishes, spring onions, squash, arugula, mesclun, jalapenos and many more veggies. The large baking rack holds still-warm loaves of whole wheat, sourdough, fruit and olive breads, and blueberry and cranberry-apple muffins. Josephine grinds all her own flour. One morning when I visited, she was a little low on bread because the power had been out for five hours the night before.

Near Christmas, Josephine takes orders for her boxes of exquisite holiday cookies. She often has samples of her baking, not that the palate needs to be tempted first. I am particularly fond of her *Spekulatius* cookies, which she kindly delivered just before the big day. She makes a wonderful range of organic jams, such as blackcurrant, Cascade berry and apple-ginger. Farm-fresh eggs are always available.

The atmosphere in the barn is warm and friendly, with a steady stream of regular, mainly local customers dropping by. They buy and they catch up on the week. Even their dogs catch up with each other. I was amused by one car that drove up with its owner's dog hanging out the window to announce his arrival to the Hills' dogs.

Josephine says it was Rob who first spotted the farm and knew she would love it; when it finally came on the market in 1995, they made the move. They had to do a lot of work to clean the place up, but now thrive in their rural lifestyle. The farm has an interesting past, having been settled by Reverend and Lady Walker. Lady Walker, daughter of Lord Seymour, Marquess of Hertford, was also related to Lady Jane Seymour. She was a noted agricultural pioneer, setting up the East Sooke Farmers' Institute around 1927 and hosting many of its meetings at Ragley Farm.

Sooke Harbour House

It's fair to say that Vancouver Island gastronomy started with Sinclair and Frédérique Philip. From their "romantic little white inn by the sea," they have heightened our awareness and raised our expectations of food in general and reawakened our taste buds specifically to the pleasure and purpose of eating fresh, local, seasonal ingredients.

There is a reason why Sooke Harbour House has become a veritable training ground for the best local chefs, including Bill Jones, David Feys, Gordon Cowan, Brock Windsor and Peter Zambri, and a mecca for gardeners such as Tina Fraser wanting to learn and apply organic methods to the cultivation of over 400 edible flowers and herbs: the inn has played a huge role in the revival of market gardening. Many Vancouver Island farmers regard Sinclair as a mentor because of the interest he takes in their operations and the knowledge he so generously shares. Tugwell Creek Honey Farm is one beneficiary of his tutelage: Sinclair encouraged Bob Liptrot and Dana Le Comte to produce honey and mead at their nearby apiary, and they now have a thriving business that includes the production of the linden honey so prized by European guests at Sooke Harbour House. The Philips also persuaded Diane Bernard to start up

Outer Coast Seaweeds, now another successful local food business. Mary Alice Johnson of ALM Organic Farm, Karen Barr of Ladybird Farm and Josephine Hill of Ragley Farm are also part of the inn's family of suppliers. Mara Jernigan of Fairburn Farm Culinary Retreat says, "What Sinclair and Frédérique have achieved at Sooke Harbour House is really a remarkable piece of Canadian culinary history."

The reason for their far-reaching impact is not only that they care; they have a long-held conscientiousness about sustainable farming and land preservation that extends beyond their own business. They want to ensure that agricultural land is used for farming, not development, and they want to see other people—growers, grocers and chefs—succeed in the food business.

In some ways, the couple's position in the local food chain was inevitable. They have plowed a lifetime of knowledge and enthusiasm into making their inn the "Sixth Best Small Hotel in the World" (*Travel + Leisure*, 2002). Its authentic local cuisine was voted first in the world by *Gourmet* magazine in 1997, and it won a Pinnacle Award for best independent restaurant in Canada in 2002. For five consecutive years, the inn has been awarded *Wine Spectator*'s rare Grand Award for having one of the world's 88 best wine lists, and in 2002, Frédérique was named a Woman of Distinction for business and entrepreneurship in Victoria. Most recently, the inn received the highest Audubon Hotel Eco-Rating in BC, garnering four green leaves in recognition of its green hotel policies, water reclamation and recycling system and "grass-paved" parking lot.

Frédérique tells me their story really began in France, when Sinclair was taking a Ph.D. in political science and international economics and Frédérique was studying economics at Grenoble. Ten years later, they went to Toronto to be with Sinclair's mother, who had fallen ill. When she passed away, the couple headed west because "Sinclair had always wanted to be by the ocean." They drove around and ended up at Whiffen Spit in Sooke, a far less populated area 25 years ago.

There, at the water's edge, was the 1929 clapboard house that would be improved incrementally, as the Philips could afford it, to become what it is today. They moved into the basement with their three children (the fourth, Rissa, was born in Sooke) and began to convert the house into an inn. They had no experience as innkeepers, but Frédérique remembers thinking, "It shouldn't be that complicated." The Philips' children grew as the inn grew, and all have worked there in various capacities. Nishka tends the gardens, Benjamin is a sommelier and waiter in the dining room, and Jasmine is the ever-gracious hostess. Rissa, who is currently in Europe, has bussed in the dining room.

What impresses me, as I have coffee by the fire with Sinclair one crisp autumn day, is how uncomplicated it all appears and how immensely relaxed both he and the inn make me feel. Intellectual, food activist, gastronome and oenophile, Sinclair is, most importantly, a very decent guy who treats his own success as a gift to give back—to his guests and to others in the local food and farming industry.

I ask about organics and Sinclair says it's the only ethical choice. He is proud to have influenced many local growers and producers to transition to organic. And he is pleased to have popularized formerly unpopular ingredients and created great interest in growing and foraging for indigenous ingredients. Those include many First Nations foods, from uncommon fish to berries, prolific local mushrooms (when we later meet up with chef Edward Tuson, Sinclair excitedly tells him about the Slippery Jack boletes he found on his morning forage), and bitter winter greens, which people used to regard as inedible. Sinclair had a pretty good idea what would grow in Sooke because it has a climate similar to where he lived in France.

I ask about Slow Food since Sinclair is the Canadian representative to the International Slow Food Council—and he tells me that he and Frédérique have "always lived by Slow Food values, as we understand them." He says it's all about

Co-owner Frédérique Philip lights the candles before dinner at Sooke Harbour House.

Chef Edward Tuson adds love and humour to the pot at Sooke Harbour House.

using and promoting "foods in their regional, seasonal and historic context," and preserving traditional foods such as First Nations dishes.

I'm anxious to see how philosophy translates into cuisine, so Frédérique offers to take me into the kitchen. En route, she shows me some images for the first of three books she is producing, *The Art of Sooke Harbour House*. These are photographs of some of the pieces in the inn's food-themed art collection. Each image has inspired Edward to create a special recipe that will be included in the book. Proceeds will go toward developing the art department at the local high school.

A great inn being the sum of its parts, it would be remiss of me to not mention the menu of spa treatments designed by Frédérique. At Sooke Harbour House, the treatments actually come to guests in their rooms (or, if preferred, they are given in the exotic Potlatch Room, where one can have a massage behind the curtains of a marquee straight out of the Arabian Nights). Frédérique recognized something that we spa aficionados have long decried: after a relaxing treatment, one is forced to get dressed and leave the sanctuary. The answer is in-room everything, from sea-salt scrubs to Swedish massage.

Before leaving me and my thousand hungry questions with Edward, Frédérique tells me, "Following the seasons is everything to good cooking." She finds it strange that chefs are making a big story about going to the markets. "We've always done that," she says, "and we didn't do it to be trendy."

Edward Tuson has a long history at Sooke Harbour House, where he loves that "every day is different." I love the fact that he is different from what one might expect of a chef with so stellar a reputation. I'm not referring to the nose ring or the tattoo; I'm impressed that he's like the boy next door, a genuinely humble guy who takes a lot of time showing and explaining things to me.

He says he's "a farmer at heart," and he lived a few other lives before coming to cooking. He delivered furniture for Sears Roebuck in Los Angeles and worked

This white clapboard house on the water's edge in Sooke has become internationally acclaimed inn and restaurant Sooke Harbour House.

on an oil rig in the Beaufort Sea before enrolling in the chef-training program at Vancouver Community College. That was the year he'd hurt his back and he figured construction jobs were out of the question. Besides, cooking had always been part of his repertoire from an early age. His mother was a hairdresser who worked at home, and he would often "try to cook her dinner."

While cheffing at places like Vancouver's Pan Pacific Hotel, Edward used to come to Sooke to snorkel for abalone. That's how he met fellow diver Sinclair. He signed on at Sooke Harbour House for five years, then took off in 1995 on an adventure across Asia (the Bangkok portion of that journey was spent with Peter Zambri of Victoria's Zambri's restaurant). Gathering culinary knowledge wherever he went, Edward finally returned to Vancouver Island in 1999, working briefly at The Aerie, Micheline's and the Malahat Mountain Inn, before settling back into the kitchen at Sooke Harbour House.

As we chat, his staff works around us: Jenny is wrapping Sooke Harbour Dungeness crab and chervil with pickled rutabaga to accompany her sea cucumber and wild porphyra seaweed fritter; Geoff is braising sculpin in a sweet cicely root, Alexander seed and wild pine mushroom broth; and Josh is preparing blackcurrant and grand fir sorbet to include with his pear and calendula-petal terrine.

There is a great deal of creativity in the kitchen and a lot of room for individuality. Edward lets his staff know what's come in fresh that day, then leaves each person to write his or her own portion of the evening's menu. The results are electrifying: spicy albacore tuna served rare on a buckwheat-noodle, root-vegetable and cilantro salad with fennel-seed duck sausage, a clam parsnip fritter and a tamari, red wine vinegar and oxeye daisy vinaigrette. As we contemplate the dish, Edward cuts me a thick slice of that albacore tuna and I'm lost for several minutes. Edward is "Entrée Dude" to his staff; he handles the creation of the main offerings and fine-tunes the rest. He also visits the local farms and markets, takes early-morning calls from fishers on their boats, manages supplies, writes recipes and gives interviews to the likes of *The New York Times, Bon Appétit* and *Canadian Living* (not to mention demanding book authors!). And yet, he is an executive chef who is always on the line during service. He tells me it's all made worthwhile "when someone tells me I've cooked them the best meal they've ever eaten in their life."

I move from back of house to the oceanside dining room to eat the best meal of my life with Toronto chef and sommelier Daniel Beiles. It is a graciously served and elegantly presented six-course dinner. The kitchen's attention to detail and relentless pursuit of excellence is evident, from the scrumptious warm albacore tuna, apple, red onion, sourdough tartlet with chickweed, oxeye daisy salad, Korean mint, cilantro yogurt and pickled ruby beet to the roasted Peking duck breast with a buttermilk and grand fir glaze, lapin cherry-fennel sauce and split-pea tortilla torte. Daniel appreciates the opportunity to sample a flight of British Columbia wines with his meal and is overwhelmed by his tour of the cellars.

"Following the seasons is everything to good cooking."

– Frédérique Philip

There's a whole lot of buzzing going on at Tugwell Creek Honey Farm.

Tugwell Creek Honey Farm

Dana Le Comte trained as a fashion designer at Ryerson University and worked as a merchandiser in Vancouver, so I'm not surprised that she manages to look fabulous in protective clothing. We're talking full beekeeper regalia: head-to-toe canvas suit, gloves and large straw hat with netting. She and her husband, Bob Liptrot, have invited me to visit them and the 3,000,000 bees that reside at Tugwell Creek Honey Farm in Sooke. No worries, I say, and pull on my own space suit.

Bob has been fascinated with bees since he was seven. He used to help an elderly neighbour with his hives and always received a chunk of sweet honeycomb in return. He went on to earn a Master's degree in entomology, then studied apiculture (beekeeping) at Simon Fraser University. He has more knowledge about his charges than most people, but I can instantly see an intuitive asset: he is completely in tune with the bees and is able to work with them without protective clothing (don't try this at home).

It's one thing to see bees in a museum setting; it's something else to stand with beekeepers as they dismantle a hive and introduce you to the clan. Each of the couple's 90 hives contains some 40,000 to 60,000 Carniolan bees. The proletariat includes 13,000 to 20,000 foraging workers and at least 26,000 workers that stay in the hive to contend with brood-rearing, comb-constructing, housecleaning, hive defence and temperature regulation. The brood consists of thousands of eggs, pupae in sealed cells and larvae being fed. Significant family members are the drones, of which there are 100 to 300, and the queen.

As I hover over the new observation beehive, Dana points out the queen (she is larger than the others and marked with a little dot of blue nail polish), and I'm fascinated by her obvious coterie of attendants. These bees are assigned to stay with her at all times to groom, feed and protect her. She's the J. Lo of the insect world, and I learn that these queens are in big demand. A good breeder can fetch as much as $150, and it is not unusual for queens to be delivered from one beekeeper to another via the postal service.

The queens breed after completing their mating flight with five drones, whom Shakespeare aptly described as "the idle bachelors." Yet there are no winners here: the drones die in the process (suffice to say, the penis snaps off), and the queens go on to lay some 2,000 eggs per day for the rest of their lives.

The workers have finely honed phonic and kinetic forms of communication. The "dance of the honeybee" is a much-studied ritual, whereby the foragers return to the hive and, through sound, taste and smell, "provide information regarding the location of a particular source of forage." The recipients of this information can then head out on their own to collect pollen.

The ultimate winners, of course, are you and I, and a visit to Tugwell Creek Honey Farm can only heighten our appreciation of one of nature's perfect foods. Dana and Bob chose their 10-acre farm for its proximity to Survey Mountain. Located 25 kilometres inland, it provides an ideal warm, dry climate and a proliferation of hawksbeard, fireweed and salal for foraging. The couple transport their hives to the mountain, as well as to nearby Muir Creek, where the bees collect nectar from linden tree blooms, and the Sooke River Potholes, where they feast on blackberry flowers.

I first sampled Tugwell Creek Honey at Feast of Fields and it has become a firm favourite. Since 2003, Dana and Bob have also operated a meadery, a first for British Columbia, where you can buy Vintage, Melomel and Sack meads. Mead was traditionally drunk in the "honey month." The father of the bride would supply his son-in-law with all the mead he could drink during what is now known as the honeymoon.

Dana says they are delighted to have control of the whole process, from hive to honey and honey wine. She is happy that their business has become a family affair: during the harvest, the couple's children enjoy the excitement and Dana's sister and mother come from Vancouver to help.

In the meantime, if you're tired of trawling superstore aisles in the city, get thee to the meadery. Dana and Bob offer a delicious and educational respite down on the honey farm.

SALTSPRING ISLAND

Bright Farm

I'm sitting on the back porch of Charlie Eagle and Judy Horvath's farmhouse, sampling juicy Italian plums straight off their trees and then chewing on the dried version—prunes that Judy proffers from one of her collection of big kitchen jars. Then Hastings House chef Thomas Render and I were spending a Sunday touring farms and food producers on the island, and this was our first stop.

Charlie and Judy came up from the Bay Area in the early 1990s and bought their 10-acre farm in about two hours, en route to the ferry. It was a fortuitous move. They had been homesteading on a remote property in California since 1980 but with their daughter, Bree, ready to begin school, they felt they wanted

Braids of Bright Farm's Korean garlic for sale at the Saltspring Island Garlic Festival.

somewhere more community-oriented. Saltspring was the answer, and Judy found the house and property so idyllic that she cried the first time she walked through the door.

I find it idyllic as well, and Charlie tells me most visitors feel a sense of wonder here. The property was originally 153 acres, bought for $153 by Thomas and Jane Mouat in 1890. It has a creek running through it that drains St. Mary's Lake and runs through to the Vesuvius estuary. It is something of a bird sanctuary. As we wander about the farm, we stop to watch a turkey vulture, a hawk and then a great blue heron soar above us.

Charlie's main crop is garlic: Chinese, Spanish, Early Red Portuguese and Korean, some of which I'd bought at the Saltspring Garlic Festival in August. He sells it in big fat braids. This was a good year—560 braids! Other crops include potatoes, beans, corn, carrots, leeks, lettuce, chard, zucchini, broccoli, winter squash and celery. There is a vast greenhouse of tomatoes, tomatillos, hot peppers and cucumbers. There are watermelons and cantaloupes and gorgeous Concord grapes (Charlie and Judy make Concord jelly together).

And then there's the orchard, an amazing planting of 200 varieties. The trees were moved to Bright Farm as a complete collection in 1993. They were just "little two-foot whips when I planted them," says Charlie. They'd been amassed by a woman from Sloan River who collected heritage apple varieties. Charlie and Judy press some 40 to 50 varieties into juice and also make cider. People buy caseloads of the farm's 20 varieties of crabapples to make jelly. Because the nights have been cold this summer, Charlie is anticipating a good, sweet apple harvest this year.

As we wander through the orchard, Thomas spots a hawthorn bush. He's just found a recipe for hawthorn jelly and a discussion ensues, mainly around how long it would take to pick enough of the tiny berries to make a batch of jelly. We pass the chicken coop, a field of sheep (Charlie counts on the neighbour's ram busting through the fence every year to propagate his herd) and a couple of hives (the bees are mainly kept to pollinate his crops, but he also harvests as much as 40 pounds of honey annually).

The orchard is watered directly from a large pond on the property. Gravity draws the water from Jane's Spring (named for original owner Jane Mouat) into a storage tank for the drip-irrigation system that waters the rest of the farm's plantings. Charlie has help in the form of a dozen WWOOFers (Willing Workers on Organic Farms) throughout the year. Some of them stay on the property in a sweet little cabin behind the house. They all sit down to Judy's hearty dinners after their working day.

Charlie is clearly proud of his daughter, who loves the farming life (yes, these young people do exist!). Bree took a degree in environmental studies in Santa Cruz but couldn't wait to move back to Bright Farm when she graduated. She worked in the gardens of Hastings House as a teenager and, like her mother, she enjoys selling at the local markets.

Foxglove Farm Retreat and The Centre for Art, Ecology and Agriculture

One day I hope to write more fully about Michael Ableman, for he is a sustainable-agriculture hero for our times, and we are fortunate to have someone of his calibre in our midst. The challenge is catching up with this internationally acclaimed farmer, author, photographer, speaker and food activist. For this update of *An Edible Journey*, I was able to chat with him by phone during his

winter sojourn at the Centre for Urban Agriculture at Fairview Gardens, the non-profit organization based on the farm he is credited with saving in Goleta, California, in the early 1980s.

He's about to embark on a writing retreat to "figure out whether I should write another book from a couple of ideas that are bouncing around in my head." And he'll do some travelling, public speaking and organizing of the faculty and programs for the Centre for Art, Ecology and Agriculture that he's establishing as the educational arm of his 120-acre Foxglove Farm on Saltspring Island. The centre's program of writing, painting, photography and culinary workshops will be taught by significant experts, and the summer concert series should be a sellout, when one considers the location. Although Michael tells me they "will start out conservatively," I reckon they'll be huge once folk hear who some of the lecturers will be.

Foxglove Farm is located on Mount Maxwell, where, as Michael says, "You can walk in any direction forever and not see a soul [sounds like perfect acoustics to me]." The farm has about 15 acres in intensive cultivation and another 30 acres of pasture and hay. The crops include fruit and vegetables, and this year, there will also be grains: oats, barley, milling corn and possibly quinoa. Michael is busy "lining up a combine, and we intend to have a mill in place by the fall." There are plans to package flour and pancake mix under the Foxglove Farm banner.

There are farm-stay accommodations on the property, charmingly decorated by Michael's wife, Jeanne-Marie. On arrival at The Historic Log House, The Green Cottage or The Red Cabin, guests check off what they'd like from a list of what's available in the fields, then cook for themselves from freshly harvested organic produce. And the couple, together with sons Aaron and Benjamin, continues to sell their amazing produce at both the Saturday and Tuesday farmers' markets.

So I have to laugh when Michael refers to their "little operation on the hill," as Foxglove Farm has become one of the largest growers on Saltspring Island, prolific in every way: agriculturally, ecologically, educationally and socially. And long may Michael and his family continue to challenge and enrich the rest of us!

The Manor House at Hastings House.

Hastings House

The winding drive to Hastings House, a member of Small Luxury Hotels of the World, takes us past fields of sheep before arriving at a charming cluster of buildings facing Ganges Harbour. There's a converted barn, an authentic Hudson's Bay Company trading post (now The Post cottage, a honeymooners' delight) and a stately replica of an 11th-century Sussex manor house built with locally quarried stone.

Received as if we've come home, my little group of foodies is invited to join the manager, Shirley McLaughlin, in the front parlour of The Manor House for morning coffee, or "elevenses" as the English affectionately call the respite. Meandering along the garden path, we are inspected by one of two resident cats, the indomitable Mr. Hastings. Some years back, word got out that chef Marcel Kauer was leaving bowls of fresh cream and tidbits of fish at the kitchen door. Mr. Hastings and Squeaky were first in line and soon took up permanent, luxurious residence here.

Inside, the perfect welcome awaits. A fire roars in the open hearth, and organic coffee from the Saltspring Coffee Company is set out in Minton china cups. There are freshly baked strawberry muffins and a selection of jams made from the inn's own heritage fruit trees. *The Gulf Islands Driftwood*, Saltspring's leading (and only) newspaper, is at hand. We sink into chintz and happily give ourselves over to our edible journey's most relaxing stop thus far.

Dining well at Hastings House.

Hastings House is located on the site of an old working farm of 25 acres. The Manor House was completed in 1940 for Warren Hastings to replicate his family home in Sussex. Features like the large inglenook fireplace in the lounge are typical of those found in Tudor homes in Sussex. When Donald Cross bought the property from Hastings in 1980, he brought in a local architect, Jonathan Yardley, to develop it into a country resort.

Hastings House faces south, overlooking Ganges Harbour, which provides a continuous show of boating activity, particularly in summer. The lush, rolling lawn, with its immaculate flower beds, is dotted with Adirondack chairs just calling guests to curl up with a book, or sit, as I did, with a glass of port after dinner and watch the sun set.

On one visit, I enjoyed a room upstairs in The Manor House, which reminded me of a hotel near Salisbury Cathedral where I'd stayed many years before. The suite's living room faces the harbour, and you can read before a wood-burning fire (remember those?). It's private and cosy with thoughtful appointments throughout. Your name is on the door, and a stuffed toy cat can be hung out to alert the housekeeper that the room is available for cleaning (its other side is a dog that appears to have bitten off part of the housekeeper's uniform, a sign that privacy is desired).

Of course the highlight for any gourmet trailblazer is dinner, and Hastings House doesn't disappoint. Many celebrities have dined here, although the inn is discreet enough to divulge only the names of those whose visits are already known, including Johnny Carson, Martin Short, Goldie Hawn and Kurt Russell.

There are several choices for dinner: the Verandah dining room, where no jackets are required and which is often booked for weddings and special parties; the Snug dining room next to the cellar, for private parties; the main dining room; and, in summer, the porch, where a lucky party of four can dine privately. Foodie fanatics can have it all by dining at a special table located right in the kitchen (this experience books up fast, so do call well in advance). It all adds up to a true English country-house feeling, where someone like me imagines intrigue in every corner.

Executive chef Marcel Kauer is Swiss-born and -trained. At the age of 16, he did his apprenticeship in his uncle's restaurant in Germany, then entered the army. When his parents were visiting Vancouver, they ate at La Raclette, and his father asked if the restaurant would employ Marcel. They agreed, and Marcel came to Canada. He worked both at La Raclette in Vancouver and at the Galiano Lodge on Galiano Island, spending half of the week in each kitchen. He said it was a busy time for him and challenging because he "had no English." He loved it when the lodge was quiet and he could go fishing.

A perfectly romantic table at Hastings House.

Marcel came to Hastings House 13 years ago and is now both chef and co-manager. He believes in cooking with the seasons, from what's available. "Wait until the food comes to you," says Marcel. What doesn't come from the Hastings House gardens, he buys from local growers, going off-island only for bulk items like potatoes and flour.

Pastry chef Carley Makela with bread just baked for the evening meal.

I'm invited to inspect the day's produce delivery. There are slender eggplants, several varieties of tomatoes and peppers, green beans, portobellini mushrooms, pattypan squashes, green-flesh cantaloupes, leeks, yams and a large tray of fragrant basil. As various members of the kitchen brigade pass by, they touch and comment, all impressed and excited by the quality. Most of it comes from Charlie Eagle's Bright Farm on the island. Sweet little strawberries arrive from Rosalie Beach's Wave Hill Farm, and saddles of venison from Broken Briar Fallow Deer Farm near Chemainus. Michael Ableman's Foxglove Farm supplies golden and red plums, as well as green asparagus and the prized white variety. Blueberries come from Cathy Bull's Bluebeary Hill Farm in Victoria. Marcel says they also buy 300 to 400 pounds of blackberries from local pickers who come to the kitchen door every summer. Many of those berries find their way into Hastings House jams and jellies, which guests can buy to take home.

Earlier in the day, sockeye salmon and snapper came in for the evening's menu. Typically, the kitchen gets calls from the boats of local fishers like Don Bemi with details of the day's catch. Someone meets the boats at the dock in Ganges, and it's seriously fresh fish for supper. Lamb, which is featured on the Hastings House menu every night by popular demand, comes from Mike Byron's neighbouring farm.

Tofu comes from Soya Nova Tofu on the island. Marcel loves the smoked tofu and includes it in delicate strudel as well as in vegetable sautés. Tempeh, the cultured soy curd that is mixed with barley and allowed to ferment, is now also being made commercially on the island and used by Hastings House.

Pastry chef Carley Makela is pulling loaves of whole wheat bread out of the oven. A graduate of the Pacific Institute of Culinary Arts in Vancouver, she originally learned how to bake from her grandmother. Following stints at Cin Cin and other Vancouver restaurants, she is now responsible for the tea trolley, breakfast and all pastries at Hastings House. Her desserts—like the dark Belgian chocolate brownie torte with blackberry ice cream that I enjoyed—are fresh and creative without being overly fussy or loaded with unnecessary ingredients. Carley recently won a top award with her Simply Grand Chèvre Cheesecake at the Grand Marnier Dessert Challenge in Victoria.

House Piccolo

Saltspring Island never fails to amaze me. You can literally cross the street from farmers' market to fine dining without changing out of your blue jeans. Even though the attire is casual everywhere, the attention to food is generally high-class all the way. Such was my first experience at House Piccolo. I arrived for dinner in jeans and was treated as if I was dressed in head-to-toe couture.

The 30-seat restaurant (which expands to 48 seats with outside seating in summer) is in a cute little blue house right in the village of Ganges. Inside, it has a homey feel, with paintings by the owner's aunt and various European knick-knacks on the walls. There is a whole display of Russian dolls that were originally owned by a Finnish prime minister interspersed with copper pots and restaurant awards, including awards of excellence from *Wine Spectator* for every year since 2000. There is also a proud certificate of membership (by invitation only) in the prestigious international gastronomic society, La Chaîne des Rôtisseurs.

The meal was one of the best I'd ever eaten, from the complementary salad and warmed house-made bread to start to the meltingly rich, yet surprisingly light Gorgonzola tart with port, toasted cumin seed and Bosc pear chutney to the Saltspring Island lamb chops with a hearty aïoli, designer vegetables and scalloped potatoes. Sticking to one glass of wine, as is my custom, I enjoyed the fruity Bacchus from Cowichan Valley's Alderlea Vineyards (Piccolo's wine list is an extensive, much-lauded collection of over 250 selections). I'm often asked where I put all the food I eat, but I had no trouble finishing my meal

Chef Piccolo and Kirsi Lyytikainen in the kitchen of House Piccolo.

with the unique lingonberry crepes with vanilla ice cream and a bottomless cup of Saltspring Coffee Company coffee. Everything was excellent and the service was friendly, but not intrusive.

Besides the local coffee, the restaurant uses Saltspring Island ingredients as much as possible. The lamb is always local; Moonstruck Organic Cheese and the Saltspring Island Cheese Company supply the cheese; vegetables come from Bon Acres Farm; lettuce comes year-round from Living Lettuce, an organic hydroponic farm nearby; and Saltspring Island Sea Products smokes the salmon. Even the beer is island-made, from the Gulf Islands Brewery in the Fulford Valley.

In 1989, Piccolo Lyytikainen and his girlfriend, Kirsi, were ready to move away from the big city—in their case, Helsinki. They had no preconceived ideas but, as an avid boater, Piccolo knew that he wanted to live by the sea. They came to Saltspring Island at the invitation of Piccolo's uncle, who lived here. It was Christmastime, and they liked the place very much. They returned in the summer to really check it out and ended up deciding to get married and make a permanent move in January 1991. Whatever happened, Piccolo tells me, they knew there would be boating 12 months of the year! Piccolo brought a wealth of cooking experience and Kirsi, bookkeeping and self-taught pastry-making skills, from their Finnish homeland.

Piccolo credits his mother with his lifelong interest in good food. "She actually had more than salt and pepper in her spice cabinet, so our food had different flavours," he tells me. Her good cooking gave him "a little kick," and he began his career as a driver for a catering company, then worked in Helsinki restaurants, "from the very bottom to becoming a schnitzel cook."

Somewhere in between, he worked in the boat electronics industry. His boss owned a small island, and Piccolo ended up becoming a cook on the island for guests of the company. He loved that "summer gig," because he could take his own boat to work and was able to cook with great local ingredients. Back in Helsinki, he decided to get some proper training under a Swiss chef at the restaurant Bellman. And then came the trip to Canada, and the beginning of Piccolo and Kirsi's love affair with Saltspring Island.

They found the little house on Hereford Avenue right away. It had been a Mexican café, then a restaurant called Carol Feeds the Planet (only on Saltspring!), and the decor needed a lot of work. They weren't sure they could afford it, but decided to do it anyway. The couple worked together and with friends to renovate the place, and opened in October 1992. They originally served breakfast, lunch and dinner on blue-and-white-checked tablecloths, but gradually honed their style to dinners-only on white linen.

When I ask Piccolo where he wants to be in five years, he tells me, "Right here. We have the one thing that everyone wants—to live on Saltspring."

Jana's Bake Shop

It's always fun to discover a culinary gem, and Jana's Bake Shop, Saltspring Island's tiny perfect bakery and coffee bar, is such a place. I try to drop in for quiche whenever I'm on the island because Jana Roerick makes the best quiche of any baker anywhere. Whether it's blue cheese, kale and jalapeno peppers, or caramelized onions and Gruyère, the combinations are fantastic, the pastry is light and flaky and each personal-sized quiche is made in a deep dish so you really get a nice portion. With a cup of Saltspring Coffee Company's coffee, this is one of the best lunches I know.

The little shop is inviting with a fun collection of coloured cookie cutters hanging on the walls, and a welcoming open kitchen from which Jana greets you as she puts another tray of baking into the oven. With only a few tables inside and a picnic bench in the garden, there is always the opportunity to meet someone and have an interesting conversation while you munch away.

Jana and her husband, Marcus Dowrich, are true islanders—he's from Trinidad; she hails from Toronto's Ward's Island—so they "couldn't have asked for a better move" when they chose Saltspring. Marcus had been raising South African Boer goats and Jana was supplying restaurants with her wonderful cakes in Tobago when the urge came to move back to Canada. "Of course, we wanted to find the warmest place in the country," Jana tells me. Marcus started studying the Gulf Islands and they decided on Saltspring. They love it, says Jana, "but Marcus does miss his goats!"

Jana graduated as a baker from George Brown College in Toronto and puts her culinary skills to use making the things people most love. Her chicken, beef and vegetarian pot pies, soups and roasted vegetable and beef lasagna portions are always on hand in the freezer for take-home dinners. The individual quiches, calzones and a great selection of sweet treats like date squares, chocolate loaves, deep-dish butter tarts and the "disappearing" chocolate-pecan junkies are consistently in demand. Jana also supplies cakes, pies and fruit crumbles to Moby's Pub.

It's good to hear that Jana and Marcus have no plans to "grow" the business (as we urbanites would say). They are delighted that Saltspring Islanders have embraced them. Customers regularly tell Jana that they love being able to watch her rolling pastry and making tasty fillings when they come in. Jana's Bake Shop is the closest thing I know to walking into my mother's kitchen and being made to feel she's baking something special just for me.

Market-in-the-Park

Nothing takes me back to the 1970s more than the weekly Saltspring Island market held on Saturdays from late March to the end of October. Market-in-the-Park, as it is now known, is a testament to community pride and an unwavering commitment to selling only items made, grown or baked on the island. With over 120 vendors at the height of the summer, the market has become a top-billed event and makes a wonderful day trip for non-residents.

In addition to produce from familiar growers and food producers such as Michael and Jeanne-Marie Ableman of Foxglove Farm, David Wood of the Saltspring Island Cheese Company, Heather Campbell "The Bread Lady," Rosalie Beach of Wave Hill Farm and Chintan and Satva Hall of Monsoon Coast Exotic World Spices, there is a plethora of handcrafted items from charming gumboots "planted" with flowers to natural soaps and hemp clothing. Many non-profit groups—from The Land Conservancy to the Raging Grannies—raise awareness at the market.

Satva Hall of Monsoon Coast Exotic World Spices discusses his spices with a customer at the Saturday market.

Monsoon Coast Exotic World Spices

Nobody is more hospitable than Satva Hall, a warm and dynamic man whose career has taken him from clothing and jewellery businesses to his real passion: creating exotic spice blends. He spent his early twenties travelling through Pakistan, and when the war ended in 1973, he walked into India. At a train station, there was a "Vegetarian Eating Room" and a "Non-Vegetarian Eating Room." As a lifelong vegetarian, he decided he had found his country. Then he found his future wife, Swiss-born Chintan, whom he met at an ashram in northern India. He says "the whole India thing touched him deeply" when he was young, and it has stayed with him.

In true Indian fashion, he first invites me for a cup of chai—in this case, his Railway Chai, "spicy and warm with ginger and pepper, fragrant with cinnamon, cardamom and cloves." We sit on the couple's sun-drenched porch, drinking the tea and nibbling papaya, avocado and pear slices that have been sprinkled with chat masala, which is based on garam masala, but goes best with fruits, and his divine Monsoon Balti Spread on crackers. Hall's spices are incredibly flavourful, complex and fresh tasting, but not over-the-top hot. He says he is mainly catering to North American taste buds, many of which are just waking up, but can also satisfy "macho customers," who want seriously hot flavour.

Satva imports spices from India and develops his own spice combinations. Traditionally added at the end of cooking, his concoctions give dishes unmistakably exotic flavours. The room where he does his mixing has a deeply intoxicating aroma of cardamom, coriander, chilies and star anise, to name but a few of the dozens of individual spices he employs.

It's both a simple and a complex process. Satva says there's a lot of experimentation, but he is gifted with a taste for layering flavours, so he doesn't make too many mistakes. He says, "It's great when the 'wow' factor happens, when it all comes together like one of Chintan's mixed-media artworks." At the moment, he is on a mission to create totally organic mixtures. He has been sent some organic spices from Orissa that he's experimenting with and is also working with Saltspring Island seed guru Dan Jason to see what spices might be grown on the island.

Monsoon Coast is receiving a lot of attention—BC's *EAT* magazine recently rated it "one of the best 100 food experiences in the province"—but for now, it is strictly a small, family-operated concern. Satva develops the spice blends; Chintan sets aside her artwork to help with packaging. When they're in full production, Chintan's mother comes over to help. Chintan says it's nice to have her mother involved; they can work and have a good chat at the same time.

"It's great when the 'wow' factor happens, when it all comes together like one of Chintan's mixed-media artworks."

— Satva Hall

Moonstruck Organic Cheese

I often order a glass of red wine and a simple cheese plate for dinner, a habit I got into when travelling in Australia one year. It enabled me to sample a great variety of local cheeses and still have room for sticky toffee pudding for dessert! At the Marriott Inner Harbour Hotel's Fire & Water restaurant in Victoria, then-chef Jeff Keenliside (now at The Marina restaurant) presented thick pieces of Moonstruck Organic Cheese's Blossom's Blue (a blue-veined Stilton-style cheese) along with thinly sliced baguette and fig compote. I enjoyed the cheese so much I resolved to visit its makers as soon as possible.

Julia and Susan Grace have been making "fine-quality, highly ripened, good-dining kinds of cheese" on Saltspring Island since 1998. Their reputation is huge among connoisseurs of good cheese and deservedly so.

When I dropped in with Cynthia Cooper on one particularly wet and muddy day in December, we were offered hot coffee and seats by the fire in the Graces' living room. It was a warm welcome and typical of those I experience in rural homes. Farm work never actually stops, but generosity always seems to prevail. I wanted to know how the business of creating what *Maclean's* magazine called "sin on a cracker" came about.

Julia and Susan weren't always in the cheese business. They began with a market garden and a brown-box program for island residents. Then Susan, who Julia says, "was always drawn to the animals," bought one Jersey cow and then another. By 1996, Julia had a lot of milk on her hands and "started to fool around with butter, yogurt and a nice cheddary kind of cheese." She would tuck the new products into her customers' brown boxes and their response was fabulous.

Eventually the women decided that "farming protein was a lot easier than growing leaves," and they considered making cheese in earnest. At that time, they had a couple of things in their favour. No one else was producing 100 per cent organic cheese commercially so they were able to obtain a provincial government licence for a dairy and cheesemaking operation, and Julia's mother had left her some money, which enabled them to get the business going.

"We don't produce supermarket cheese," says Susan. "Our cheese sits on your tongue and makes you go 'Oohhh.' We want the flavour to be there, the

Julia and Susan Grace and one of their prize Jersey cows.

taste to last in your mouth in a pleasant way." Those great tastes, such as the nutty creaminess of White Moon, the peppery, woodsy flavour of Savoury Moon or the sweet, buttery blue bite of Baby Blue, are, says Susan, "all about the milk." And that milk is from the famed cows first bred on the British Channel Island of Jersey. As someone who was Jersey-born, and raised on its cows' milk, I can heartily attest to the milk's superior quality.

Twenty-five of the Graces' 28 Jersey cows are "dry" when we visit, leaving 3 producing milk "to keep the soft cheese accounts going over the winter." By March, the calving will begin. Lisa Lloyd of Saltspring's Stowell Lake Farm raises the "youngsters" for Susan, returning them to the herd when they are ready to milk. Susan credits Lisa with teaching her how to milk in the first place, and she also mentions fellow cheesemaker David Wood of the Salt-spring Island Cheese Company as having been "a great help to us over the years." David, who has a delivery van, regularly delivers Moonstruck cheeses for the Graces, while the women, who own the requisite lab equipment, do cheese testing for David. They all benefit by "shouldering one another along."

Towards the end of March, Saltspring's Market-in-the-Park gears up for the season, and the Graces go into full-scale cheese production as they have a booth at the market every Saturday in addition to wholesale and retail orders. They were able to take a short break one fall to attend the biannual Slow Food Terra Madre conference in Turin. Afterwards, they "rattled around Italy" visiting other cheesemakers, an experience they found "uplifting and humbling at the same time." Julia says that they came back to Saltspring "feeling really good about our cheese."

Ultimately, they credit their animals with creating such a good product. Says Susan, "The integrity of the cheese comes from the good milk." Even though it's an expensive process to be both producing the milk and making the cheese, they say the Jerseys give such high-quality milk that they want to keep it all going. Julia also wants to experiment more, to get "wilder and funkier" in her cheesemaking. She ripens the cheeses on open shelves, "letting those huge moulds grow, washing them down and developing the flavour." That is real cheese to her, and she makes us laugh when she tells us, "When I see a cheese without a good rind, it looks naked to me."

You'll find Moonstruck organic cheeses on the menus of Café Brio, the Marriott Inner Harbour Hotel's Fire & Water, Spinnakers, the Hotel Grand Pacific's The Mark, Butchart Gardens and the Temple in Victoria, and at Sooke Harbour House, where an entire course is created from these truly world-class cheeses.

Morningside Organic Bakery and Café

Alan Golding and Manon Darrette have created a café that not only serves "everything organic, all the time," but also provides a comfortable venue for good conversation—an outlet for talking things over. Says Alan, "There are a lot of scary things happening in the world. We've been disconnected. We need to be bold, to reconnect with each other." Those reconnections are regularly made over cups of excellent coffee, house-made muffins and pizza.

Alan is a gentle man, with a lifetime of mindful thinking and responsible action, who has created a modern-day salon in a little adobe building at Fulford Harbour. The café came about at the right time, after he had looked for the ideal situation on some of the other Gulf Islands.

Alan and Manon had been living in Victoria, and came to Saltspring in 2002 to take in the Market-in-the-Park. Getting off the ferry at Fulford Harbour, Alan had an instant wonderful feeling about the place and said to Manon,

"We're not going to the market. We're staying here." They looked around, discovered that the little café on Morningside Road was vacant, and signed a lease that day.

The café menu is focussed on nutritious, organic fare made from mostly local ingredients. The Caffè Fantastico coffees and Wildfire Bakery breads and pastries, delivered daily from Victoria, are exclusive on Saltspring to Morningside. There is also a wide range of organic fine foods available for purchase, including olive oils, balsamic vinegars and teas. In spring and summer, local organic produce is sold in the café's courtyard. Alan has also been working with island farmers to grow some special vegetables for the café's menu. Eventually, they hope to grow herbs on the roof of the building, an urban-gardening concept that would be well suited to this little place.

Alan's aim to provide "food for the stomach and food for the mind" has already been more than fulfilled here. I find myself returning not only for the good eats, but also for the inspiring conversation.

Salt Spring Flour Mill

What must be the world's smallest flour mill is located at the north end of Saltspring Island. As I approach the architect-designed home of Pat Reichert, I find myself looking in vain for a water wheel. The actual mill is in a tiny yellow room in the back of the house. Its main feature is a wood-framed stone mill that's beautiful enough to be a piece of furniture.

Pat greets me at the door of the mill and asks if I'd like a demonstration. Once the mill starts grinding the grain, which she brings in from her partner's family-owned, certified organic farm in Saskatchewan, I can see her passion for milling. This is a second career for Pat and one she hadn't exactly planned, but which seemed like the right thing to do at the time.

She's always baked. When she was working as a social researcher, she travelled a lot and found herself coming home and baking bread "to ground myself." A few years ago, she saw a photograph of a stone mill and felt herself connecting to it. It wasn't long before she started looking for her own mill, which turned out to be more difficult than she had imagined.

Her research finally led her to the only person who still makes mills in Canada, and he agreed to make hers. It's constructed of untreated solid pine and the wood's natural resin prevents bugs from developing in the flour. Pat tells me that grain and flour should never be milled against metal as it destroys nutrients. Inside the mill are two specially tumbled granite stones from the Tyrol that work together to grind the grain.

Pat produces only about 15 to 20 pounds of flour at a time, using a cool-milling process where the stones turn very slowly; fast action creates heat and heat reduces nutrition. She estimates she has personally ground 12,000 to 15,000 pounds of flour in the last three years, most of which is distributed through the weekly Market-in-the-Park, and at Nature-Works health food store in Ganges. Local restaurants like Hastings House also use her flours.

Pat says she is pleased to be doing something useful for the community. In the old days, people would take their grains to the local mill to have them turned into flour. She says she would love to "bring that quality back to Saltspring." She is proud to be offering fully certified products that are distinguished in the marketplace.

In addition to various flours, Pat also has some delicious cereal combinations, as well as mixes for quick breads, muffins and pancakes. When I visited her at her home, she was working on an expanded line of heritage-grain products as well as cake mixes, including a tempting double-chocolate cake. Later in the year, I ran into Pat at Saltspring's Seedy Saturday event, where she was launching Hearty Seed, Lemongrass and Cilantro and Mediterranean bread mixes. For those wanting organic baked goods without having to start from scratch, these products are a godsend.

Pat Reichert would love to "bring that quality back to Saltspring."

Salt Spring Island Bread Company

Heather Campbell's mother always said, "It doesn't matter about your china; it's sharing the food you have with other people that counts." She would divide whatever she had for supper by the number of people at her table, and Heather does the same today. On Friday nights, before she bakes 400 to 500 loaves of bread, she cooks and leaves her porch door open. Neighbours and friends know they can just drop by. Some eat, some drink; all contribute to the lovely sense of *joie de vivre* that Heather exudes.

When I arrive on a Saturday afternoon, the week's work is done. Heather has just returned from the Market-in-the-Park, where she regularly sells every loaf she bakes. She and her architect husband, Phillip van Horn, are looking forward to a sunset picnic with friends that evening. There's a beautiful salmon lying on the butcher block, about to be cooked. Phillip has gone off for a swim. Heather and I sink into a couch and talk baking.

Unlike many people I've met who have changed careers to become food producers, Heather always sought an alternative lifestyle and always baked bread. It was a natural evolution for her to turn a passion into a business. She says she likes doing hands-on things, loves "making something that I really like and passing it on to others. It's a way to pass your energy around."

"It doesn't matter about your china; it's sharing the food you have with other people that counts."

– Heather Campbell's mother

For 15 years, she and Phillip lived "in the bush" on 25 acres in the Ottawa Valley. There was no power or running water and no phone. When they came to Saltspring in 1991, the locals warned them that the lifestyle was quite rustic. To them, it was practically luxurious.

A friend of Heather's had heard Alan Scott, author of *The Bread Builders*, speak at a conference and Heather liked the sound of his wood-fired bread ovens. She bought plans from Scott (which Phillip revised somewhat to make the oven stronger) and had a local mason build her a four- by six-foot oven. The oven holds 35 loaves at a time, and she bakes up to 700 loaves of bread a week. She mixes and hand-shapes every loaf, but has help loading the oven—from Phillip and from Mark Stevens, who produces seeds for Dan Jason of Saltspring Seeds. People are very much connected on the island. Heather says it's one of the most caring places she's ever lived.

Heather's bread is sold at the seasonal Saturday market and year-round at Admiral's Sushi Bar and at NatureWorks in Ganges. One day a week, she and other producers sell at a small organic market in Ganges (Tuesdays, 10:00 a.m. to 2:00 p.m., 112 Hereford Avenue). People who know her phone ahead to place their orders.

The bread is made with certified organic flour and mainly organic ingredients. I find it impossible to choose from 95 per cent rye, 100 per cent spelt, whole wheat levain—plain, or with walnuts, raisins, apricot/hazelnuts, dates/ginger or rosemary. Heather is always experimenting, and one week, produced a bread combining cranberries with white and dark chocolate. Her customers couldn't get enough.

When I finally get up to leave, Heather invites me to come back for dinner "any Friday evening." I'm truly touched and reminded of something Fairburn Farm Culinary Retreat's Mara Jernigan once said, "You can go to Italy and eat in all the best places, but if an Italian family invites you into their home, you'll remember it forever."

Saltspring Island Cheese Company

I was introduced to David Wood's famous goat's milk and sheep's milk cheeses in Victoria at Ottavio's, and found them not only delicious but also beautiful. Each perfect mound of chèvre is decorated and flavoured with different edible flowers (from Rosalie Beach at Wave Hill Farm), peppercorns (David recommends the peppercorn cheese with a nice Scotch, "There's something so right about that combination"), white truffles or roasted garlic. They make a notable addition to the cheese tray. David also makes Marcella, an aged soft goat's milk cheese, and a crottin chevrignon, which holds its shape when baked. In addition, there are creamy Camembert types, including a delicious blue version, an aged sheep's milk cheese and a hearty feta. The thing about sheep, though, is they take the winter off, so the goat's milk cheese is really Wood's bread and butter.

Before visiting the *fromagerie* and meeting the cheesemaker himself, I have been invited to picnic atop the island's 1,975-foot Mount Maxwell. At its lookout, we open a lovely, wicker picnic hamper to reveal a cornucopia of delights packed this morning by the chef at Hastings House. There is a tasty chicken salad, fresh fruit, bread, a root-vegetable terrine with onion confit and an assortment of David Wood's cheeses, some freshly baked gingersnaps, chocolate cookies and almond shortbread. The wine is the popular Millefiori 2000 produced by Venturi Schulze Vineyards on Vancouver Island. After this lunch, I couldn't wait to see how the diverse range of cheeses we'd tasted was produced.

David's story is not untypical of the kinds of people who settle on Saltspring. He paid his dues in Toronto, running the highly successful David Wood's Fine Foods shop and writing a couple of cookbooks, and then, nearly 20 years ago, picked up the family and bought a peaceful sheep farm on Saltspring. He says the change in lifestyle has been good for family life, "You get to do things with your kids like milking the sheep." It's hard work, but they are making a living and loving their new life.

David considers himself a "gumbooter," one of the hardy and hearty south-end Saltspring Island residents whose outdoor lifestyle requires them to keep gumboots at the ready. (There is also an implication that these are the "real" Saltspringers, the kind who collect oysters, clams and seaweed.) As I tour the *fromagerie* with David, I sense a quiet pride of accomplishment. The goat's milk cheeses are made from milk brought in from "goat people" in Abbotsford on the mainland, and from Mill Bay on Vancouver Island. They're mostly fresh cheeses; because of the smaller fat globules in goat's milk, they have a great silky texture—not gritty or grainy in the mouth. I happily learn from David that the higher the moisture content, the lower the fat. His soft goat cheeses have only 19 per cent fat content—what a pleasure!

The milk is pasteurized (heated to 145°F for half an hour, then cooled), then a culture is added and it's left to ripen. This, says David, is the curds and whey or "Miss Muffet" stage. The whey or water is drained off, leaving behind the curds—the fat and protein. "Differences in time, temperature and acidity make a huge difference to the finished product," says David, so these aspects are closely monitored. His soft goat's milk cheeses age for four days; the Camembert-style take 25 days. He makes 280 soft cheeses per day and 120 Camembert-style.

After the tour, we gather around the Sweet Heart stove in David's kitchen and sample his beautiful cheese. It's a food memory I recall each time I buy Saltspring Island Cheese in Victoria—another rewarding link from "field" to feast. And now, the charming shop on the farm is open seven days a week in the summer.

Saltspring Island Garlic Festival

Garlic ice cream, anyone?

From early August until the end of September, that distinctive waft is in the air at the many garlic festivals across North America. West-coasters can celebrate on Saltspring Island, where the island's garlic growers come together for a real love-in on the first August weekend. There's also the odd off-island grower, like the exuberant Ken Stefanson of Gabriola Island, who brings his Russian Hard Neck, Porcelain and Purplestripe varieties—fresh, pickled or made into chutney and potent chocolate bars. Dozens of vendors set up tents at the Farmers' Institute Grounds on Rainbow Road in Ganges, and people come from as far away as the mainland to stock up on the season's first juicy harvest.

Yes, there is lots of garlic ice cream on offer, but it's a bit too early in the day for that, so I buy a braid of Korean garlic from Charlie Eagle's Bright Farm, and wander from stall to stall absorbing the festivities. Garlic has come a long way, baby, since its odour offended those unaccustomed to Mediterranean flavours, and it's now firmly embedded in the North American culinary lexicon.

Salt Spring Vineyards

Happy, who trained to be a seeing-eye dog but ended up failing the course, appears to be greeting us with great enthusiasm when Cynthia Cooper and I open the gate to Salt Spring Vineyards. But it's really Cynthia's adorable Lhasa Apso, Jasper, who has caught Happy's eye and the two of them become fast friends. We are warmly greeted by the Janice Harkley and steered straight to the tasting room for a welcome glass of 2004 Christmas Release Blackberry Port, which Janice describes as "alcoholic blackberry pie." It makes a delightful mid-morning refreshment.

Janice and her husband, Bill, are new to the winery business, but then so is Saltspring Island. In 2002, they were granted the island's first-ever licence to operate a winery. Pragmatic folk, Janice said they felt they had "done every-thing they wanted to do" in their previous business, the River Run Cottages bed and breakfast in Ladner, and decided to make their next project a winery. They chose the Fulford Valley on Saltspring because it was on the same lati-tude as Vancouver Island's Cowichan Valley wineries. Saltspring has a long history of successful orchards so they knew the climate would be conducive to grape-growing. Their vineyards sit high up on Lee Road, which ensures that late spring frosts are unlikely to harm the grapes. The location also gives them great visibility for attracting customers.

They began to clear and groom the property in 1998 and planted two acres of Pinot Gris, Pinot Noir and Chardonnay in 2000. The following year, they added another acre of Pinot Noir and an early-ripening red, Leon Millot. When they were granted their winery licence in 2002, their neighbours Elaine Kozak and Marcel Mercier were granted a licence half an hour later for their Garry Oaks Winery. The Fulford Valley is emerging as an interesting wine area on the island. The Harkleys' winemaker, Paul Troop, has subsequently launched his own vineyards of experimental varieties across the road (see Dragonfly Hill Vineyard).

Janice tells me the Pinots are very well suited to the area because they like a longer, cooler ripening period. She feels "they have a better flavour than the Okanagan, maybe because of the higher mineral content in the soil here." I'd wager their dedication to organic growing practices also contributes to the improved taste. Says Janice, "We believe that grapes free from herbicides produce healthier and tastier wines." On offer the day we visit were the winery's 2004 Ortega, Blanc de Noir and Christmas Release Blackberry Port as well as its 2003 Pinot Noir and Merlot Bin 537 (the latter is made with fruit from Oliver, BC, and won a silver medal at the All Canadian Wine Championships). Janice was particularly excited about their 2004 wines because "we had fabulous weather."

When I ask what she is most proud of at the winery, there is a curious pause. Janice says she associates pride with its "seven deadly sins" meaning, so we laugh and I reword the question. What fulfills her here on her five-acre vineyard? She tells me she "always feels happy when I walk out into the vineyards." Believing that "we are here to be stewards of the land," she is pleased that they have been able to utilize what they've got. She enjoys the sense of community on Lee's Hill and appreciates it all the more when she comes back from a visit to the city. "It's always nice to come home to our Slow Islands in the gulf," a term that has recently been adopted by some Gulf Island residents to express their idyllic lifestyle (and, inherently, express their desire to keep it that way!).

"We are here to be stewards of the land."

— Janice Harkley

Bill Harkley is a pilot who also teaches flying in Vancouver. Janice is a certified accountant who also teaches a course in entrepreneurship for Royal Roads University's School of Business in Victoria. When they decided to go into the wine-making business, they both took courses in oenology at the University of California at Davis. She says that she and Bill "work really well together. The winery is fun and people are happy to be here." She teaches her students the process of planning for success that makes such a venture possible and often brings them to the vineyard to see for themselves the fruit of her business model.

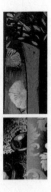

Cynthia and I buy blackberry port (we love the fanciful, award-winning labels designed by Vancouver wine rep Bernie Hadley-Beauregard) and jars of chow-chow, a relish made by one of Janice's friends on the island, before collecting Jasper and heading back to Fulford Harbour to catch the ferry. As we leave, Cynthia turns to me with a smile, "It's always impressive to see what education, foresight and planning produce."

In June 2008, the vineyard had a change in ownership. Devlin and Joanne McIntyre are the new owners, although Janice and Bill have retained a minority share, live nearby and continue to be involved.

Soya Nova Tofu

I consider a visit to Soya Nova Tofu a quintessentially Saltspring Island experience. There's something wonderfully communal about the operation, which is also home to owner Deborah Lauzon. Located in one of the island's old orchard areas, Soya Nova Tofu has been in production for 20 years.

Deborah invites Thomas Render and me to join her in her "office." She sets out real sofas and tables on her patio in summer and receives visitors in the sunshine. All around her, employees are coming and going. They're just finishing off a long day of production and the place is really buzzing. All her employees are young; many sport interesting dyed hair and tattoos. All seem wildly passionate; Deborah calls it "energized enthusiasm."

When there's work to do, she has a policy of "hiring whoever walks through the door," and she is proud that all three of her children—Zoltan, Nova and John—are seasoned tofu makers.

What, I ask, is her secret? I mean, how is it that these young people are so obviously turned on to tofu? She laughs. When her own kids had parties, she always cooked something for them. Being a vegetarian for 30 years, she often made tofu burgers and they loved them. She says the kids of Saltspring eat tofu: burgers, soy-sausage rolls and her famous Zed Spread. Now, her grandchildren are enjoying the benefits of tofu. When they are "strung out on candy from a birthday party," she feeds them tofu with nutritional yeast and tamari, and watches them "mellow right out."

Deborah gives the okara (the pulp by-product of tofu production) to local farmers to feed their animals. She would like to see more farmers using this high-protein organic feed.

Wave Hill Farm

Rosalie Beach's rosemary sprigs and edible flowers sit atop the artisan chèvre made by the Saltspring Island Cheese Company, and her jewel-like strawberries and figs are on the menu at Hastings House, yet this enterprising woman is actually best known for her flowers.

Today, I have a bouquet of Rosalie's dahlias on my desk: globes of deep fuchsia, purple and pink that take me back to the tranquillity of her flower garden every time I look at them. The garden itself is overwhelming, both in colour and in variety: dahlias, tiger lilies, Casa Blanca lilies (Rosalie's favourite) and daisies. Giant purple and golden cardoons have also found their way into the flower beds. The day I visit, Rosalie is about to make up a special order for the International Federation of Organic Agriculture Movements conference in Victoria: 200 handmade bouquets that she will deliver herself.

She takes me on a rambling tour of her orchard, greenhouses and market garden. I soon see that not only did she and husband, Mark Whitear, save this property, but she is deeply passionate about growing and wholly committed to their new life in Canada. The couple spent 25 years in England where they raised three children and Rosalie lectured on holistic health care.

Forty years ago, Rosalie's parents bought a 575-acre property on Saltspring Island. Twelve years ago, when they were forced to sell off a few acres to pay off an enormous tax bill, Rosalie and Mark decided to try to keep the place. The couple moved to Saltspring, converted some of the land to organic farming, started a natural-selection timber business and felt they were finally home.

The flower garden meets up with the vegetable and fruit gardens, where Brussels sprouts and broccoli are underplanted with mizuna, and companion planting is used extensively. There are strawberries, Cascade berries (a cross between a wild trailing blackberry and a loganberry), figs, asparagus, grapes, watermelons, Ogen melons, St. Nick melons (they keep until Christmas), plums, potatoes and herbs. There are also greenhouses for tomatoes, cucumbers, peppers and eggplants.

Theirs is the oldest orchard on the island, planted in 1855 by pioneers Trage and Spikerman. It originally had 1,600 trees. Rosalie loves the Braeburn apples for their taste. Her Wolf River variety is well known for its flavour and for the size of its fruit ("One apple, one pie," says Rosalie). She also grows the King of Tompkins County, Baldwin, Wadhurst Pippins, Gravenstein, Mann and Fallow Water varieties. As we wander through the orchard, "the slug patrol" marches by: a family of Rouen ducks. The sheep regard us from a distance. Rosalie and Mark press and sell apple and grape juices in the fall.

As many as 20 WWOOFers (Willing Workers on Organic Farms) work on Wave Hill Farm every year. Once, one of them asked Rosalie why they never eat citrus fruits. She replied that, with so many fruits and vegetables in season on the farm, they had no reason to buy oranges from some place else. One night, she and Mark counted 23 vegetables, herbs and fruits on their dinner plates. To me, theirs is an enviable, self-sustained existence.

Rosalie and I walk back to her barn (actually, it's underneath her house), passing the fence lined with grapevines, lavender and rosemary and she tells me how these plantings remind her of holidays in Provence. She loves gardening and loves Saltspring Island, and, gazing at the dahlia bouquet on my desk in Victoria, I reflect on her enviable state of contentment.

PENDER ISLANDS

(yes, there are two: North Pender and South Pender)

Aurora at Poets Cove Resort

There have been some changes at Poets Cove since I was last there in 2005, including, quite recently, a new general manager and a new executive chef. As far as I can tell, these changes are going to make something good even better.

Walter Kohli, the new general manager, is Swiss-born and has managed resorts all over China. He bought a property on Pender Island a few years ago and was just about to return to China to commence work there when the owners of Poets Cove asked if he would run the resort. "So I did a U-turn," he laughs, "and now we are delighted to be known as locals on the island." Walter has high praise for executive chef Steven Boudreau, in particular because he runs an immaculately clean kitchen. Which coming from a Swiss hospitality expert is high praise indeed.

Steven takes time one afternoon to answer my many questions. He's a wiry, high-action kind of guy, who seems pleased to now be making Pender and its more laid-back lifestyle his home. He's originally from Cape Breton, Nova Scotia, and did his cook's training at the Canadian Culinary Institute on Prince Edward Island. He and four others were hired from his 1999 graduating class to work for the Nantucket Clambake Company, which specializes in hosting clambakes on the beach. Bill Clinton and the Boston Pops Orchestra were among the clients he cooked for during his two seasons with the company.

Chef Steven Boudreau has taken over the helm at Poets Cove Resort.

Then a friend persuaded him to go west, and the two of them landed in Vancouver. Steven worked at Raintree at the Landing, then helped

 another friend open The Ordinary Café. He credits that work—both as *garde manger* and *entre métier*—with "making me the chef I am today. My passion is for the details and I believe that what makes a plate is what's with it." Indeed, he has a flair for the sides, for reading a customer and then doing a chef's tasting menu "on the fly. It's when I'm most creative."

The other big influence for Steven was the time he spent in the kitchen at Cioppini's in Vancouver's Yaletown. "Chef Posterero instilled a proper chef's work ethic in me!" he says (and those of us who have met Pino Posterero don't doubt it). Along the way, Steven worked for Painter's Lodge and April Point (four kitchens at once!), and worked in Montreal for a bistro and catering company that catered events like Fashion Week. Steven has a range of experience that he "wants to give to the food. I want the customers to see the detail and love that goes into our food."

I certainly saw and tasted it in Dungeness crab cakes with a tangy red pepper and caramelized onion relish and gentle rouille that was served with mixed lettuces. And I saw it in spades in the chef's roasted sablefish with endive that had been sautéed in maple syrup and shallots, and the accompanying red onion and fennel tartlet, served atop a du Puy lentil and diced vegetable salad—such precision in presentation and fresh tastes against the rich fish! But then, Steven tells me, "You know, I'm always looking at a dish and trying to figure out how it could be even better."

Like his predecessors, Steven is attempting to source locally. It's a bit difficult on Pender where output is never quite enough for a restaurant that can do 200 to 300 covers a night, but he has already found a supply of local walnuts (Shepherd's Croft Farm), garlic (Don Charman) and Moonbeams coffee. And he's pouring Morning Bay wine as well as working towards using it in compotes and sauces. Mussels are coming from Saltspring Island, although "it took me a while to get past thinking PEI had the best mussels," and he's buying chicken from Cowichan Bay Farm. We had a good discussion about local cheeses, and I left him with a suggestion of trying the Moonstruck Organic Cheese company's Beddis Blue with his steaks.

A big part of what Steven brings to his food comes from his travels. He tells me, "My belief is that there is so much to learn in the culinary field, so why not get out and learn it?" He and his fiancée travel extensively, so he brings "outside-the-box" thinking from Argentina, Peru, Vietnam and, most recently, Turkey to his cooking style. "You will notice my Montreal-deli influences on our Syrens Bistro menu," and indeed, there are great traditional choices like steak frites and pulled-pork sandwiches alongside fresh-sheet offerings like the prawn and chickpea-vegetable sauté.

Both Walter and Steven emphasize the importance of having good service to complement the food, and I am charmed to be served by one particular member of the international staff. Dining room captain Eduardo Brandao has been sponsored for another two years at the resort, and his professional but friendly demeanour sets the tone here.

Since Poets Cove came onto the scene, I've spent time in the spa and overnighted in the very comfortable guest rooms (all with fireplaces and oceanfront balconies), but true to my foodie nature, these are just foils for the restaurants. Sitting in Aurora's gracious-but-not-pretentious dining room, or out on the deck overlooking the cove (there are often up to 300 boaters in port), always feels like a real getaway — and it's only a 40-minute ferry ride from Victoria.

Iona Farm

As I attempt to stroll casually by Ellen Willingham's vegetable stall at the Pender Island Farmers' Market, apparently I'm not casual enough. "Taking notes this morning?" is her friendly enquiry. The old notepad has blown my cover, but it leads to a great chat over samples of her divine goat's milk cheese with fresh herbs and garlic.

Ellen and Rob Willingham are both Anglican priests and crisis counsellors who came to Pender Island seeking a healthier lifestyle. They had been practising in separate parishes in Winnipeg, their youngest daughter had been diagnosed with leukemia and they felt they had a lot of stress to deal with. On a visit to the West Coast, the family visited a cousin on Pender Island. Amazingly, after having coffee with his cousin, Rob bought her house and the Willinghams went back to Winnipeg to sell their home there.

Ellen says they have never regretted the move. Eventually, Tekla Deverell told them about the Iona property and they decided in earnest to try farming. The 20-acre farm is mainly forested, but they have five large vegetable gardens and pens for their goats, sheep and chickens. Ellen and Rob first began farming to feed themselves and later started selling at the Saturday market. They've been certified organic since 1995.

Ellen tells me they are essentially "boat people," who used to enjoy sailing on Lake of the Woods in western Ontario. The Gulf Islands reminded them of that. "We feel like seals, torn between wanting to be on land or water," she jokes. She and Rob are always on the water on Sundays, heading out together on their diesel-powered boat but spending the day apart. One of them gets off on Mayne Island, to conduct the Sunday service there; the other carries on to Galiano Island to lead that congregation. When they're not leading services, farming or at the market, the Willinghams provide crisis-counselling services on the island.

I buy a big tub of chèvre and some of Ellen's green peppers, and then move on to speak to her tablemate. Tekla Deverell, formerly a psychologist living in Vancouver, is the island's undisputed doyenne of organic gardening and wife of the famous crime writer Bill Deverell. From Tekla, I buy the freshest walnuts and ask what brought her to Pender. She smiles and tells me, "I followed Bill." Now, Tekla owns one of the island's most beautiful and prolific organic gardens, and she loves bringing her produce to market.

Jane's Herb Garden

It's absolutely appropriate that my cellphone packs it in halfway through my conversation with Jane Gregory just as I'm driving off the ferry. After all, Pender Island is a relatively small place and everyone knows everyone else. I shouldn't have to rely on big-city technology to get directions to her garden. A helpful walker at the side of the road points me right and, minutes later, I find Jane waiting at her front gate to greet me.

I'd remembered seeing her sweet little rosemary plants on the tables of Aurora restaurant at Poets Cove Resort, and decided I wanted to meet her. Born in Buckinghamshire in England, Jane was working in a legal process-serving company in White Rock before moving across to Pender Island. As we survey her raised beds of herbs (all grown without sprays or fertilizers), she tells me she has always loved gardening. "Herbs are wonderful to brighten up a meal or transform vinegar or a bar of soap into something special."

With her two daughters, Samantha and Melanie, "now in school mode," Jane has expanded her business of fresh herb plants and cut herbs to include a full herbal product line of preserves, soaps and sweets. She rises at 3:00 a.m. on market days (the Pender Farmers' Market is held Saturdays from May to October) to make her famous glazed orange buns. When she has fruit available— apples, plums, strawberries or rhubarb—she makes pies, which have garnered just as loyal a following as the buns.

Jane makes wonderful soaps using organic goat's milk from Ellen Willingham of Iona Farm. I tried rosemary and orange, from a range made with such enticing ingredients as raspberry, lavender, oatmeal and almond. The soaps are made from scratch and take six weeks to cure. Her preserves include hot pepper jelly, kiwi jam with pine nuts and cranberries, and an amazingly complex and addictive fig, walnut and brandy conserve. Jane recommends serving the fig conserve with pork or turkey, but mine didn't last beyond the cheese course that night and a midnight nip to the fridge to eat the rest directly out of the jar!

On the sweet side, Jane's rich Dundee Christmas cakes are shipped all over the world. She also makes a terrific toffee and vanilla fudge, which she tells me is "really creamy and not terribly sweet." Its popularity meant there was none left for me to try, but it certainly has given me a good reason to return.

Morning Bay Vineyard and Estate Winery

They say that on the Gulf Islands, the proverbial "six degrees of separation" is only two degrees. My husband and I ventured down a very long and winding dirt road to find a picture-perfect cabin with smoke coming out of the chimney

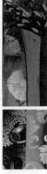

and a stunning view across to Saturna Island at its back door. We knocked and a couple I had met before answered the door. Keith Watt and Barbara Reid had been at the Marley Farm Winery one hot summer's evening two years ago, and I had remembered that they were going to start a winery on one of the islands. Now, here they were, with that winery about to open its doors to the public.

Keith invites us to join him on an invigorating walk around the vineyards, which he calls "the most difficult thing I've ever done." It's not hard to see the work that went into clearing the land, installing a drip irrigation system and planting the vines. Says Keith, "We were able to make good use of what we cut down," with wood from the land going into the house and new winery building.

Keith is a former CBC Radio journalist; Barbara worked in wholesale clothing for the April Cornell Trading Company in the United States. When they bought their 25 acres, they thought it would suit apple orchards, because Pender Island has a history of apple growing. They decided to start with a market garden and sold their bounty of lettuces, purple cabbage, Oriental greens, Brussels sprouts, eggplant, watermelon, herbs and saffron at the Pender Farmers' Market. Last year, they grew 3,000 pounds of veggies for the market, making them "the largest organic farm on Pender Island."

One day, Keith was looking across to Saturna Island and thought he spotted grapevines. He soon discovered that he lived directly across the pond from Saturna Island Vineyards. After calling on Eric von Krosigk, consulting winemaker to many local wineries, to appraise Morning Bay Farms, he got the green light for grape growing.

"In 2001, we planted Schönburger and Marechal Foch here on the east side, and Pinot Noir, Pinot Gris, Riesling and Gerwürztraminer on the south-facing upper bench." It seems the upper bench can get as hot as 40°C in the summer, which suits the white varietals perfectly. While the grapes grow, Keith has been taking courses at the University of California at Davis, and experimenting with winemaking, using grapes sourced elsewhere.

Keith hasn't been able to find out too much about the property, except that it's never really been farmed. There is an old barn and cabin where a woman lived and kept goats in the 1950s. Keith and Barbara have restored the buildings and moved them to the upper bench. One-quarter of their property is in the Agricultural Land Reserve, and that's the section where they were given permission to build the winery. "We're fortunate that winemaking is being encouraged as a sustainable agricultural industry," Keith tells us.

The winery and tasting room are now open, with the first Morning Bay vintages released in 2007. Morning Bay hosts special events with music and food throughout the summer, so you may want to call ahead in order to include one in your visit.

Pender Island Bakery Café

Dorothy Murdoch is a long way from hotel management in Vancouver, and she's a lot happier. "I'd had my eye on this bakery for a couple of years," she tells me, "and when it came up for sale, I was ready to buy."

She is delighted to finally be working for herself and providing employment for Pender Islanders. While Dorothy operates a bakery and catering company, she is not a baker, and many people thought she was crazy to operate her business from the same plaza as the island's main grocery store with its in-house bakeshop. However, it seems Dorothy saw something they didn't: a craving for back-to-basics, made-from-scratch baking. She hired the shop's original master baker, Dorian Wilde, and took on a pastry baker and several assistants. From the day she opened, Dorothy has put the Pender Island Bakery Café on the map. Her impressive range of breads and buns—many organic—literally walk out the door. We took Cornish pasties (a nod to Dorothy's English roots), spanakopita and the biggest cinnamon buns ever back to the cottage for lunch, and it was thumbs up all around the table.

Dorothy is very attuned to baby boomers' desire for organics and interest in knowing what's in their food. She serves only organic coffees from Reingold, a German roaster in Vancouver, and uses organic ingredients in baking whenever possible. Sitting at the window on a sunny Sunday morning, my niece and I enjoyed our Americanos and, yes, just one more of those sinful cinnamon buns.

Pistou Grill

As I journey forth for the third edition of *An Edible Journey*, I'm aware of a certain self-consciousness about what we're doing with food on the islands. Don't misunderstand me: local, organic and seasonal really must be the focus or we will never achieve food sustainability here. However, we don't want to become too precious, as in, "I'll never eat anything that isn't grown within sight of my back door." And I feel we have chefs who are, to a certain degree, just paying lip service instead of taking a real stance.

It may have to do with a lack of experience and confidence in some of the younger chefs, qualities of which Pierre Delacôte, owner and chef of Pistou Grill, has no shortage; I find his approach refreshing.

As I drive to his bistro in the dark of night, deer leap across my path and the local constabulary stops me for driving as though I'm in Paris not on Pender so it's something of an accomplishment to arrive intact. I am instantly relaxed by the simple but warm decor: golden walls, wooden wainscotting and basic wooden tables and chairs are the foil for colourful local art (some of it, I later learn, finger-painted by Pierre himself) and a display of wines.

A friendly if brusque gentleman comes out of the kitchen and sizes me up. We sit and talk and it doesn't take us long to realize that we understand each other. When I compliment Pierre on his five-star review from Victoria *Times Colonist* food critic Pam Grant, he says (though not without some obvious pleasure in having achieved that rating), "She didn't even introduce herself!" But of course that is the difference between a food critic and a food journalist like me. Pam operates anonymously and critically and writes honestly—about good and bad; I operate critically and honestly but write only about places that I like. So I pay an anonymous visit to Pistou once, and then I'm ready to reveal my identity and get my story. I am also a devout fan of Pam's, and it was because of her excellent review that I landed on Pierre's doorstep.

Pierre has a bio that one might not expect to find in this some-what isolated place: he's part of a generation in France that was still allowed to leave school at 13 and begin a trade. He tells me that he "had fun at elementary school, but couldn't see the point of going on." When his sister, with whom he was very close, managed to

Chef and owner Pierre Delacôte of Pistou Grill.

find him an apprenticeship at a friend's restaurant, he was delighted to "do whatever it took to take me out of school."

Though the apprenticeship road was hard, he calls it "character building" and seems grateful for having developed so thorough a background in classic French technique. He learned to be "fast, tough and creative," but not without some abuse along the way. Once, when he moved a large, boiling copper pot of pea soup and burned his arm so severely that he had to take two weeks off work, his superiors were relentless: "You're abandoning us. You loser, you traitor!"

In those days, he was making 11 francs a month for putting in 70-hour work weeks, preparing breakfast, lunch and dinner. "Things have changed so much," he tells me. "We cooked with coal and without a temperature gauge. Fifty kilos of mussels would arrive straight from the sea—still attached, not cleaned and ready for use like today. We learned to cut everything with a knife as nothing came in pre-sliced, and naturally we made all our own stocks and sauces—even puff pastry."

Pierre's character is evident in the rigorous pace he sets for himself in the restaurant. "I don't change the chef here. I *am* the chef, and every plate that goes out is made by me." While the industry is often heard to comment on how much more educated the public now is about food and dining, Pierre turns that sentiment on its head: "The public has a lack of education because they are often demanding in a way that doesn't fit the industry. We should be held responsible for what we *do*, not what we don't offer." Nevertheless, the Pistou Grill menu is sensitive to some aspects of today's demanding clientele in that it offers lower-fat entrées, uses no trans fats and indicates which items are vegetarian.

Other customers are arriving, so Pierre goes into the kitchen and I order my supper. A classic pistou soup is so good that I spoon every drop. It's thick with diced carrot, celery, tomato and zucchini and enriched with basil pesto (made from local grower Dan Charman's hydroponic basil and garlic) and Parmesan. A 12-inch piece of toasted focaccia is perfect for dipping into the steaming bowl.

Slow-cooked organic buffalo short ribs ("as in Jakarta") are everything they should be, but so much better. The ribs, crusted in white and black sesame seeds, arrive in a still-bubbling sauce of garlic, lemongrass, kaffir lime leaves, coconut and whole peanuts, sided with a potato croquette and nine vegetables (well, a couple of fruits) in the French style: asparagus, tomatoes, red and green peppers, zucchini, snap peas, apple, squash and Brussels sprouts. I eat as much of the buffalo as possible and, for the first time in my life, ask for a "doggy bag."

Pierre's cooking gives West Coast ingredients the benefit of 40 years of French technique. He brings such impressive credentials to his craft that I am forced to ask him for highlights. He was chosen to cook for the 1993 Vancouver summit President Clinton hosted to honour President Yeltsin, and he prepared the feast for Sarah McLachlan's wedding, but his personal favourite was cooking for nine years for the Penske racing team competing in Vancouver's Molson Indy.

SATURNA ISLAND

Haggis Farm Bakery

I follow Priscilla Ewbank by car to Haggis Farm Bakery, which she co-owns with her husband, Jon Guy. Partway there, an oncoming car stops in the middle of the road, and Dottie, Priscilla's dog, is transferred to her car. Seems Dottie has been out for a walk with another dog, and her play date is now over.

The bakery is a clapboard building a kilometre or so from the Saturna General Store, which is also owned by Priscilla and Jon, in partnership with Hubertus Surm. As we walk in, we enjoy the residual aroma of the 600 loaves that were baked the day before. Priscilla shows me the walk-in cooler ("refrigeration is very important here"), the stacks of grains that are milled on-site, the big mixer, oven and cooling racks. Behind the bakery is a greenhouse where tomatoes, basil and peppers are grown for the store's café.

Besides the bread, cookies and cereal that are baked twice a week for customers all over the Gulf Islands, and in Victoria and Vancouver, the bakery produces pasta and some special-order cakes. Priscilla attributes the success of the bakery to Jon, "He's an excellent baker—he's a Virgo. It's really his heart and head in the whole operation."

My conclusion is that both Priscilla and Jon, together with their dynamic, extended family, are all responsible for the success of Haggis Farm Bakery and the Saturna General Store and Café. And their success is a reflection of their commitment to the land and to each other.

Saturna General Store and Café

The hub of the island's food and social scene has to be the big ol' general store, which offers everything from a post office to groceries and video rentals. There's also an excellent selection of BC wines and a café where I could happily eat every meal.

Co-owner Priscilla Ewbank takes me to an outside table, telling me she needs some air after packaging a bread order for Vancouver and Victoria until four o'clock that morning. Her husband, Jon Guy, is now making the off-island deliveries in their new refrigerated truck. Bread deliveries have come a long way since Jon started baking a decade ago and their two eldest daughters took the loaves door-to-door on horseback.

Today, Priscilla and Jon appear to have it all—a thriving store, bakery and café that together employ 23 islanders—but, understandably, it's been a long journey. They met as students at Berkeley during the heady 1970s, and came to Canada when Priscilla decided she "didn't want Jon to be cannon fodder in Vietnam." She tells me that the suburban values she was raised with, but never embraced, collided with the activist scene at Berkeley. She and Jon then attended Simon Fraser University, but Priscilla thought it restricting, and found herself looking across the pond to Saturna Island.

Co-owner Priscilla Ewbank enjoys a hearty breakfast at the Saturna General Store and Café.

When they first arrived on the island, they lived and worked on Jim Campbell's farm. They milked cows and helped with the haying, and Priscilla spun and wove wool from the sheep. Today, she says she is "so grateful to have experienced that way of life, and realize how it informs my own."

The evening's dinner menu reads like a gastronome's dream: Organic Mayne Island Greens with Buttermilk Feta Dressing and Summer Vegetables; 40-clove Roasted Chicken Breast with Roasted Vegetables; Haggis Farm Pasta with Basil Pesto and Parmesan; Tagliatelle with Roasted Eggplant; and, for dessert, the blueberry tart, cheesecake or their specialty, big, luscious fruit pies.

One by one, café staff members drop by our table, each one hugging Priscilla, and introducing themselves to me. I find myself in the centre of a warm and loving extended family. Katie often stays with Priscilla when she works evenings, as her family lives on the other side of the island. Amy divides her time between the café and the Saturna Lodge & Restaurant. Kolton is working in the kitchen before heading off to university on the mainland in September. Priscilla says she believes in "teaching the kids well" and giving them something meaningful to do. I think about how a lot of city teenagers I know would turn around in this hugely nurturing environment.

Priscilla says their philosophy includes "organic wherever we can," "feed people well" and "keep bread affordable." She is proud to be a significant employer on the island, and enjoys buying organic products from many on- and off-island growers. Ron Pither of Mayne Island supplies vegetables, and Flora House of Saturna Herbs supplies herbs. Four local wine connoisseurs advise on the store's selection.

There's an impressive symbiosis between the store, the bakery and the café. The café produces pesto and other things for the store's deli. Priscilla says when the café recently had a corned-beef sandwich on the menu, the bakery produced "really big rye bread." Leftover crumbs from the bakery go into Hubertus' famed Go-Nut Burgers that are sold in the store.

I stock up on spelt bread, whole wheat croissants, giant Loon cookies and Date Crunch Cereal, before following Priscilla by car to the bakery. Those exceptional Loon cookies, and many of the Haggis Farm Bakery breads, are available in Victoria at Seed of Life, Lifestyle Markets and Planet Organic.

 *Saturna Herbs*

Twenty-five-acre Breezy Bay Farm is located in a sheltered valley, just across the road from the Saturna Lodge & Restaurant. The property is mainly forest with about 10 acres of pasture for sheep, together with greenhouses and an acre under cultivation. There's also a bed and breakfast, where guests stay in a pretty 1892 farmhouse surrounded by orchards and scented lindens. I learn that the farmhouse was built by Gerald Fitzroy Payne, the grandfather of Noël Richardson of Victoria's Ravenhill Herb Farm.

It's a co-operative farm, owned by members of the Saturna Freeschool Community Projects (SFCP). The SFCP was named for a freeschool that operated on the property in the early 1970s. Member Flora House says, "Since then the farm has been run by members and a number of 'newcomers'—that is, you've only been on Saturna for 20 years or so!"

Flora and some of the others grow culinary herbs including thyme, sage, oregano and basil. The basil greenhouse is a beautiful thing to look at, and I stand inside for a long time just inhaling. All the drying and packaging of the herbs is done on-site, and they're sold through the farm's website, and at the Saturna General Store. You'll also find them on the menus at the Saturna Lodge & Restaurant and the Saturna Café.

Flora says the SFCP members have farmed organically for over 25 years, feeling "it's better to feed the land to feed ourselves." They have recently also become organically certified.

Saturna Island Vineyards

A relative newcomer to Saturna Island, the vineyards have made a big impact on 60 acres of south-facing waterfront, and their wines have made quite an impact both regionally and nationally. At the 2000 Northwest Wine Summit, winemaker Eric von Krosigk won a Crystal Rose award for his 1997 Vancouver Island Riesling Brut and silver awards for his 1998 Gewürztraminer Rebecca Vineyard and the 1997 Okanagan Valley Riesling Brut. At the 2001 All-Canadian Wine Championships, the vineyard won "Best Dry Riesling" for its 1999 vintage.

In some ways, it's all happened very quickly for the Page family from Vancouver. Larry and Robyn Page had been looking for a retirement property on Saturna when this spectacular property became available. They bought it and, with encouragement from their friend and viticulturist Jean-Luc Bertrand, decided to begin growing grapes in 1995.

Daughter Rebecca is the general manager, and I chat with her between tastings in the winery. She loves Saturna and is used to a small community, having lived previously in Pemberton, BC, where she ran the gas station and deli, and she is delighted to have her young son in the local school. Rebecca tells me the vines have been planted to take advantage of sun trapped on the property by vast sandstone cliffs. The cliffs act as a sort of heat radiator that "keeps the soil warm—several degrees warmer than the rest of the island." The land slopes, so it's ideal for drainage, and the soil is well fertilized "from nearly a century of sheep farming."

Michael Vautour is the cellar master who runs the convivial wine tastings and gives tours of the vineyards. It's a fairly hot day when I visit, so he suggests a tour by air-conditioned van. A former Vancouverite himself, he tells me how much he enjoys living in a small community now: "I feel everyone is family on Saturna."

The vineyards are magnificent. The Rebecca vineyard produces the award-winning Gewürztraminer, as well as Pinot Gris, Pinot Noir and Merlot. The two Robyn vineyards produce Chardonnay and Pinot Noir. The Long Field vineyard also produces Pinot Gris, and in the Falcon Ridge vineyards, 14 experimental varieties  include Muscat, Cabernet Sauvignon and Syrah. Because of its age, the vineyard has been using some grapes from the Okanagan, but it will eventually be self-sufficient. (Eric, "the flying winemaker," actually lives in the Okanagan, so he is able to make the grape selections personally.)

I stand in the Rebecca vineyard and catch my breath. The sun beats down. The grapes hang heavy with mellow fruitfulness on the vines. At the end of each row there is a pretty rose bush that "attracts aphids and provides early warning signs of any mould or mildew." Eventually, the Pages will plant olives and produce oil, but for now, their days are full with the vineyard, the winery and the casual bistro.

I enjoy a nice antipasto plate and glass of Riesling on the patio and take my time leaving.

MAYNE ISLAND

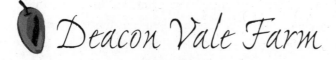

Deacon Vale Farm

Shanti McDougall asks, "Have you ever had the divine pleasure of eating a sun-warmed tomato fresh off the vine?" and then picks me a handful of her best cherry tomatoes. We're touring her greenhouse, and she's pointing out some of the special varieties that she grows for her famous (but still only in small production) tomato sauce: San Marzano (she brought the seeds back from Italy); Alicante (considered the best tomato by the British Horticultural Association); and a heritage variety called Brandy Wine.

Shanti will harvest up to 3,500 pounds of tomatoes, and then go into serious sauce production in her commercial kitchen. Her tomato sauce is in hot demand, mainly from private customers in Vancouver who buy it by the caseload. Local Mayne Islanders can buy it, and her jams, chutneys and relishes, at the Saturday Farmers' Market and Tru-Value store; in Victoria, these products are available at the Market on Yates and Planet Organic. Shanti says she will move beyond direct marketing once her production levels are higher. Eventually, she would like to be able to hire local residents because she believes the island needs more small-scale industry.

Sun-warmed tomatoes from Deacon Vale Farm

When Shanti and her husband, Don, started out, tomatoes were their main crop, but they now produce more of a variety. They grow 800 pounds of Spanish Roja garlic, Pinot Noir grapes, raspberries, artichokes and greens. There are also damson plums and yellow plums, from which Shanti makes jam. They harvest 500 chickens a year, and sell some 20 to 24 sides of beef. Shanti says some people will buy a whole year's supply of chicken from her and freeze it.

Deacon Vale is a magical, certified organic farm of 95 acres, co-owned by the McDougalls and the Abbotts (Shanti's brother is Vancouver doctor Bill Abbott). About half of the land is used for hay or pasture, and another large section is a woodlot. There's a large, 20-foot-deep pond in the centre of the property, surrounded by fruit trees. Closer to the McDougalls' house is a one-acre market garden, and another half acre of new plantings, including the grapes. Shanti is thinking about putting in some hazelnut trees because organic nuts are hard to find. Saltspring Island breadmaker Heather Campbell had told me that she couldn't find organic hazelnuts for her bread, so I introduce them—the grower and the baker—and, perhaps, organic hazelnut bread will one day be coming out of Heather's oven.

The farm operates on a closed-cycle system, producing what it needs to operate. To keep the soil viable, Shanti and Don maintain a hot compost measuring about 25 feet by 8 feet by 6 feet that is turned four times a year. The soil gets a good dose of micronutrients from local seaweed that is collected by the Village Bay Improvement Association and scattered over their plantings.

Mayne Island Farmers' Market

Shanti and Don McDougall were instrumental in starting the farmers' market on Mayne Island "to forge a closer bond between people and the food they eat." It's held in Miners Bay at the "Ag Hall," built around 1900 and the place where things happen on the island. The hall and its grounds offer an ideal setting. In the middle of the grounds, Shanti and Don have built a quaint pole structure, used as a stage for local performers.

The market offers a stunning array of the island's bounty: goat's milk cheese, produce, sauces and chutneys, jams and jellies, pies, soft lamb pelts and yarn made from mohair goats. It's a great day when Peter Renner comes across from Galiano with his superb wood-fired-oven-baked breads to sell. Deacon Vale Farm cooks up a delicious lunch (homemade sausages, hot beef sandwiches, salmon burgers, etc.), so many people spend the morning shopping, eating and chatting with their neighbours. The lunches are delicious, not surprising when one discovers they are prepared by a chef trained at London's Dorchester Hotel—that's Don McDougall! Market organizers hope to develop a complete food court in future.

Shanti says she values the quiet and privacy of her farm, but also enjoys the social aspect of the market. There are usually 10 vendors, and this increases to 20 stalls for the annual Fall Fair. The market runs on Saturdays, 10:00 a.m. to 1:00 p.m., from July to October.

Oceanwood Country Inn

Romance and food are always a good combination, and English country-house gentility provides a relaxed setting. I arrive at the Ocean Country Inn alone to find a lovely, rambling home set in the caress of the aptly named Dinner Bay, and ring the doorbell. Jonathan Chilvers, looking dapper in khaki shorts, greets me with, "Are you planning to come in, or have you just missed the bus?"

Jonathan is a long way from his birthplace "in the shadow of Wandsworth," but his dry, particularly English humour is fully intact. An expat myself, I take an instant liking to my host and ask him how he came to own this charming place.

He and his late wife, Marilyn, were living in Vancouver, working in advertising and public relations, respectively, when the idea to have a weekend place in the Gulf Islands emerged. The couple bought a low-maintenance cottage on Mayne Island and began escaping for long, Friday-to-Monday weekends as often as they could.

In 1989, a realtor friend suggested they look at a property that had just become available, and Jonathan agreed on the understanding that he and Marilyn were only looking. When they returned to see it a second time, they took along friends. Their friends said, "All you could do with this property is open a bed and breakfast," so they did.

While Jonathan excuses himself to change for dinner, I take a leisurely tour of the grounds. There's a prolific vegetable-and-herb garden overlooking the bay, and comfortable nooks and seating areas, all situated to take in the view. An impressive flagstaff sports the British Columbian, Canadian, American and British flags. Through an open window, I can see the kitchen in the full flutter of preparations for dinner.

As I wander around the side of the inn, I chance upon chef Steve Kruse taking a brief coffee break before service. He worked extensively in restaurants as a waiter and dishwasher before "getting serious and going to school in 1994." A graduate of the Stratford Cooking School, he worked at Sooke Harbour House and owned his own Mayne Island bistro, the Miner's Bay Café, before landing the big job at Oceanwood.

He loves living and working on the island, and appreciates the opportunity to use high-quality, refined ingredients in the Oceanwood kitchen. He says he tries to keep his cooking "straightforward and honest" and believes that the best food is "pulled out of the ground."

He relies on the inn's own gardens for much of the spring and summer, but also buys from some of the local cottage growers including Helen O'Brien and Naralaya Farm's Ron Pither. While the menu is planned a week in advance and posted on the inn's website, it can change daily, like last Thursday when no fisher had caught the anticipated skate that day. For chefs working on these somewhat remote islands, menu planning is both a challenge and a joy (the joy being when something fresh and inspiring arrives unexpectedly at the kitchen door).

Jonathan greets me again in the library with, "Would you like a beautiful martini or a nice, delicate sherry?" As I settle onto chintz with a glass of Harvey's Bristol Cream, Tony Bennett croons in the background and a kitchen helper passes by the window with a bowl of fresh-picked salad greens from the garden. An American couple joins us for a drink while their teenage daughter "completes her makeup" in their room upstairs. Returning guests, they ask Jonathan to recommend a local Chardonnay: "Something we haven't tried before."

Jonathan later tells me that British Columbia wines are in great demand, and he is pleased to be supporting the local economy. I enjoy his comments on the restaurant's wine list, such as what he's written for the popular Venturi Schulze Millefiori: "Enjoy it here because it is unique and you won't find it back in Kansas, Dorothy."

We all head downstairs to the oceanside restaurant for dinner, where a window seat has been reserved for me, although I can see that every table in this dining room commands a sea view. There is a rather large yacht in the bay tonight, the owners of which are dining at the table next to mine. When I mention that I will be overnighting on Pender Island, they point to it across the bay and we contemplate whether or not it's within swimming distance.

When the prix fixe menu is presented, I drift away into foodie heaven. One can choose from two appetizers and two mains, and the rest of the menu involves no effort on the part of the diner, other than emitting a few "ooohs" and "ahhhs" when the food arrives.

This evening's *amuse bouche* is a simple (or "honest," as Chef Steve would say) cucumber slice topped with smoked Sooke trout mousse. What follows is an amazingly good soup: Mayne Island lamb broth with white beans, zucchini and tomatoes. A fresh sage leaf from the garden adds to the delicious, earthy taste. The lamb was delivered from the island's Iredale Farm. The accompanying breads—calendula (edible marigold) and whole wheat walnut—are both excellent.

"Are you planning to come in, or have you just missed your bus?"

— Jonathan Chilvers

I have chosen the Pacific Octopus in Carrot Broth with Thai Basil, Daikon and Nasturtiums, a brilliantly coloured presentation that reminds me of a Chagall painting. I ask for a soup spoon to finish every last drop of the broth. A raspberry and fennel sorbet cleans the palate, and then I move on to albacore tuna loin seared rare served on lemon couscous with rosemary-caper butter sauce. Jonathan has paired this dish with a Tinhorn Creek Merlot.

My waitress, Candida, is a charming woman who also looks after the inn's gardens, and paints and decorates in the off-season. Like many Gulf Islanders, she has embraced the necessity of employment diversity. Working two or three different jobs is the way many are able to sustain life on the islands.

Alas, the ferry calls, and I take my leave. Jonathan opens the big gates and waves me off into a dark night. I foolishly tell him I know the way. With no sense of direction and only the moon to guide me, I somehow avoid all three deer that leap across the road en route, and find myself the only passenger boarding the 9:10 p.m. ferry from Mayne Island.

GALIANO ISLAND

Daystar Market and Market Café

Since *An Edible Journey* was first released, I have had the good fortune to spend extended periods of time on several of the Gulf Islands. During a three-month sojourn on Galiano, I did my grocery shopping at the Daystar Market—a store, café and community gathering place all in one. I was always impressed by the quality of ingredients that were available on what is arguably one of the least populated and remote of the Slow Islands in the gulf.

Stopping by before the place opened one morning to meet the sisterhood that runs it, I began to understand the difference passion can make to business. Tahirih Rockafella is a 28-year-old beauty who could easily walk the Milanese fashion runways if she was the least bit interested in that lifestyle. She isn't. In fact, she tells me she "could easily fall into the easygoing lifestyle" that her parents originally shared at Primal Point Commune on Galiano in the 1970s. Her boyfriend, Gabriel, a carpenter on the island, who has joined us for the interview, smiles at this.

Indeed, the lifestyle of Tahirih's parents, Lony Rockafella and Johanna New Moon, was in many ways idyllic in those early days. They picked fruit in the Okanagan and trucked it to the Lower Mainland. Later, they started Wild West, an organic food-distribution company, before selling it and moving to Galiano Island. On their nine-acre property, Lony and Johanna cut the trees that would be used to build their house and the Daystar Market store.

The café came later, built around the four-tonne reefer truck they had once used to transport fruit. Tahirih tells me that when she and her three sisters were younger, they "used to hang out in the truck's cubby above the café." The truck is now the café's cooler—seeing is believing!

Although Johanna and Lony eventually divorced, the family remained tightly knit. The girls lived with Johanna in Cobble Hill on Vancouver Island, but "we came home faithfully to our father [on Galiano] every weekend." Tahirih went on to work at Capers in Vancouver for a year, returning to Galiano to run the Daystar Market with her 26-year-old sister, Josli, for two years. They leased out the cafe, but Tahirih also did a waitressing stint there.

Gradually, all four sisters took on specific areas of responsibility in the store and café. Seventeen-year-old Cecia comes across from Cobble Hill in the summer to wash dishes; 23-year-old Oleann runs the produce department; and Josli works in the office. Tahirih runs the Market Café, with great enthusiasm. From her work at Capers and in the Daystar Market, she "got a good front-end idea of what people like to eat and what they are willing to pay." She attracted to the café Martine Paulin, a terrific island chef, whose wholesome cooking is a big draw.

My sister and I, still on the urban clock, stopped in for coffee and fresh cranberry muffins one morning. We were joined by islander John Scoones, who was just taking a break from excavating a nearby building site to tuck into the Farmer's Lunch, a hearty vegetarian pie with whole wheat crust, served with salad. There is a great community feel in the café. It's common to share a table, and interesting conversation is always on the menu.

The store and café depend on a wide range of suppliers, with "as much organic as possible" from local growers like Erik Nelson, Sutil Lodge and Doug Lhatta, and from Mayne Islander Ron Pither. Tahirih says "we grew up organic because of our parents." What better gift to pass on to one's children?

# Donna Marben

Just when I think I've met most of the dynamic organic farmers around these parts, Donna Marben invites me to enter paradise. Her farm, located way off the road at the north end of Galiano Island, has an amazingly diverse topography, allowing her to grow almost anything from kiwi to kamut.

Donna and her life partner, Hans Bongertman, met at the Primal Point Commune on the island in the early 1970s. Disillusioned with the Vietnam War, she had left her home in Minneapolis "to find a wilderness, a quiet space to live and work." Hans is a carpenter from Holland, who Donna says has farming in his blood; his surname means "man of the orchard." I learn that Hans is the linear planter; Donna the free-form artist who plants all over the place.

They both loved the communal life, but in 1984, with their two children in tow, they set out to carve their own piece of paradise out of a five-acre forested property. Their farm began as a way to sustain their family. When Donna realized she was buying a box of fruit every week, she quickly began to plant her own. Today, their orchards comprise 400 apple, pear and plum trees.

My tour begins at the upper bench, the property's rockiest area, where Hans and Donna have established raised beds. There are leeks, French heritage pumpkins and prolific grapes for making wine and raisins. A small greenhouse holds 25 varieties of tomatoes. Says Donna, "The important thing is to diversify. That way, if one kind doesn't take, another will."

The property dips way down into a three-acre valley that is naturally boxed in by huge trees, creating a microclimate. As we climb down what feels like hundreds of steps, Donna tells me she goes "up and down six times a day," often accompanied by her black Lab, Lucy. There are two vast, 25-foot-deep ponds in the valley, one of which is covered with the most fragrant lotus plants. From the valley's upper garden—the sandiest part, and therefore the first tilled every spring—Donna often gets two or three successive crops. Today, there is a profusion of lettuce, corn, potatoes, sunflowers and squash. The latter has been planted around the perimeter so it can wander. There are also echinacea and St. John's wort plants that Donna makes into tinctures.  She picks me a few delicious raspberries and tells me the local goldfinches visited here a couple of nights before, "learning to sing and eating the seeds of the sow thistles."

What Donna calls her "mid-garden" contains onions, broccoli, cauliflower and cabbages. Here also are the many grains that she hand-grinds into flour: Tibetan barley, kamut, golden flax and Mandan corn. The garden in the lowest part of the valley is given over to winter carrots, parsnips, potatoes, turnips, beets and several kinds of radishes. These are the crops she digs out to trench under a foot of soil in the upper bench area for winter storage. Last year, the family was still eating trenched carrots in June. Donna lifts some of the floating vegetable row covers to harvest arugula and a host of Oriental greens. The tenting provides warmth and acts as a great bug barrier.

From a garden designed to sustain one family, this property has grown to feed many in the Galiano community. Donna rises at dawn every day to prepare brown boxes, each one made to order. As with many other brown-box programs, her customers choose from a daily "menu" of fruits, veggies, preserves and juices. Donna tells me that some people are very specific ("too specific, and they run the risk of being cut off from paradise!") and others love getting a box full of surprises.

During a sojourn on Galiano, I loved the adventure of receiving a box from Donna. Ordered the night before, it was waiting for me in the morning, having been tucked behind a rural mailbox by her son on his way to work. Being a greedy foodie, I couldn't wait to open it: a just-picked bouquet of Oriental greens, four succulent varieties of tomatoes, tiny jewel-like beets, spicy arugula, small new potatoes, hard heads of the season's first garlic and a big bottle of mellow apple cider. Breakfast never looked so good.

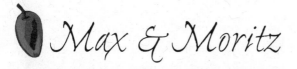

Max & Moritz

Christian and Lucy Banski are the smiling faces behind the little red catering cart with the German fairytale characters painted on its side that parks at the Galiano ferry dock in the summer. The intoxicating aromas of Indonesian (her background) and German (his) foods are hard to resist—no matter what time of day it is. I have often picked up a portion of *bami goreng* (stir-fried noodles with vegetables, tofu and peanut sauce) for breakfast, particularly if my ferry is about to leave and I know I won't be back to the island for awhile! Even though Lucy cooks a great all-day breakfast omelette, it didn't take much convincing from her to get me to try the noodles before 9:00 a.m.

The service is fast and friendly, and the lineups first told me that this was a good place to eat. The Indonesian side of the menu offers either rice or rice noodles with delicious combinations of veggies, chicken, beef, sausage or tofu. The house-made spicy sauce is so popular that Christian and Lucy now sell it by the bottle. German fare includes Bratwurst with sautéed onions and Sauerkraut on a toasted bun, and *Schaschliktasche*—grilled beef or chicken with green peppers and onions in a pita-bread pocket.

Good coffee, cookies made by the Haggis Farm Bakery on Saturna Island and Mario's Gelati bars are also on offer. There are seats scattered about, which make it another of the important "meet-and-greet" spots on the island.

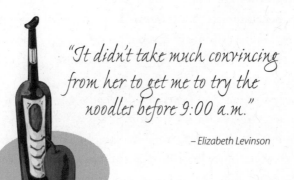

"It didn't take much convincing from her to get me to try the noodles before 9:00 a.m."

– Elizabeth Levinson

MID-ISLAND

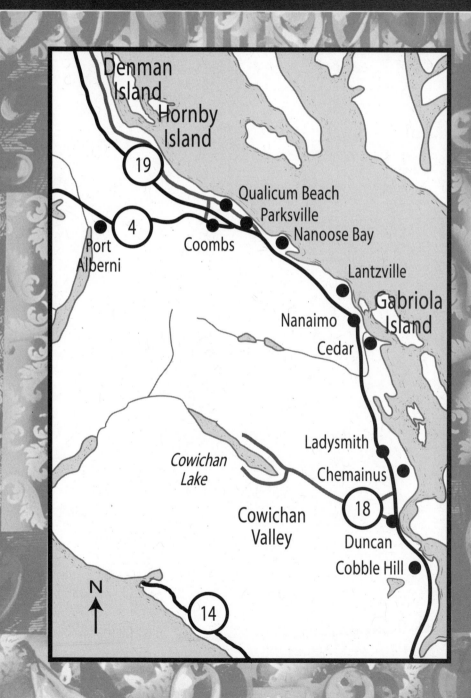

Denman Island

Hornby Island

19

Qualicum Beach

Parksville

4

Nanoose Bay

Port Alberni

Coombs

Lantzville

Gabriola Island

Nanaimo

Cedar

Ladysmith

Cowichan Lake

Chemainus

Cowichan Valley

18

Duncan

Cobble Hill

N

14

Amusé

I'd heard about Amusé from Mara Jernigan, chef and owner of Fairburn Farm Culinary Retreat, and was eager to see what had settled into that cute little spot in the heart of Shawnigan Lake Village. Driving home from the north end of the island one Sunday, I decided to call ahead for a table.

One enters from the back of the building—past the raised beds of fava beans, radishes, chard and arugula and across the patio—and the door opens almost directly into the kitchen, which

Owners Leah Bellerive and Bradford Boisvert before the dining room fills up at Amusé.

makes for a warm impression. Greeted by owners Leah Bellerive and Bradford Boisvert, I'm shown to a table in the dining room, which is upstairs. It's small, very cosy and nicely appointed with local original artworks.

The couple's intent to "intrigue the senses, amuse the palate" is evident in the *amuse bouche* that begins my meal. A potato, leek and celery roulade in a petite pastry shell is beautifully presented with a slice of beetroot and a sprig of dill. Creamy, earthy, vibrant: my eye is titillated and my palate is awakened. The True Grain bread from Cowichan Bay is warm (a simple step far too often overlooked by fine dining rooms) and served with a delicious white bean spread.

What follows is by far the most delicious treatment of chanterelles I've ever eaten: whole mushrooms picked in the Valley are served in a brandied cream sauce over True Grain Bread toast and finished with fresh thyme.

I'm not drinking tonight because I'm driving back to Victoria, but I can vicariously enjoy the selections of those sitting around me. One party has ordered a bottle of Okanagan Merlot, but it's great to see so many Cobble Hill and Cowichan Valley choices as well, including wines from Glenterra Vineyards, Venturi Schulze and Blue Grouse.

Leah and Bradford have endeavoured to reflect "the abundance of produce in this area" on their menu. Bradford and co-chef Steve Elskens, who formerly cooked at Shawnigan Lake's Steeples restaurant, are drawing on an impressive number of neighbouring producers. There's venison from Broken Briar, cheeses from Hilary's Cheese Company and Moonstruck Organic Cheese, beef and lamb from Quist Farm, oysters from Evening Cove and emu from Code's Corner Emu Farm.

Having never before tried emu, I went for the carpaccio with horseradish aïoli, parsley oil and organic greens. It was sliced thinner than rice paper and absolutely gamey and delicious with the tangy horseradish. There was a sorbet of Yellow Point Cranberries' signature fruit to cleanse the palate, followed by a classic, red-wine-braised bœuf bourguignonne made of Quist Farm beef, served with Parisienne potatoes, chanterelle mushrooms and roasted shallots. What could be finer than dining on local fare presented by chefs respectful of their ingredients?

Bradford is originally from Rhode Island and was schooled in cheffing and restaurant management at the Culinary Institute of America in New York. He's been on Vancouver Island for a while: he worked previously at The Aerie Resort and at Amici's, and co-owned The Sunshine Café in Ladysmith for five years. Leah grew up in Cowichan Bay, took a B.Com. at the University of Victoria, and thought she'd just be keeping the books at the restaurant until "he wore me down." She is now working full-time at the restaurant and "loving it."

Elford Farm Bakery

My edible journeys are made richer when someone gives me a tip, and then I feel like I'm also having an adventure. Elford Farm Bakery was suggested to me by Bradford and Leah of Amusé, who buy bread there, and I'm glad to have made its acquaintance.

My parents and I drove clear around the lake, and eventually landed in Shawnigan Lake village. I didn't have an address for the bakery, but the village is so small that it was easy enough to find. Elford Farm Bakery was formerly a wholesale business that baker and owner Gerald Billings operated from its namesake farm (the farm was originally owned by the fellow who owned the mill at nearby Mill Bay).

Today, Gerald runs a thriving retail pastry shop that attracts locals and visitors for authentic croissants, ginger and chocolate tarts, "apple" pies made with Asian pears, cinnamon buns and specialty breads like the multi-grain *jaggar loaf*, potato bread and French baguettes. Gerald uses organic flours, local eggs and seasonal fruits, and there is no doubt he's offering the "wow" factor. His pastry displays have a certain Continental flair that he picked up when travelling through Munich, Vienna and Budapest.

Gerald's fascination with baking goes back to when he was 14 years old and working as a "pot scrubber" in Victoria's legendary Dutch Bakery, eventually helping with the pastry making. But he tells me it was his stint driving through Europe "in a VW van" that propelled him to go to Malaspina University-College in Nanaimo to learn the art of pastry.

Gerald had his own shop, Whistler Peak Pastries, in Whistler, BC, and also worked at the Bellaggio Hotel in Las Vegas, but he soon "tired of big cities" and came home to the island. His love of the artistic end of pastry-making is evident, and he is "booked every weekend in summer to make custom wedding cakes."

Later that day, I ate one of his spinach and goat's milk cheese croissants, which have a little rock salt sprinkled on top, and wished that I'd bought more. The bakery is also a great spot for soup and sandwiches, which can be enjoyed on the deck in summer.

Steeples

Steeples was born when locals Daphne and Michael Francis realized the village of Shawnigan Lake needed a proper restaurant. They weren't restaurateurs, but they had the vision necessary to renovate the former Sylvan United Church. Despite a change in the nature of its business, the building has somehow retained a sense of spirituality. The dining room soars with light and colour. The altar is now a modern open kitchen and the pews have been

Chef and owner Darren Cole prepares to flambé at Steeples.

replaced by tables and chairs at which patrons can dine on divine creations like roasted duck breast with blackberries, grilled vegetable and goat's milk cheese *torta* and prosciutto-wrapped filet mignon.

Formerly a partner, and now sole owner, Darren Cole describes the renovation and decoration of the former church as "one big art project." Experienced in starting restaurants from scratch (including Mill Bay's Fridays and Sidney's McGinty's), he clearly enjoyed the process. His cooking experience has come in handy, too— from stints at Victoria's Fogg 'n' Suds, the Six Mile Pub and the short-lived but brilliant Classical Pig Café. Before Darren worked in the restaurant industry, he was a motivational speaker, and I expect that training stands him in good stead in a business where not everyone knows what to order.

Like Brasserie L'École in Victoria, this is a very social room. I always enjoy dining by myself when the dining room is abuzz with interesting conversation and table-hopping. I can feel part of the action around me without actually having to engage in conversation. All the more time, I gleefully think, for enjoying my food and drink.

What impresses me immediately is Darren's commitment to showcasing local producers. Chicken here comes from Cowichan Bay Farm, free-range turkey from Kilrenny Farm, vegetables from Apple Bear Farm, mussels from Saltspring Island and oysters from Fanny Bay. The wine list reads like a wine route for this book: an entire section is devoted to the best of Alderlea, Blue Grouse, Cherry Point, Glenterra, Godfrey Brownell, Vigneti Zanatta and Venturi Schulze vineyards. And Darren has gone one important step further: he has noted on the menu which wines are produced entirely from grapes grown in the Cowichan Valley (versus those that have been made with grapes imported from the Okanagan). Darren tells me he loves selling Vancouver Island wines, and I take great pleasure hearing him turn other diners on to a new Merlot from Alderlea and the refreshing Millefiori from Venturi Schulze.

I start with a fabulously flavourful thin-crust pizza with duck confit, goat's milk cheese and red onions and then try Darren's favourite: grilled prawns and Digby scallops atop avocado, with a summertime salsa of pineapple, mango and cilantro. The ultimate filet mignon served with a portobello mushroom topped with meltingly sinful Cambozola and mashed potatoes, whole carrots and asparagus spears is one of the restaurant's most popular entrées. I end with a chocolate pâté with orange custard from local patissier Gerald Billings' significant repertoire.

There's a lot to like at Steeples, including the heated deck where it was warm enough for dinner on Valentine's Day; the enclosed garden with its pretty pond and kiwi vines, where diners can play croquet before or after their meal; and the sense of occasion that seems to permeate every table in the place. I particularly like the fact that servers actually serve the excellent house-made focaccia one beautiful, warm slice at a time, and don't need to be asked to bring more, and that they take the time to prepare Caesar salad and a host of dessert flambés tableside.

Steeples may no longer be a church, but food is sublime here and the service is appropriately divine.

MAPLE BAY

Grapevine on the Bay

Several years ago, chef and food consultant Bill Jones recommended a tiny restaurant in Genoa Bay to me. When I was finally able to check it out, it had moved to the next bay over! Grapevine on the Bay had a huge reputation for seven years in Genoa Bay, then reopened in Maple Bay in December 2003.

One cold afternoon that month, my husband and I had a long wait for the Crofton ferry to Saltspring Island and decided to take a drive, which happily brought us to the Grapevine. Daniel and Ruth van den Wildenberg were in the throes of reopening their restaurant in a space no bigger than a breadbox, but there were enticing pastries and organic coffee on offer and many locals were popping in to order from a takeaway dinner menu.

Fast-forward to the summer of 2004, when my parents and I were heading to Qualicum Beach for a little break and decided to see what was cooking at the Grapevine. The restaurant had by then expanded into a back room with breathtaking sea views and we had a Margherita pizza and salad lunch that my very dear but very particular mother is still raving about.

"Now," says Daniel, when I drop in to see the fully renovated space in 2005, "we have what we want: a nice sunny feel, a restaurant where everyone can be comfortable, whether you've jumped off your boat in shorts or feel like dressing for supper." The transformation is impressive. Walls have been knocked down and larger windows installed to capture "those picture-postcard orange moon-rises in summer." There's a large, open kitchen positioned so that both diners and cooks can enjoy the view, unique driftwood furnishings and a revival of the full, seafood-focussed menu of Grapevine's Genoa Bay days.

Local customer Liv Finch, who has dined every month at the Grapevine (on both bays) drops in for coffee and tells me, "Nobody cooks seafood like this guy." Although Daniel describes himself as "old school," having been formally trained in the European hotel and restaurant management style in Bruges, Belgium, he also admits to "breathing some fresh air into the basics." Ahi tuna, salmon, halibut and Arctic char appear on the menu—as do oysters, but only those from Union Bay, which he claims "have the lightest beards. The farther you go up the island, the cleaner the water, the cleaner the beards, so the cleaner the oysters."

Ruth is a chocolatier, also trained in Bruges. When they came to Canada, Daniel worked front of house in Vancouver at the William Tell and at Hy's at the Mansion. In those days, there was more tableside cooking involved, "but then nouvelle cuisine came in and cooking and presentation went back inside

"Nobody cooks seafood like this guy."

– Liv Finch, Grapevine on the Bay customer

the kitchen." Ruth reminisces about the days when "dessert and specialty coffees were prepared at the table," and says the couple hopes to introduce some of that style at the Grapevine.

Big supporters of the local food producers, Daniel and Ruth buy from farmer David Wiebe, Providence Farm and Hilary's Cheese Company, and also go slightly farther afield to Saltspring Island for David Wood's cheese and to Parksville for Little Qualicum Cheeseworks cheese. A customer grows their herbs, and they offer several wine selections from nearby Alderlea and Blue Grouse vineyards. Ropey Fish on Saltspring custom cold-smokes halibut and tuna for the Grapevine, which is presented as part of a Nordic plate along with smoked salmon, herbed cream cheese, garden greens and horseradish dressing, and served appropriately with aquavit.

GLENORA/DUNCAN

Alderlea Vineyards

Frances Sidhe and I find vintner Roger Dosman pruning the canopy ("the curtain of leaves and shoots that is formed by the grapevines," Frances tells me). He agrees to give me a lesson. As it's January, he first removes the clips that attach the vertical shoots to the wire fencing—there are some 100,000 clips among his eight acres of vines. Then, aiming to keep the shoots separate so that when the clusters of grapes appear, they won't touch each other and create rot, he chooses two or three of the shoots to salvage, and clips the rest. The tiers will come along after him and tie the shoots down. Ideally, one wants to leave two vertical shoots from the previous year for renewal (Roger sometimes leaves a third as the shoots are susceptible to breakage when they are tied down).

He explains that it's all about allowing sunlight and air to get to the fruit. Mid-June to the end of July is the heavy-labour period when he and his workers will be "deleafing in the fruit zone" of each vine. Roger is a lot like the Venturi Schulze clan: he does everything the hard way, beginning with propagating his own plants. Says Roger, "Higher quality canopy management gets a better fruit."

Roger had an automotive shop in Vancouver, but didn't want to live in a big city anymore. He took note when the provincial government passed legislation in 1989 to allow small farm wineries. Frances jokes about how to make a small fortune in the wine business: "Start with a large fortune and wait a few years. She and Roger agree. Roger did not start with a large fortune but, after searching in the Okanagan and on Vancouver Island for two years, he found a lovely, sloping, 10-acre parcel in the Cowichan Valley that faces southwest, and set to work.

He has stuck to his mandate, "to produce wine only from grapes grown in our vineyard." Beginning with 30 varieties, he has narrowed that down to 15 that perform well. Roger describes the business as "slow as you go," meaning that you don't know until you try if things will work or not.

What certainly has worked for Roger and his wife, Nancy, who runs the wine-tasting room, is that they have created a viable business and a healthy (from all that hard work and fresh air) lifestyle. They are also contributing to the local economy by providing jobs for five workers in season, and they are giving wine connoisseurs, and even amateurs like me, the benefit of their considerable skill.

Frances and I stopped by to taste the talk of the town, the vineyard's fruity, ruby-style port called Heritage Hearth. Roger set out a nice piece of Stilton and some fresh filberts from a farm down the road, and we quietly imbibed. Frances declared the nectar "rich and lush, with good acidity," and immediately ordered a case. I bought a bottle that I have practically hidden at home to enjoy with my next cheese course.

Other offerings at Alderlea include Bacchus (a Riesling/Sylvaner cross), Angelique (a blend of Optima and Siegerrebe), Pinot Auxerrois, Pinot Noir, Pinot Gris (partial French oak-barrel fermentation) and a Claret that Frances describes as "a big, fat, juicy, fruity" wine.

We talk about defining Vancouver Island wine, and Roger suggests that "it will take at least another 10 years to see what the island industry really is." He points out that, even within the Cowichan Valley, vineyards "vary greatly in their ability to grow grapes" due to their location. One day, say Frances and Roger, it will be nice to see a flavour profile, to be able to say what's typical of the area.

For now, we can enjoy the journey from vineyard to vineyard and wine-maker to winemaker, and make our views part of the exciting evolution of this area's style.

Black Coffee and Other Delights

Okay, it's true. Coffee is what fuels the urban hunter-gatherer, which is probably why the people who know me best know to find me in the island's cafés. One

Black Coffee beckons at Whippletree Junction. Don't forget to order a cinnamon bun!

favourite refuelling stop is Black Coffee and Other Delights at Whippletree Junction, south of Duncan. Even when I'm pressed for time, I still stop for a takeout giant cinnamon bun and an Americano—such is my addiction.

Located in Cobble Hill's former general store/post office building, which was moved to the Whippletree Junction site along with buildings from Duncan's old Chinatown, Black Coffee has been in business since March 2001. It's run by baker Andrew Simonson, coffee maven Morris Cleveland and Morris' wife, Corrine Wilson, a local pharmacist who is involved "behind the scenes."

Andrew and Morris are brothers who grew up in Calgary. As teenagers they worked for Heartland, a busy general store/bakery/café in Kensington, a well-established coffee district. Corrine tells me that it was at Heartland that Andrew began to hone his baking skills "under the watchful eye of Alice Kichik," the cook who, it seems, really kept him in line ("No soup served before 11:30 a.m. even if it is ready! No cutting out the centre cinnamon bun before the side ones!"). Andrew bakes all those amazing "other delights"—hearty food made from scratch like the soup, chili, muffins, date squares, big cookies and even bigger (and quite sinful) cinnamon buns. Morris is the coffee guy, using great Caffè Fantastico beans from Ryan and Kristy Taylor in Victoria.

In summer, the place hums with tourists who love shopping at Whippletree Junction's antique and curio shops. Part of the attraction of Black Coffee for me is that you can also stop there in the middle of winter, early in the morning, when most Whippletree shops are closed, and have a coffee with the locals and the truckers. It has great warmth and charm.

Corrine says they support local producers for dairy, berries and produce in season. They have copies of the cookbook Andrew contributed to during his time at *Heartland: Heartland Country Store Cookbook* (Centax Books, 1995) by Alice Kichik and the restaurant's owner, Nonie Sundstrom. And let me know if you've ever tasted a better cinnamon bun!

The Community Farm Store and Corfield's Coffee Shop

For those who believe that there are no coincidences in life, consider the grey day in February when I decided for no particular reason to pull off the highway at Duncan and see what might be new in town. Surely the Duncan Garage was put there for me to find.

The bright yellow building across from the railway station caught my eye and the sign on its side ground me to a halt: The Community Farm Store—a name from the past, a whole foods store that I'd written about when it was located in Glenora, just outside of Duncan. I instantly remembered its notable baker, Susan Minette, and the ginger scone recipe she had so kindly parted with, and I went in to investigate.

The old Duncan Garage, now beautifully restored, houses Ulla's bookstore;

an outlet of The Udder Guy's Old-Fashioned Ice Cream (whose original shop is in nearby Cowichan Bay) that's been designed to look like a 1950s-style diner; Long John's musical venue, which hosts all kinds of performers; and The Community Farm Store and its offshoot, Corfield's Coffee Shop. What a find! Nourishment for stomach and soul all under one roof!

The Community Farm Store is just as it was in its previous location, only larger and with a more extensive stock of organic fresh produce and dry goods. This time, however, there were things I'd never tried before, like goat's milk butter, refried bean mix and black japonica rice. A great cheese selection included Mountain Meadow sheep's milk feta, several Quebec cheeses and Courtenay's Natural Pastures cheeses. Cowichan Bay Farm's chicken pieces and sausages, candied chum salmon from Cortes Island and organic French chocolate truffles were also among the new offerings. Since I was heading north for the weekend, I couldn't shop for groceries, but I had no difficulty buying "road food" from the selection at Corfield's Coffee Shop next door.

With a commitment to organics and many vegan selections, the deli offers irresistible snacks like a Brie, tomato and sweet red onion sandwich; a yummy hot strata of eggs, cheese and vegetables served with what appears to be just-picked salad; and millet, cheese and herb croquettes with a creamy curry dipping sauce. There are heavenly treats (again, many are vegan or are made with alternate grains like spelt or rice and sweetened with rice syrups or orange juice) such as Double Dutch chocolate cookies, spelt carrot cake, caramel nut squares and a pineapple cheesecake topped with fresh and candied pineapple slices that I tried very hard to share but just had to polish off myself.

I look forward to returning for breakfast when the offerings include cheesy scrambled eggs with veggies and organic toast; a fried egg sandwich with onion, cheese, mustard and mayo; and rice or oatmeal porridge with raisins, cinnamon and cow's or soy milk. The mention of that porridge alone takes me back nostalgically to a shack on Hermosa Beach, California, in the 1970s—a restaurant whose porridge I still crave. But after eating her pineapple cheesecake, I'm convinced Susan's porridge will at last provide Hermosa Beach's match.

Deerholme Farm and Cottage

I'm heading into the hills behind Shawnigan Lake with Bill Jones, geologist, former chef at Sooke Harbour House and other superb restaurants from Alsace to Vancouver, author of six cookbooks and busy food consultant. We're going way off-road to stalk the much-lauded chanterelle, the trumpet-shaped wild mushroom that emerges after the rains from mid-August through mid-November—or until the killing frosts begin. Not being too specific about our location is all part of the adventure: once a picker has found good foraging ground, he is not about to tell the world. I agree to keep the code.

It's a beautiful day in the woods. We've waited the requisite three days since the last rain to ensure there will be lots of new mushrooms, so we grab our bags and Swiss Army knives and make our way through the underbrush. It's fun, and a highly aerobic process. Bill steers me towards the mossy beds where chanterelles are most likely to be found, telling me that where I find one, I'll certainly find more. The yellow-orange ones (*Cantharellus cibarius*) are fairly easy to spot, and today there are white ones (*Cantharellus subalbidus*) as well—a real treat. I'm quickly hooked.

This is perfect territory for chanterelles, which, it turns out, are one of the hardiest mushrooms. Bill tells me that pharmaceutical companies are looking at the chanterelle's composition in their antibiotic research as they are almost never attacked by insects or worms, and don't tend to rot.

Picking mushrooms, I discover, is a tactile, organic experience. Once the specimen has been identified as edible, you knock off any debris that may have settled on it. Then, firmly holding the stalk, you pull the whole plant out of the ground, cut a small slice off the bottom of the stalk to perfect it, and pop the plump, spongy mushroom into your bag. It feels like a grown-up Easter egg hunt. With the retail price of chanterelles in my head, and the prospect of a mushroom feast that evening, I have no problem staying out in the woods for the rest of the afternoon—my eyes roaming the forest floor, knife at the ready.

By the time our bags are full, we've spotted at least two dozen of the 2,000 or so varieties in the world including the Zeller's bolete (*Boletus zelleri*) and honey mushroom (*Armillaria mellea*). On an old nurse log, we spy a bouquet of angel wing mushrooms (*Pleurocybella porrigens*), so named because of their shape. We eat them right away, their disarmingly fresh, nutty taste bringing the beauty of the forest to our palates.

At the end of our hunt, we climb back up to the logging road and snack on organic apples from Bill's farm. Later that day, Bill will cook up Phyllo Packets of Roast Chanterelles, Farm-cured Bacon and Leeks; Mushroom Risotto with Saltspring Island Cheese Company's Montana Cheese; Cured Salmon on Three Kinds of Kale and Porcini Mushrooms in Tomato Sauce; and a grand finale of Heritage Apple Tart with Vanilla Rosemary Ice Cream.

With a menu like that and a chef like Bill, I'm devastated to be double-booked and missing the meal. Still, I have a bag of fresh chanterelles and within hours they're merrily sautéeing in a little olive oil with garlic, thyme and a splash of cream and brandy. Since I'd picked them myself, they were of course the best I'd ever eaten.

Bill Jones has been busy since we last crossed paths in the forest. He and his wife, Lynn, have renovated their five-acre property in the rolling hills south of Duncan to accommodate her vast production gardens and his workshop and demonstration-cooking facility.

Bill's goal of making Deerholme Cottage "feel comfy and natural" has been realized from the highly polished concrete counters in the kitchen to the art nouveau-style motifs of fungi on the walls and the Charles Rennie McIntosh-inspired furnishings throughout. His concept of offering workshops on mushrooms and other local seasonal foods as well as professional chef-training classes was influenced by Michael Stadtländer, whose eclectic farm and restaurant outside Toronto, Eigensinn Farm, regularly garners international attention.

The Jones' goal is to provide "a beautiful space to think about agriculture and food—where it comes from and what the difference is in growing organic." Lynn offers tours of her gardens and Bill leads inspired culinary workshops that are followed by barbecues in summer and cosy meals in the kitchen in winter.

"Our goal is to provide a beautiful space to think about agriculture and food."

– Bill Jones

The farm is situated above Glenora Creek on the Trans Canada Trail, which "goes from here all the way to Newfoundland." Bill and Lynn are actively involved in the stewardship of the creek through the Community Land Trust.

The water buffalo roam at Fairburn Farm and Culinary Retreat.

Fairburn Farm and Culinary Retreat

"This year will see more change at Fairburn Farm than there has been in the last hundred years," says Mara Jernigan, who is wielding a paintbrush and flashing her characteristic impish smile. The farm's 111-year-old family home is where Mara has moved her agritourism operation (previously, she and Alfons Obererlacher owned and operated a similar business, Cobble Hill's Engeler Farm). The farm's owners, Darryl and Anthea Archer, have relocated into a new home on the property and are focussing their energies on *mozzarella di bufala* production.

Mara, a chef who parlays her considerable knowledge and talent into educating people about eating well, practises what she preaches. She has always been proud to "do everything the Slow Food way—I can say where everything on my table comes from." As Slow Food's Canadian coordinator of the Ark of Taste and founder of southern Vancouver Island's Feast of Fields, she is well known for her strong advocacy of our local food-security system and sustainable agriculture.

What people may not realize is that she is also known for her aesthetic taste and decorating abilities (I can't forget that gorgeous appetite-inducing, red dining room at Engeler Farm). Her bold colour schemes and attention to details like fine linens, silverware and china reflect her goal "to give Fairburn Farm's accommodations and dining room elegance paired with down-to-earth hospitality."

Fairburn has offered farmstays for over 50 years, and Mara is honoured to be continuing that tradition. She tells me that the Archers were the first people she met when she came to the Cowichan Valley and "they are very special people to me." She says that between them, they now have the potential "to take the farm to the next level, from both a culinary and a farming point of view." Mara says she is excited to be working with the buffalo products from the Archers, "While the products are in very small supply, I am the first to get my hands on them, so my guests enjoy specialties like buffalo-milk pannacotta, ricotta for ravioli and ice cream."

Mara's guests can participate in cooking classes taught by her and her coterie of distinguished guest-chefs (including Karen Barnaby, Peter Zambri, Sean Brennan, Edward Tuson, Christophe Letard, Michael Stadtländer, et al.). Not to be missed are "Sunday lunches on the farm," when Mara presents six-course, leisurely lunches in the European tradition, but using all local ingredients. Served on the veranda, these "events of the day" encourage urbanites to take a drive into the country and experience both the cuisine and the farm itself.

"What always appealed to me about agritourist accommodation in Italy," says Mara, "is the emphasis on dinner." I couldn't agree more. The North American bed and breakfast focus on elaborate five-course breakfasts may look great on the websites, but often those breakfasts can be excruciating. Mara is excited to be offering bed-and-dinner ("of course, farm-fresh breakfasts are on offer every morning, but there is more focus on the occasion of the evening meal").

In addition to the Sunday lunches, cooking classes and farmstays, Mara continues to offer Cowichan Valley farm tours, which culminate with lunch at Fairburn Farm. On Saturdays, in season, people can arrive at Duncan's Farmers' Market by train (the train from Victoria stops right in

Thanks to these chickens, there are always lovely fresh eggs for breakfast at Fairburn Farm.

Chef and owner Mara Jernigan slices freshly baked pizza at Fairburn Farm Culinary Retreat.

the middle of the market at 9:30 a.m.), where they are met by Mara to gather produce for lunch later at Fairburn. After spending the day on the farm, they are returned to the train station for the pleasant journey home. In the shoulder and quiet seasons, Mara offers more cooking classes as well as her popular culinary tours of Italy.

Mara Jernigan has indeed taken Fairburn Farm to a whole new level and has been recognized by the international culinary and agritourism media, yet she remains true to her roots and her philosophy. My nephew Nicholas and I spent a night at Fairburn this past summer, doing all the things we love to do there: walking miles to find and then commune with the herd of water buffalo, gathering eggs from the chickens, waking from heavenly sleep to the rooster crowing (try to find that experience in the city!) and charging downstairs for Mara's hearty farm breakfast.

Feast of Fields

Vancouver Island's foodie event of the year highlights the strong links between our local growers and chefs, and dishes up some of the best food you may ever eat. Hosted by a different island farm each time, the event is the ultimate gastronomic walkabout. Ticket-holders are greeted with a plate, a wine glass and a large linen napkin and invited to stroll from stall to stall to eat (all items are designed to be eaten by hand) and imbibe over the course of a long, leisurely afternoon.

The area's best chefs and vintners purvey their wares: one moment, you are savouring ostrich kebabs straight off the grill, the next you are enjoying the bouquet of a lively Pinot Gris from Cobble Hill's Glenterra vineyard or cooing over an almond johnnycake drizzled with poaching sauce, enhanced with a dollop of cinnamon crème fraîche with lemon verbena and a rosette of slivered caramelized poached pear, and sprinkled with candied ginger and a confetti of pansy blossoms, created by David Feys of Feys + Hobbs Catered Arts.

Tasty bites at Feast of Fields.

Feast of Fields is a fundraiser for Farm Folk, City Folk (FFCF), a non-profit organization that recognizes and promotes "the connection between those who grow our food and those who eat it, and the interdependency of all living things." Among its many projects, FFCF is active in the development of food policy around food security, supporting sustainable agriculture and conducting a broad public-advocacy campaign to project awareness of food issues in British Columbia.

The indefatigable Mara Jernigan is Vancouver Island's representative for FFCF. She has organized successful Feast of Fields at many of the island's stellar farming operations including Oldfield Farm and Ravenhill Herb Farm in Saanich, Cowichan Bay Farm and Duncan's Providence Farm. It's a sell-out event every year, so if you are planning to be on the island in mid-September, call for tickets well in advance.

Godfrey-Brownell Vineyards

There is something deeply satisfying about meeting a vintner and discovering that, in addition to making great wine, he or she is also a "character" as it somehow adds to the flavour. I mean this in the nicest possible way in the case of Dave Godfrey, a gentleman I have known for some time and whose intelligent, engaging company I enjoy—particularly over a glass of his jammy 2002 Maréchal Foch Reserve, which I am doing this afternoon in his living room several months after the annual harvest.

Dave has spent most of his life in academia, but it's obvious that he's always had a farmer's heart. He was a professor of creative writing from 1976 to 1998, both at the University of Toronto and at the University of Victoria.

Dave Godfrey, the jovial vintner and owner of Godfrey-Brownell Vineyards.

He and his wife, Ellen, also founded and operated publishing houses. In Toronto, their House of Anansi, launched in 1967, published then-unknown Canadian writers such as Margaret Atwood, Michael Ondaatje and Dennis Lee. When they moved to the West Coast, they ran Beach Holme Publishing, working with similarly "unknown" authors like Robin Skelton and Susan Musgrave.

However, Dave and Ellen always managed to find time for farming. They ran a 100-acre cattle farm outside Toronto, and now their focus is grapes (although Ellen also works "in computers" for the BC government).

Dave's French Huguenot background gives him a sort of new-world homesteading quality, and he's really made a go of vineyards on his property in Glenora. He's planted 14 of the property's 60 acres with "Burgundy grapes plus an acre of Foch and one of Bacchus because people told me Chardonnay wouldn't grow here [which he's already proven is incorrect]." He and Ellen also own a vineyard on Mount Prevost where they grow Pinot Noir, Pinot Gris, Merlot and Gewürztraminer.

Their wines are estate grown, although they did buy some grapes in 2002 from their neighbour, the late, great Dennis Zanatta (see Vigneti Zanatta), and I remember that they also bought some from the Okanagan a few years ago. Dave and Ellen's grapes are grown without pesticides and herbicides, although they are not fully organic because, as Dave says, "Look, we grow grapes in a rainforest where we're susceptible to powdery mildew. If I only grew Foch, we could be organic!"

Godfrey-Brownell (the Brownell name is for Dave's grandmother Rebecca whose second cousin, Aaron Alonzo Brownell, bought the Glenora farm in 1886) produces some excellent wines and certainly puts to rest the theory that we can't grow grapes for red wine on Vancouver Island. In fact, their Scarlatti Sisters, a classic, somewhat spicy Merlot/Cab Franc blend, is one of my favourite pours and Dave points to a favourite of his: William Maltman's Double Red, which has the deep body of Foch and the sparkle of Gamay and was named for the uncle who "taught me to drink red wine."

And there's even more to be jazzed about at Godfrey-Brownell. In September, Jazz in the Vineyard is a much-anticipated annual event that includes barbecue feasts by Duncan's Equinox Catering. And soon—olives! Dave takes me out to the greenhouse, where he's growing Pendolino olive seedlings for planting on a half-acre of the property. "Once I get six acres planted, I'll buy a centrifugal press!" he enthuses, and I don't doubt that Godfrey-Brownell olive oil will become a household staple before long.

Providence Farm Community Lunches

I first visited the kitchen of Providence House in 2004 with Mara Jernigan, now owner of the Fairburn Farm Culinary Retreat. She shared with me her idea of restoring the old kitchen to provide a facility for people in difficulty—including low-income mothers—to cook together for their families in a healthy, supportive environment. With the help of the late "Urban Peasant" James Barber, Deerholme Farm's Bill Jones and the generosity of organizations like Farm Folk, City Folk and many individuals, Mara was able to realize her dream.

Today, the Providence House kitchen is bustling with activity under its warm and compassionate kitchen manager, Kori Kelloway. Kori guides a kitchen crew of staff and volunteers, most of whom have mental and physical challenges. They make jams, preserves and other products from Providence Farm's organic produce, which are sold in the on-site Farm Store. They also rustle up a buffet-style lunch that is served to staff, volunteers and the general public at 12:30 p.m., Monday through Friday.

I took my parents to the farm on a bitterly cold day, and we were warmly welcomed by a community of hard-working people whose happy spirits we found infectious. We lined up with the farm and kitchen workers for a hearty lentil shepherd's pie and mixed salad and ate with them at one of the convivial round tables. Our dining companions were blind, deaf and cognitively challenged but nothing stopped us from having a great conversation and finding many subjects of mutual interest.

My parents and I were pleased to be taken out of our relatively comfortable world and shown the Providence Farm philosophy manifested in its clients: "We believe that caring for the land together is by nature healing and therapeutic." I would add only that cooking together, as these people do on a daily basis in the farm's kitchen, is also an important part of that therapy.

The 400-acre Providence Farm has been owned since 1864 by the Sisters of St. Ann. The Vancouver Island Providence Community Association has leased the farm since 1979, and offers a wide range of therapeutic programs from allotment gardening and woodworking to animal husbandry and cooking.

If you're in the area, take advantage of the privilege to drop in for lunch and a self-directed tour of this impressive, historic facility. Just remember that you will need to call the farm by 10:00 a.m. the morning of your visit to book a spot. Lunch is $5 per person.

Vigneti Zanatta

A visit to Vigneti Zanatta should properly be combined with a meal at the vineyard's farmhouse restaurant, Vinoteca, so Daniel Beiles and I make time to do both. In fact it is hard to find a more idyllic setting than its veranda, where one can easily while away an afternoon eating and drinking and mistaking the scenery for the Loire Valley in France.

Loretta Zanatta is the kind of thoughtful, intelligent vintner you want making your vino. The care and pride she puts into

what she does, and her obvious depth of knowledge, are inspiring. We ask how she got into the business in the first place.

"We're an Italian family," she tells me, "so we have always grown grapes and made wine." Her parents emigrated from Treviso, which is north of Venice, in the 1950s. They found a 120-acre dairy farm just south of Duncan and decided it would be "a great place to raise kids," so they raised dairy cattle and their own children. And the family always grew their own vegetables and grapes.

By 1981, Loretta's father was experimenting with grapes in earnest. The family turned an acre of land over to the Duncan Project, a government-sponsored effort to determine which grapes would really grow well in these parts. Loretta says she spent a lot of time "testing the acids and sugars" of what was planted. She and her husband, Jim, had acquired degrees in plant science from the University of British Columbia. Loretta had also obtained a Master's degree in winemaking from the university in Piacenza, Italy. They were more than prepared when the provincial government introduced the legislation that permitted farm wineries.

In 1992, Vigneti Zanatta became the first licensed commercial vineyard on Vancouver Island. Loretta is known for her sparklers, which she makes "in the Champagne style." She calls sparklers "the cleanest wines," because they contain no sulphur and are based on unadulterated wine fermented only with naturally occurring yeast and sugar. At Vinoteca, you can enjoy a Champagne tasting of Loretta's three sparklers paired with an appetizer plate, and I can think of no merrier way to begin a leisurely afternoon on its veranda.

Daniel tastes but, as I'm driving, I opt to take the three sparkling beauties home and create a dinner around tasting them—one of my more delicious excuses for a party. So, at a later date, my friends and I happily imbibe Glenora Fantasia Brut (made from 100 per cent Cayuga grapes, aged up to six years); Alegria Brut Ros, (Loretta's personal favourite, a light rosé, made from Pinot Noir and Pinot Auxerrois grapes); and Taglio Russo (made from Cabernet Sauvignon grapes, a deep red sparkler that's based on the still wine Loretta used to make for her grandmother). All of us are most taken with the Fantasia Brut, the sparkler Daniel described perfectly as having "a fine, light pale yellow complexion with thin, persistent streams of bubbles; a nose of fresh bread and Granny Smith apples; followed by a medium mouth feel with a crisp and tangy citrus finish." The Zanatta winery also produces Pinot Grigio and Damasco, an appetizer or sipping wine that's made using Auxerrois wine refermented on Ortega skins.

Loretta is proud of what her family vineyard produces. They only make wine from their own grapes and will not bring in product from other grape-growing areas like the Okanagan. She recognizes that wine is a new industry in the Cowichan Valley, but would prefer to see more estate-based operations. "Ideally," she says, "all vintners in the valley will grow all their own grapes or buy them from other Cowichan Valley growers, and then we'll have a true sense of what Vancouver Island wine is."

COBBLE HILL/ COWICHAN BAY

The Asparagus Farm

Charles Ford and his dog, Asta, are just returning from picking up mail at the end of the road as I pull in to The Asparagus Farm. It's still early in the year, but my visit is partly designed to add to my own anticipation of the short, six-week-long asparagus season. Standing at the farmgate, I visualize myself right at the front of the long lineups that occur here every day from about mid-April through May. People travel from as far away as Vancouver to buy the Fords' asparagus, and Charles says it's not unusual to have 50 cars parked at the gate before he opens it at 10 o'clock in the morning. One man, crossing the Atlantic on the *Queen Elizabeth II*, complained to his tablemate that he couldn't find white asparagus in North America. The tablemate sent him to Charles.

What is all the fuss about? To me, it's two things: you can't get asparagus any fresher (it's picked daily in season and only hours before the gate opens), and you can buy white asparagus here. Freshness and the way the asparagus is handled mean everything to the connoisseur: the tenderest shoot can become woody from being stored too long or stored in the wrong conditions. That "woodyness" can actually climb up the stalk after it has been picked, and if the asparagus is not chilled immediately after picking, its sugars turn to starch.

The white asparagus is a whole other story. Long prized by Europeans, white asparagus or *Spargel* arrives with great fanfare every year. It is traditionally served with a white sauce and boiled potatoes. Charles has answered the prayers of many here who grew up in Europe with a taste for white asparagus.

We take a walk across the 10-acre property. Asta bounds ahead and has a wonderful time chasing the California quail out of the asparagus patch (Charles encourages the quail, as they eat many of his weeds). I ask how he got into this much-sought-after product in the first place.

Charles has always farmed, but mostly cranberries in Pitt Meadows on the mainland. He says he was lucky to be growing cranberries "during the boom time when Ocean Spray was buying tons of fruit." When his wife, Carole, accepted a teaching position at the University of Victoria in 1989, the couple decided to look for land on Vancouver Island. The Cobble Hill farm fit the bill, and Charles planned to grow asparagus and apples. He planted the apples first, but they got blight, so he focussed on the asparagus.

Charles is also experimenting with growing the coveted black truffle, as well as black elderberries, which are known for their health properties. As he collaborates with a botanist on the truffle project, Vancouver Island chefs are holding their collective breath.

Blue Grouse Vineyards

It's one of those heart-stopping, big-blue-sky days in the Cowichan Valley, as Daniel Beiles and I pull into what is arguably Vancouver Island's prettiest vineyard. In the tasting room, we are warmly greeted by Sandrina Kiltz, who introduces herself as the "D.O.B.—daughter of the boss."

The boss is Dr. Hans Kiltz, microbiologist, biochemist and former United Nations veterinarian, who brought his family to the Cowichan Valley in 1989. The timing was ideal: provincial legislation was just changing to allow small

Sandrina Kiltz offers wine tastings at her family's Blue Grouse Vineyards.

farm wineries to operate commercially. The Kiltz family began to test different varietals for suitability, eventually settling on Ortega, Bacchus, Pinot Gris, Siegerrebe, Pinot Noir, Gamay Noir and others suited to the relatively cold climate, and planted in earnest in 1992 and 1993.

The vineyard is truly a family affair: Hans and his son Richard, both European-trained winemakers, make the wines; Hans' wife, Evangeline, lovingly tends the vines by hand; and Sandrina, a graduate in international business, is responsible for the marketing and daily public wine tastings. Sandrina tells us it was wonderful growing up at Blue Grouse, "My brother and I did the weeding, thinned out the grape clusters and learned how to drive a tractor before a car. I think it's given us a really good work ethic, and the kids at school thought it was cool that we lived in a vineyard."

Before we turn our attention to the business at hand—wine tasting—we catch a parade of white swans on one of the lower slopes. Then, a couple from North Carolina drops by, and all eyes and ears are fixed on Sandrina, who pours the first selection: 2000 Ortega. Daniel notes the "tropical fruit in the nose—lychee, as well as fresh, ripe peach; low acidity on the palate; and a clean fruit-driven finish."

Next up is the winery's 1999 Müller-Thurgau, a relation of Riesling, from which Daniel gets "soft, white peach and Bosc pear on the nose; petrol [typical of fine Riesling] on the palate, and a faint herbal, lemon balm finish." He tells me it would pair perfectly with a light fish (Sandrina recommends halibut) or shellfish.

The 2001 Pinot Gris is a big hit, and the entire tasting group appreciates what Daniel declares its "floral aspects and figginess." He identifies geranium, white peach, ripe cantaloupe and even a slight nuttiness, and suggests its low to medium acidity would pair well with lamb or fatty fish such as salmon. We learn that Blue Grouse was the first winery in the valley to produce Pinot Gris and they have been winning awards for it in the prestigious Oregon Wine Festival ever since. This is the wine we stock up on before reluctantly saying our goodbyes.

Broken Briar Fallow Deer Farm

The very first fawn David Groves raised was called Briar, and she became a family pet. Unfortunately, she lost her life to a careless hunter, but her name lives on.

The farm, originally called Barkley Farm, was a whistle stop on the Canadian Pacific Railway line. David's father, Tom, bought the farm from Kitty Barkley. Tom's father, whom David describes as "a genuine remittance man," also had a farm in the area. "He did anything for sport, including logging and fox hunting." He used to say to Tom, "No Englishman ever got up at 4:00 a.m. to milk cows." Tom wasn't afraid of milking cows, but he ended up taking a degree in forestry engineering at the University of British Columbia, then built bridges all over the country.

Owner David Groves offers an afternoon snack to one of his fallow deer at Broken Briar Fallow Deer Farm.

Later, David took a Ph.D. at Purdue and became an animal nutritionist. He began to study protein synthesis and mammary tissue culture, and taught animal physiology and biochemistry at both the University of Alberta and the University of Victoria. He'd always been interested in farming and enjoyed applied research.

David believes in raising animals under conditions that are as natural as possible. The number of fallow deer he raises is "in direct proportion to the capability of the land to produce feed." While their ancestors came from the Middle East, these hundred or so fallow deer are offspring of David's original herd, which were brought over from Sidney, James and Saltspring islands.

His neighbour had trapped some of the deer on those islands and sold them to both David and to the Douglas Ranch near Merritt.

I tasted David's venison at The Aerie, and liked venison for the very first time. The meat is very tender and mild-tasting, lacking that strong gamey flavour. Other restaurants have standing orders, including Saltspring Island's Hastings House, the Inglenook in North Cowichan and the Mahle House in Cedar. The First Nations also buy hides from him, and "there are always roasts in the freezer for people who just drop by."

With the restaurants demanding the saddles for ribs, Dave says he and his wife eat a lot of bone-out shoulder. He barbecues it, always serves it medium rare and only sometimes adds a glaze such as maple syrup and garlic. It's delicious meat on its own, so he doesn't advise marinating or drowning it in sauce.

David and I take a walk out to see the deer. He picks a bunch of burdock, and only has to wave it once before they come leaping over for their "candy."

Cowichan Bay Farm

Mara Jernigan loves the fact that she can grocery-shop by "just going from farmgate to farmgate" in the Cowichan Valley. This doesn't mean only fruit and veggies, but also local wines and cider, and top-quality pastured chicken, chicken sausage and duck at Lyle and Fiona Young's Cowichan Bay Farm. When we arrive at the farm, we are treated to the sight of a movie being shot. The juxtaposition of actors in Second World War attire and crew running around against the original farm buildings on a pastoral 43-acre backdrop is quite fun. We stop to chat and discover that this is a locally based production company of young people who are shooting their first pilot, which they hope to sell to Hollywood.

The farm buildings are fascinating. There is the 1920s butcher shop erected by Lyle's grandfather, Nigel Kingscote, to process his own pork. It has a wooden walk-in fridge, sloped tables for ease of cleaning after rolling the pork into sausages, and earthenware urns for immersing special cuts of meat in brine. Behind the building is the wooden smokehouse where the hams and bacon, as well as Cowichan Bay salmon, were cured. The butcher shop is still in operation,

One of the rustic heritage farm buildings at Cowichan Bay Farm.

and this is where local customers come to pick up the farm's pastured poultry, lamb and beef.

There's the newlywed cottage, where Lyle's grandparents lived after their marriage in 1935. Across the way is Nigel's workshop, where Lyle spent many hours straightening and sorting bent nails for his grandfather. He says he "remembers fondly the subtle lessons of an old man passed on to a young boy, simply by being fortunate enough to be there." Other original buildings include the Chinese labourers' shack, the granary, the horse barn, the dairy and the cow barn. The creamery boasts Lyle's grandmother's interesting collection of milk bottles.

Every Father's Day, the Youngs host a wonderful art show, with over 30 local artists represented. It's always thrilling to walk through the old farm buildings, their walls laden with the impressive talent of painters like Grant Leier, Adam Noonan and Wendy Bradshaw, and to sample delicacies such as gelato from Victoria's Italian Bakery and sausage dogs containing Cowichan Bay Farm's own chicken sausage.

We trek out to the fields to see the pastured-poultry operation and run into Jerry, one of the farmhands. He used to work for Lyle's grandfather and still enjoys his work on the farm. He shows us the method the Youngs use to raise their birds. First developed by Joel Salatin, a Virginia farmer, it's a model that Lyle chose to use for its humane practices. The chickens are housed in large moveable pens that are set out in the pasture. Jerry demonstrates how the pens are moved every day, thereby giving the birds an always-fresh source of food. They stay together and behave in a natural way, in contrast to chickens caged indoors. Whereas many chicken farmers follow the modern agricultural model of getting the animals to market as fast as possible, the Youngs are focussed on taking the animals to their own food in a natural environment. Birds that are allowed to develop naturally turn out happier, healthier and tastier.

The Youngs' chickens and ducks are featured on some of the area's top restaurant tables, including Victoria's Café Brio and Brasserie L'École and Tofino's Long Beach Lodge, and they can be purchased from the island's better butchers. When I'm in the area, I make a stop at their farm store to load up on birds and sausages for my freezer. Mara Jernigan calls Cowichan Bay Farm "simply the best for roast chicken, clean healthy liver, delicious handmade chicken sausages with no mystery meat or additives and pasture-raised duck, which many chefs consider the best they have ever had."

When the Youngs first took over the farm, they raised veal calves in addition to the poultry, but they felt they were looking for something else. On a trip to England some years back, they began to take an interest in rare breeds of live-stock, and when they returned to the farm, decided to invest in a few San Clemente goats, Navaho Churro sheep and Dexter cattle. The goats were brought by explorers from Spain to the coast of California, and left there as a food supply for whenever they returned to that part of the world. In Spain, the goats became extinct, but they lived for another 200 years on San Clemente Island until the American army used the island for bombing practice. Most of the stock was moved, and the Youngs ended up getting theirs from Boston. Today, there are probably only a hundred San Clemente goats in the world.

Drum Roaster Coffee

I'm not a long-distance trucker, but one day I will write about all the coffee stops on our island highways because they are essential to the enjoyment and safety of drivers and their passengers! Given the many miles I do travel, I have come to appreciate the new coffee shops that are springing up at the side of the road, and Drum Roaster is one of the best. Of course it caters to the Cobble Hill and Cowichan Valley communities, but Drum Roaster means that travellers like me never have to compromise on the quality of their coffee when they're on the road.

Carson, Patricia and Geir Øglend show off their mighty roaster at Drum Roaster Coffee.

Geir Øglend has been establishing serious coffee shops on Vancouver Island since 1988 when he opened Café Giovannini in Victoria. That was followed by Coffee's On in the Strathcona Hotel, Bean Bandits, Castello, Café Misto and Serious Coffee at Mill Bay. Geir sees his latest venture as part of coffee's "third wave." It's a "community-oriented coffee bar with a roaster and bakery," designed so that customers can view the whole process of roasting and grinding that goes into preparing their cup of coffee. Says Geir, "We do it all in the open so it is educational but also creates some theatre at the same time." The 1948 Vittoria roaster is a showpiece, while the new 30-pound Diedrich roasts up to 120 pounds of fragrant beans an hour.

My husband and I pulled off the highway early one morning to find Geir and his son Carson cupping an Ethiopian natural-processed Mistry Valley coffee that they were excited to share with us. Their interest in sourcing and serving unique organic coffees is infectious as we pore over the huge sacks of "clean, sound and new" coffees from Uganda and Brazil and admire the Dutch Technivorm coffee machines for sale.

The Øglends have come full circle in establishing their newest shop near Cowichan Bay, for that is where Geir's merchant marine father first came into port on Vancouver Island. When Geir's own family settled on the island in 1966, they brought with them a tradition of coffee drinking. "Scandinavia is the largest consumer of coffee in the world," he tells me.

The in-house bakery, run by Geir's wife, Patricia, has a scrumptious selection of muffins (make mine a Chunky Monkey!), blueberry scones, orange-coconut brioche, espresso brownies and frittata sandwiches that, together with the caffeine in your cup, will keep you alert on the road.

Glenterra Vineyards and Thistles Café

Winemaker John Kelly and his wife, Ruth Luxton, a Dubrulle-trained chef who cooked for the fabulous Meinhardt food store in Vancouver, decided to make a move. John had been commuting for two years to Okanagan University College to complete a diploma in viticulture and oenology and had also been volunteering at several Okanagan vineyards to learn the trade. When a 17-acre parcel of land became available on Vancouver Island, they moved their family across the pond.

While John tends the 4.5 acres of vines and makes the wine, Ruth runs Thistles Café and a busy catering business. They are both involved in the promotion of their vintages.

I first met Ruth at the Harvest Bounty Festival where she turned me on to Glenterra's Pinot Noir. Even though the property was originally a vineyard, John has done his share of experimentation. Early on, he determined that the Alsace varieties would do best: Gewürztraminer, Pinot Blanc, Pinot Noir and Pinot Gris. He tells me about the Duncan Project, a practical research project in the early 1980s where vintners from the island's first wineries did a range of test plantings to determine the suitability of various grape varieties.

It's a very cold day when Frances Sidhe and I visit John in his tasting room, but we are soon warmed up with good conversation and samples of his 2002 Vivace, a blend of Ortega, Auxerrois, Bacchus, Siegerrebe, Schönburger, et al.

Owners John Kelly and Ruth Luxton at their tasting bar at Glenterra Vineyards and Thistles Café.

that Frances finds to be "almost sweet at the start with a kick of acidity." We both enjoy the 2002 Gewürztraminer straight from the barrel with its lychee, rose-petal and grapefruit notes. Frances is impressed with the acid in the wine, as she is looking for a good structure to stand up to Peter Zambri's dynamic cooking. Another tasting is of the 2002 Brio, again from the barrel. John says its herbaceousness comes from the Dunkelfelder grapes. He will add some Cabernet Sauvignon to round off the flavour.

Glenterra won a silver medal for its 2000 Pinot Noir at the prestigious Northwest Wine Summit. John says they are producing 400 to 600 cases annually now, and will eventually expand production to 10 acres and increase their output to 1,200 to 1,500 cases.

Since I last visited Glenterra Vineyards, John and Ruth have built a wonderful new winemaking room, tasting room and restaurant. I stopped to chat with John and taste his estate-grown 2007 Pinot Gris before joining my husband for brunch in Thistles Café (named for the thistles in John's native Scotland). Twenty-five per cent of the wine had been fermented in French oak, the balance in stainless tanks, resulting in a very light-tasting pour with "lemon, lime and mineral notes, a core of tropical fruit and a polished elegant texture."

The restaurant is a light, modern room with an open kitchen in the centre and all of the windows facing the vineyard. In fact, the light is so amazing here and the building so well situated, that one feels like one is sitting among the vines (the windows themselves deserve a mention as they came from the

Park Royal Hotel in Vancouver when it was demolished; many customers remember the hotel and are charmed when they discover that association).

Our server is Ruth's sister Helen, who helps out in the restaurant, as does Annie, Ruth and John's daughter, who is the café's "ice cream-making expert" (her homemade lemon ice cream is on today's menu, served with fresh blueberries). Helen recommends "everything" but we choose what turn out to be a perfect spinach and aged cheddar omelette with pan fries and a pretty fruit presentation for me and vegetarian moussaka for Clive. The moussaka has an intriguing sauce made with quinoa and comes served with a hearty mixed salad. I also enjoy a glass of John's crisply acidic 2007 Gewürztraminer.

Ruth pops out of the kitchen to tell us how much she loves living in the Cowichan Valley with its profusion of food producers. She buys organic produce from Kilrenny Farms, "pops over to buy eggs and herbs from Mia on Cameron-Taggert Road" and gets her meat from Quist Farm. She suggests we finish our late-harvest meal with the tall, lighter-than-air pumpkin cheesecake on a gingersnap base with marshmallow sour-cream topping and roasted pumpkin seeds. It proves to be the best cheesecake I've ever eaten!

Hilary's Cheese Company

I've been invited into the aging room at Hilary and Patty Abbott's Cheese Pointe Farm to see for myself the many monastery-style cheeses they produce. Stacked up are their well-known St. Clair, a cow's milk, Camembert-style cheese with a white rind bloom that was named in honour of Vancouver Island's sultan of Slow Food, Sinclair Philip; St. Michel, the goat's milk version of St. Clair with a similar creamy texture and nutty, mushroom-like rind; Red Dawn, a French-style Tomme whose rind has been washed and massaged in Merridale Ciderworks' traditional cider to break down and ripen the cheese from the rind towards the centre; and Belle Ann, another French-style Tomme that has been bathed in Cherry Point Vineyard's blackberry port.

That ingredients from neighbouring farms and vineyards show up in the Abbotts' cheeses reflects their strong commitment to being part of a regional culinary identity in the Cowichan Valley. As members of Vancouver Island's Slow Food convivium, they believe in actively promoting the regionality of their products—their milk comes from local dairy farmers David Lestock-Kay and Joan Wilkinson of Shin Cliffe Farm, whose cows are pastured and allowed to graze naturally.

Co-owner and cheesemaker Hilary Abbott of Hilary's Cheese Company offers tastings at Feast of Fields.

Hilary and Patty haven't always been in cheese. He was a school administrator and fundraiser; she, a banker and gardener. When Hilary's father had a client who wanted to open a cheese factory, the Abbotts thought it sounded interesting and got involved. The Cowichan Cheese Company was founded in 1998, but it eventually fell victim to too many investors with different visions. However, the Abbotts had caught the bug of taking their cheese to farmers' markets and meeting their customers face to face. They decided to continue on their own and eventually bought the 10-acre Cheese Pointe Farm in the bucolic Cowichan Valley.

A visit to the farm provides an opportunity for a tour and viewing of the cheesemaking process (due to provincial sanitation regulations, visitors watch through a window) and to purchase artisan cheese at its source. Tours are available for groups of 10 or more, or one can visit on a Travel with Taste tour (see Travel with Taste).

For those with limited time, the Abbotts' cheese shop and café in Cowichan Bay provides a delightful introduction to their cheese. There, they sell both their own labels and cheese from other parts of Canada, such as maple-smoked Canadian cheddar and blues from Quebec, Swedish vodka *kasse*, Spanish Manchego and aged Italian Asiago. Hilary's Cheese Company also supplies many Vancouver Island restaurants, including Long Beach Lodge and Clayoquot Wilderness Resort in Tofino, Steeples in Shawnigan Lake and Sooke Harbour House.

Since my last visit, the cheese shop has moved from its original location inside True Grain Bread to where the Mellow Side Arts Lounge used to be. The space is perfect in that one can shop up front, then retreat to a waterfront table for a delicious lunch of homemade soup, a sandwich and a glass of wine. And I always enjoy the buzz here because even in summer, when there are many tourists in the Bay, it still feels like a local scene.

Merridale Ciderworks

In the tasting room at Merridale Ciderworks, I join a family visiting from Mexico to sample six of the cidery's eight beverages. I discover that what owners Rick Pipes and Janet Docherty say is true: there is "a taste for every palate" here. From the very dry Cidre Normandie to the award-winning, strong and sharp Scrumpy to the sweet and velvety port-style Winter Apple, we all find something to enjoy.

As Andrea Butler pours, she describes the qualities of each style of cider and expertly advises on food pairings. For example, Scrumpy, the robust blend of crab apples and cider apples, "pairs well with strong-flavoured meats and blue cheese"; Winter Apple, with its aroma of baked apples and brown sugar, "is great with melon, dark chocolate and aged cheese."

After the tasting, I sit down to chat with co-owner Janet, who was named "Rural Woman of the Year" for 2004 by the Women's Farmers Institute of southern Vancouver Island. Recognized for her contributions as chair of the BC AgriTourism Alliance and her tireless efforts to promote the Cowichan Valley's culinary tourism, Janet says she was "deeply honoured" to be chosen by women whom she herself admires for their own hard work and commitment to the rural life.

Janet previously worked in the construction industry, as a realtor and accountant; her husband, Rick, is a lawyer specializing in commercial real estate law. They bought the existing cidery five years ago "because we were looking for something to do together and a change in lifestyle. This opportunity came across Rick's desk and we said to each other: 'How hard can it be?'" She laughs as she tells me that, as the cidery has turned out to be both idyllic and a lot of hard work, but she "loves creating things and loves the people aspect" of the cider business.

From where we sit in the tasting room, we can see across to the experimental orchard where they are growing some apples on the vine using the Swiss *dispelier* method, which has never been tried here. A self-guided tour takes visitors through that orchard and down to the pond, where they learn not only about apples but also about the indigenous flora and fauna in the orchard. Woven into the tour of both the orchard and the plant is a story about apple-blossom fairies and their involvement in the process. I was charmed by the fairy-sized doors and portals, the mining village and even the Mad Hatter that have been placed around the cidery to "bring the magic into the orchard" and captivate visiting children.

There are also guided tours, which are particularly interesting during the autumn harvest when it is possible to view the massive picking, sorting, washing, pressing and fermentation process. Merridale Ciderworks "makes all of our cider for the coming year when the fruit ripens." They do not use concentrates, which allow commercial ciders to make cider on demand. They believe that using estate-grown, cider-specific fruit, following the seasons and "letting nature control the cidermaker" is the way to make great cider.

Visitors can book a tour that "unlocks the vault door to our barrel room" and includes sampling the new cider releases. In 2007, the cidery embarked on a mission "to make North America's best Calvados-style brandy," so there are now also tours of the distillery.

The cidery has a stunning casual restaurant, La Pommeraie, and extensive covered and open decking where weddings and meetings can be held. In season, lunch paired with ciders can be ordered for groups of up to 100 people. Designed by chef and restaurant consultant Bill Jones (see Deerholme Farm and Cottage), these meals showcase many of the Cowichan Valley's culinary delights, from Fairburn Farm water buffalo sausage and True Grain breads to The Udder Guy's special apple sorbets and the Hardy Boys' candied smoked salmon. Janet makes sure their business supports other culinary ventures in the Cowichan Valley because she believes "we've got something special here."

This summer, Nicholas and I celebrated his 13th birthday on the deck of Merridale Ciderworks with an amazing Blue Moon Pizza of caramelized onions, Beddis Blue cheese (see Moonstruck Organic Cheese) and spinach with house-made tomato sauce and mozzarella. We first watched it being cooked in the open-air brick oven, and then Nick declared it "the best pizza ever."

Saskatoon Berry Farm

On a summer Saturday, I join one of Mara Jernigan's popular farm tours. I feel like a real tourist as the van pulls out and our host begins to tell us about the day's program: "We'll stop by a cidery, a vineyard, a pastured chicken farm and how about a mystery stop this morning?" Naturally, we all agree. The mystery stop is one Mara hasn't been to yet, either, and it turns out to be a highlight.

It's the Saskatoon Berry Farm, which has become something of a mecca in the area. Alwin and Connie Dyrland moved to the Cowichan Valley from Edmonton, thinking it would be a great hobby to grow the berries of their native Prairies, but the farm's popularity has exceeded their expectations. With so many Prairie folk having moved to British Columbia and an annual influx of "snowbirds" every winter, the farm's namesake berries are in high demand. "On any weekend, you can meet most of Alberta and Saskatchewan at our farmstand," Alwin says.

The Dyrlands bought the farm six years ago and started the six-acre orchard with 1,400 to 1,600 seedlings from southern Alberta. The plants take eight years to fully mature. Alwin shows us the extensive drip-irrigation system he's devised for the fields ("That was about the fourth mortgage," he jokes). Connie keeps busy producing jams and the best saskatoon-berry pies this side of Edmonton. Every weekend, they sell from their farmstand, and the cars never stop pulling in. Even though the season is short, it's a year-round operation and, as Alwin says, "We don't get off the farm much."

Across Canada, saskatoon berries go by a variety of other names including chuckleberries or Indian plums. As Alwin says, "They don't like wet feet, so that's why you don't usually see them out here [on Vancouver Island]." He is lucky to have land with a 20-foot slope from one end to the other. Also, the land has been covered with weeping tile to ensure good drainage.

Alwin takes us straight to the fields where the berry bushes are ripe with fruit, and invites us to "eat and enjoy." We are like kids in a candy store, and soon our mouths and hands are stained from the succulent, dark purple fruit. Mara suggests picking a quantity, promising us sabayon to go with the berries, which she later prepares in her farmhouse kitchen. We pick with gusto, everyone thoroughly enjoying this real hands-on farm experience.

The fresh saskatoon berries are available from early July for three to four weeks. While they last, frozen berries are available direct from the farm.

True Grain Bread

Living on an island that produces less than 10 per cent of its own food supply means the majority of what we consume has to be brought across the pond, inevitably by truck, burning carbon all the way. How refreshing, then, to be visiting a 50-acre farm in the Cowichan Valley where David and Nancy Clegg and their son Tom are reinventing the idea of local farming to feed local people.

The Cleggs, in partnership with Metchosin farmer Tom Henry ("We're providing the land; Tom's providing the equipment and marketing know-how") are growing 15.5 acres of certified organic Red Fife wheat. This hardy, disease-resistant heritage grain was brought to Canada in 1842, and flourished as no grain had done before. However, it was later hybridized so severely that it eventually fell out of favour on the Prairies. In recent years, a few passionate organic farmers have

The Vancouver Island Slow Food Convivium held a discussion evening at True Grain Bread.

Leslie and Bruce Stewart are the new owners of True Grain Bread.

begun once again growing Red Fife, and it is being baked to nutty, rich-flavoured perfection by artisan bakers.

It was Tom who initially planted a half-acre test plot of the grain on his Metchosin farm last year. That crop was stone-milled by the True Grain Bread bakery in Cowichan Bay and baked into the now-famous 30-Mile Loaf, named for the relatively short distance between farm and bakery. To devout locavores, the 30-Mile Loaf, together with True Grain's 20-Mile Loaf made from Durham wheat grown by Saanich farmer Mike Doehnel, tastes like manna from heaven.

Jonathan Knight, who founded True Grain Bread four years ago in what was then a very sleepy fishing village, gets to take credit for introducing Cowichan Bay taste buds to this certified organic "real bread." He landed in town on a snowy day and had the good foresight to locate his new bakery in a vacant shop in the centre of the village. His daily offerings of organic breads, pastries (including an authentic apple strudel and *pain au chocolat*) and cookies were well received by locals and by many, like me, willing to journey from other parts of the island simply to eat well in a happy, healthy environment.

Jonathan's bakery rose in popularity as quickly and effectively as the natural leavening in his breads, and soon he was employing three full-time bakers and a friendly front-of-house crew. Yet the baker who had started it all found himself increasingly "without my hands in the dough" and he felt it was time to pass the baguette to someone else. Today, Jonathan and his bride, Emily McGiffin, are cycling across Canada looking for their next adventure.

True Grain Bread is now owned by Bruce and Leslie Stewart, a young couple who left sales and human resources jobs in Calgary to follow Bruce's long-held dream of running his own business in a small town. When he spotted an ad for True Grain on the Internet in December 2007, he could hardly have imagined that he and Leslie would be operating the place come March 3, 2008.

Entering the shop incognito for the first time, Leslie says they both responded positively, "It's a magical, busy, friendly place." Bruce finishes her sentence, "... serving second-to-none baking in the middle of the small community we were looking for." The Stewarts have high praise for Jonathan, who Leslie says, "let go gracefully," and they are delighted that the original 12 staff have all stayed on. The Stewarts, who pledge that they "won't change a thing" at the bakery, have been well received by the locals.

Of course, True Grain famously dishes up more than just great baking. "We're known as a place that's supportive of local sustainable food initiatives," Bruce tells me. The Vancouver Island Slow Food Convivium recently held a series of discussion evenings on sustainable agriculture at the bakery, and Bruce welcomes any opportunity to educate people about the importance of making Vancouver Island's food supply homegrown. "There's a real appetite [for these initiatives] now because people are more concerned with food security, with where their food comes from," says Bruce.

True Grain Bread welcomes community agricultural initiatives such as the local production of certified organic wheat. Every morning, Bruce jogs the bucolic 4.92 km from his bakery to the Cleggs' farm, where he takes a photo of the Red Fife to record it progress. By September, it will be ready to harvest, and if the crop is successful at generating the projected yield of one tonne per acre, True Grain stands to bake some 30,000 loaves from it. "That's an exciting prospect," says Bruce, who will be milling the grain himself in the bakery's grist mill.

Venturi Schulze Vineyards

We all know that there's balsamic and then there's *balsamic*. Venturi Schulze produces Aceto Balsamico, a nectar that attracts calls from all over the world. I first sampled it with a group of travel writers one overcast day, and I swear the sun came out.

Michelle Schulze tells us that the family's vineyards were originally planted for vinegar, and "then we found we were able to make wine. You see, for vinegar, we need to use grapes that are as high, if not higher, quality than for wine. If you have faults or a mouldy taste, it is so huge after 12 years that you have to throw it away. You can't use pesticides, or the poisons end up in the vinegar. We like to do things the difficult way, and if there's a harder way, well, we'll find that, too."

She passes around samples of the vinegar on silver spoons, and tells us, "You're looking for sweetness, and you have to have some acid in there. These can be fairly high in acid, say 5 to 6 per cent, but you won't be able to tell because they're so sweet. This one can be almost 50 per cent sugar. A lot of people expect something quite acid, but they say, 'Wow, it's so good. It's sweet!'" I find it delicious—a dessert in itself. We all want to buy bottles to stash in our purses.

Michelle says they like their balsamic vinegar because it maintains some of the flavour of the grape. "We really enjoy a lot of the Italian ones, but they don't taste quite as alive. Our woods are younger than theirs. You're looking for some wood flavour, and often people don't recognize that. If you put your nose in there, you can smell cherries."

Michelle recommends serving it over strawberries or on really good ice cream. If you're going to use it in a sauce, she advises adding it at the end, as it's already so concentrated. One doesn't want to boil it down and destroy the flavour. We also learn that the Venturi Schulze vinegar is not as black as some of the commercial vinegars because there is no added colouring.

We wander out to the vines to admire the healthy clumps of Madeleine Sylvaner, a white grape variety used for the vinegar. Says Michelle, "We'll go through there seven times in a certain season. You can basically tell by July how your fruit is set and how it's going to ripen. Sometimes you can pick

Barrels of the famed Aceto Balsamico in the vinegary at Venturi Schulze Vineyards.

everything at once in one or two days; sometimes it's over three weeks. You get in there, and start picking those bunches that have ripened first. Giordano [Venturi, her stepfather], will say, 'I need more acid,' so sometimes we even pick portions of bunches."

Sometimes they have to let the grapes overripen because they need higher sugar and lower acid to make it work. Once picked, the grapes are crushed as they are for wine, and the juice is simmered in 60-gallon pots for about three days. Michelle says, "It's really kind of a fun process. It's like making a broth, and the proteins come to the top. They have to be skimmed off or they'll turn brown and have a bitter flavour. We're looking for a clear product."

When Michelle opens the door to the vinegary, the aroma pulls us inside. The neat rows of barrels represent more than 30 years of work. Giordano made his first barrel of vinegar in 1970. He comes from a very poor family and had never had the real stuff. His first batch went mouldy and had to be thrown out. Michelle tells us, "He ended up going back to Italy and bringing back a live culture. He put it in a barrel and basically forgot about it. It was many years later that he tasted it and that was it! It was just sort of a fluke that it happened that way, and it took off from there. That's the little barrel right there—the mother barrel. We didn't make another vinegar until 1986." Although they've slowed down the evaporation from that original barrel, basically, the whole stock comes from it.

Michelle laughs as she points to the flowerpots on the property, barrels cut in half with geraniums in them. "Each represents $30,000 in lost revenue. When there's mould, you just have to throw the vinegar out and that's all they're good for. It's hit and miss, really."

Michelle's mother, Australian-born Marilyn Schulze, received a National Research Council grant to obtain certain Italian documents regarding vinegar production. She was able to make sense of them, and worked side by side with Giordano to create their special vinegar.

The current release is a blend of vinegars between 6 and 32 years old from various barrels. Barrels are laid on their sides, side by side, and holes are cut in the top for evaporation. It gets fairly warm in the vinegary, so there is intense evaporation. They can lose up to 30 per cent volume a year, depending on how hot it is.

Each barrel gets topped up from the barrel beside it. That's why each barrel is slightly larger than the one next to it; it's also a year younger. The vinegar moves down the whole line, which is why they have to keep the grape production up. It takes a long time. Vinegar barrels are traditionally made from mulberry wood, but it's a protected tree so it's now unavailable. Venturi Schulze uses oak, acacia, cherry, chestnut and ash barrels.

Michelle puts the whole production into perspective: "If you start with 1,000 gallons of juice, in 12 years you will have between 25 and 30 gallons, which is why it's so expensive. This is Giordano's dream, and it's working out. We're the only ones who are doing this commercially in North America."

Venturi Schulze is also highly regarded for its wines: a Brut Naturel that was chosen for the Queen's 1994 visit to the Commonwealth Games in Victoria; Millefiori, the ultimate tropical fruity Siegerrebe; and Brandenburg No. 3, a rich dessert wine that pairs perfectly with my favourite course, the cheese course. They are all estate-grown, and Marilyn is adamant that this is the only way to develop a regional identity for wine. She is concerned that some local winemakers are buying their grapes from other parts of the province and not declaring their origin. She sees huge potential for the Cowichan Valley wine area, and just wants it to be true to itself. Venturi Schulze has become the exclusive distributor of an amazingly authentic Grana cheese that's made in Alberta. "This natural, aged cheese gives off explosions of flavour that we have found in the past only with fully aged Parmigiano-Reggiano," says Marilyn. Leoni Grana Cheese is available in 2.5-kg and 300-g pieces.

CEDAR/ YELLOW POINT

Cedar Farmers' Market

The Cedar Farmers' Market features mainly organic growers from the surrounding area, including Yellow Point Orchards, Bensons' Olde Tyme Farm, Limberlost Orchard, Golden Maples Farm, Big D Emu Farm and Munro Creek Farm. There are also some crafts and great bread and baked goods from the Cedar Women's Institute.

To make a wonderful day of it, combine your visit to the market, which is located in the field next to the Crow and Gate Pub, with a nice pub lunch and afternoon visit to the nearby Barton & Leier Gallery, featuring the paintings of Grant Leier and Nixie Barton, and their magical, whimsical garden and gift shop.

The Crow and Gate Pub

I've drunk enough Pimm's No. 1 Cup and lemonade in English country pubs to know the real thing, and The Crow and Gate Pub's *is* the real thing. It's included in *An Edible Journey* not because it is a proponent of the 100-Mile Diet or because its wines are reflective of the local *terroir*, but by virtue of its authenticity and charm, which, for the 25 years I've been a grateful patron, are reasons enough for me.

Whether one is visiting Yellow Point for the afternoon or weekend, or simply passing through en route to other parts of the island, the pub makes the most delightful stop. On many occasions, my parents and I have driven to The Crow and Gate expressly to have lunch, and returned thereafter to Victoria.

The pub is housed in a Tudor-style building set on peaceful green lawns on 10 bucolic acres. I have never stepped inside at lunchtime without being greeted by a gentle bustle of happy patrons, their plates loaded with genuine pub fare like Melton Mowbray pies, oyster stew and Stilton ploughman plates of cheese, salad, pickles and bread and their tankards frosty with ale.

Mahle House Restaurant

I arrive early for dinner, and Maureen Loucks bounds out of the kitchen to greet me. "You must see our gardens first," and she walks me around the colourful vegetable and herb beds, stopping to show off various plants ("Look, have you ever seen white borage? Juliet tomatoes. Aren't they just perfect? Every kind of carrot, Maxibell French filet beans, Florence fennel"). She shows me zephyr, Costa romanesco and pale green pattypan squash, saying, "A chef can't create something wonderful out of inferior products."

Maureen established the kitchen garden to ensure she would always have high-quality organic veggies. The garden has been tended by Kate White, who also gardens for the folks

Chef and co-owner Maureen Loucks of the Mahle House offers freshly picked tomatoes at the Harvest Bounty Festival.

at Hazelwood Herb Farm. She's off to Arizona to take an herbalist course, and in her absence, Scott, a local orchardist, will take over.

We wander over to the house itself, a Queen Anne beauty built in 1904 and surrounded by immaculate flower beds. These gardens are cared for by Maureen's sister-in-law, Ginny Horrocks. In July, Mahle House holds its Summer Wine and Garden Party. Maureen's brother, and partner in the restaurant, Delbert Horrocks, organizes a dozen or so wine reps to proffer their wares, and a huge alfresco brunch is set out for guests. I immediately mark my calendar for the second Sunday in July.

Once inside, I am impressed by the hominess of the restaurant and the clubbiness of its patrons. Fine dining takes on an appealing friendliness in the country, and the air is vibrant with greetings. It really is a close-knit place. Not only is it run by a brother and sister, but the next generation is also involved. Delbert's daughter waits tables and Maureen's daughter worked in the restaurant before moving to Victoria, where she now runs the venerable Bengal Lounge in The Fairmont Empress.

I take a seat by the window with a lovely view of Ginny's flower beds, and then count six of Grant Leier's richly textured food paintings on the walls around me. One can only hope that food emulates art here.

It seems I've timed my visit well because tonight is the famous "Adventurous Wednesday," when ordering from the menu is thrown out the window, and the chef gets to surprise diners with things they might never have considered ordering before. The concept took off from day one. People come from all over the island with friends and family, and everyone at the table is served something different for each of their four courses.

Even though I'm dining alone, I can vicariously enjoy the reactions from tables around me. The two couples opposite are obviously thrilled as their appetizers are set down: prawns with cannellini beans for one man; Kataifi-wrapped prawns with wasabi sauce for another; steamed mussels and calamari Dijonnaise for the women, one of whom says, "I can see a food fight coming."

I've given Maureen a bit of a challenge with my request for "no pork or shellfish," but she certainly rises to the occasion. I begin with a salad of tomatoes from her garden, topped with melted Fontina and shredded basil and follow with a delicately flavoured carrot-ginger soup. The accompanying molasses bread is made locally for the restaurant.

My main course, lamb tenderloin with a basil and Dijon mustard sauce, is served with some of those beautiful baby zucchini and red cauliflower from the garden. Delbert, winner of a whole wall full of wine awards, also gets to have fun on Wednesdays, pairing new wines with the food. I enjoy Lang 2001 Pinot Auxerrois, Hogg Fumé Blanc (from Washington State) and Wolf Blass Yarra Valley 2000 Pinot Noir and Yellow Tail Shiraz (all in very small amounts, as I'm driving myself back to Victoria).

The pièce de résistance is a chocolate triple sec pâté, with raspberry purée and a good cup of coffee. Earlier, Maureen told me, "I am really happy when I'm cooking." Her food is a winning reflection of that feeling.

Yellow Point Cranberries

I remember being surprised to discover kiwis growing on Vancouver Island, and now we have cranberries!

When Grant and Justine Keefer were married, they received a gift certificate to stay at Yellow Point Lodge. Just down the road from the lodge, they came across a 43-acre farm for sale, which turned out to be exactly what they'd been looking for. It had once been a potato farm but was dormant for some 30 years. Grant's family grew cranberries in Richmond and he was aware that Ocean Spray was looking for more growers, so everything fell into place for the couple to buy the farm and plant cranberries.

And plant they did: 15 acres are now under cultivation with the crop, and the Keefers produced some 50,000 pounds of fruit last year. "The potential is here to harvest up to 300,000 pounds of cranberries from these plants," says Grant, as we take a tour of his demonstration field. It's mid-November but there are still a few stray, deep-red jewels peeking out from the foliage. To show me how the fruit grows, he picks an "upright," which is the portion of the plant that grows perpendicular to the ground.

Around June 23, the farm hosts a blossom festival to celebrate the plants' pollination by the Keefers' bumblebees (neighbourhood bees also help out). Tiny, pale-pink flowers appear on the plants, signifying the fruit to come. The Keefers prefer bumblebees because they work harder than honeybees, and they encourage their proliferation by planting early flowering plants such as heathers, geraniums and daffodils.

Beginning in September, the dry harvest begins wherein the berries are picked by a machine that literally strips them off the plant. Later, a wet picking is done involving flooding the fields and corralling the berries. The wet-picked fruit is used for juice.

In addition to shipping fruit to Ocean Spray, the Keefers make and sell a delectable range of cranberry products in their on-site Cranberry Cottage Kitchen. There are lovely jams and jellies, including the unique and delicious Cranberry Horseradish Jelly, which I've discovered goes very well with a little chèvre or cream cheese on crackers.

Cranberry Cottage Kitchen really comes to life at the end of November when Justine packs the shop with all the wonderful preserves she's been putting up for the annual Cedar-Yellow Point Artisans Association Country Christmas Tour.

LADYSMITH

Hazelwood Herb Farm

Sitting under the arbour with the heady fragrances of clematis, ahebia, cidergum eucalyptus and passion flower lulling me, watching the fantastical mating dance of hummingbirds and looking across a gentle lily pond to the herb gardens beyond, I am transfixed. This peaceful place is a dream come true for Richard White and Jacynthe Dugas. He is originally from Leeds, England, and was a maintenance mechanic for the Ladysmith sawmill; she hails from Val d'Or, Quebec, and previously worked for the federal government. Richard says that once he had fixed every piece of equipment at the mill many times, it was time to find a new challenge.

It was his idea to start growing herbs for local restaurants, but that didn't work out. In those days, the restaurants were only looking for a little bunch here and there, so the venture didn't pay. Not one to be deterred, Richard quit his job and the couple began growing herbs in earnest, improving the gardens and buildings as their budget allowed. Jacynthe soon left her job, and the two have since thrown themselves into creating a multi-faceted business whose success, they say, is sometimes overwhelming.

Owners Richard White and Jacynthe Dugas and their delightful nursery and gift shop at Hazelwood Herb Farm.

By the end of May, there are over 400 different culinary, landscape and medicinal herbs proliferating—everything from what Richard calls the "Simon and Garfunkels" (parsley, sage, rosemary and thyme) to some very unusual varieties. Many people come looking for alternative health cures, and what the couple don't already grow, they are always game to try. Richard says if a medicinal herb hits the news, they are flooded with requests. Evening primrose, St. John's wort and milk thistle are in constant demand.

Word of mouth brings people from all over Vancouver Island, and there are many out-of-country visitors in the summer. It is not unusual for people to bring in plans for herb gardens to seek Richard's advice and stock up on plants. Everything is conveniently labelled to help people orient themselves to the many types of herbs. There are historical herbs like germander to treat gout; camphor for the stomach; every imaginable variety of thyme; Tucson blue rosemary; calamint; lemongrass; angelica; sweet cicely, a sugar substitute appreciated by diabetics; red bugle, a styptic; bloodroot, a native plant for medicinal purposes; red-flowered comfrey to rejuvenate skin cells; and lavender, which finds its way into Jacynthe's soaps and soothing eye masks.

The formal garden is just the beginning. Beyond it are raised beds of herbs and a lath house—an open-slatted nursery with a plastic roof that allows watering to be manually controlled. The building is full of herbs, lined up row upon row. We are joined at this stage of the tour by Saffron, the resident golden Lab who politely leads us to the first greenhouse. Here, many plants begin their growing cycle heated by the wood-burning stove. The greenhouse's thermostat is set at 60°F, and when the stove cuts out, an oil furnace kicks in. Richard says this hothouse makes a wonderful place to hang out in winter with a glass of brandy.

In addition to their generous free advice, Richard and Jacynthe have hundreds of potted herbs for sale, and there is a fabulous gift shop brimming with all things herbal.

Kiwi Cove Lodge

When I arrive, Peggy Kolosoff is saying goodbye to some of her bed and breakfast guests. They are six women who have been kayaking down the coast for two weeks and are singing the praises of her bathtubs and showers. There are 12 rooms at the inn, all of them facing the orchard, and beyond it, Ladysmith Harbour.

It's a lovely fall morning, so we take a walk through the vines. Peggy and Doug Kolosoff bought this 10-acre property in 1994 with the intention of making it into a campground. The rezoning didn't happen as planned, so they built a lodge and planted a thousand Christmas trees.

They gave a lot of thought to producing a crop that "would be fairly low-maintenance and would create a nice ambiance on our property." Kiwi fruit vines came to mind, and the result is seven varieties on a .75-acre vineyard of immaculate design. Doug, a forestry worker who has kept his day job, chose the site wisely and has developed an irrigation system that waters the plants while ensuring that the leaves don't get wet. He created slight valleys between the rows of vines and the whole orchard slopes toward the shore, which is essential for runoff during heavy rains.

There is no spraying and very little threat of predators. Peggy says the deer don't like kiwis (finally, something they don't like!), and the birds could not

care less about the fruit. Only the rabbits are interested, but Doug has wrapped the bottom of the vines in chicken wire to prevent any major damage.

The Kolosoffs grow the well-known Hayward variety of kiwi as well as other "fuzzy" varieties like the Elmwood and Saanichton and three types of Arguta (smaller, grape-like) kiwis. Yellow kiwis will be available in the future. The Argutas ripen on the vine and are available in October. The fuzzies are handled differently. They are picked unripe in the first week of December, then placed in cold storage.

When Peggy needs some to use at the inn or for a buyer, she simply brings them to room temperature and lets them slowly ripen. Guests enjoy a variety of "kiwi cuisine," from kiwi glaze on homemade yogurt and pancakes to kiwi cheesecake, jelly rolls, chutney and salsa. The night before my visit, Peggy's kiwi-jalapeno topping received rave reviews from the kayakers.

Page Point Inn

The best food experiences are often revealed, not anticipated, and such was the case at Page Point Inn. I'd heard about the 1940s charm of the place, the classic cooking of John Grove and the friendliness of the staff. I enjoyed it all, but was particularly blown away by a sailboat—or, more specifically, by the prospect of dinner on a sailboat under a starry sky.

The inn has a long and colourful history dating back to 1873, when David Page homesteaded 160 acres at what came to be known as Page Point. Page raised oysters in Oyster Bay (now Ladysmith Harbour). It's amazing the chap lasted as long as he did, given the cougar dens on his property and the Natives who regularly threatened his life, but he lived at Page Point until 1911 when he moved to Ladysmith. The property was bought by an American doctor, who subsequently leased it to the Krjivitsky family. The family's daughters, known as the "Russian Marys," rowed across the bay every day to attend school in Ladysmith. Their father planted asparagus, flowers and fruit: cherries, peaches, currants and apples. When he died in 1938, the family moved to Vancouver and Page Point fell into disrepair.

Harry and Zella Olmstead bought it in 1947 and built Manana Lodge the following year with help from a local artist, Ron Grouhel. Ron was responsible for the totem pole art still on display in the older guest rooms and an interesting rolled copper mural that was uncovered in 1999 during a renovation of the dining room. Zella had a pet deer called Bambi that had the run of the lodge's dining room, and it was Zella who claimed there were singing fish in the bay.

Fortunately, much of that colourful past lives on in Page Point Inn's new incarnation. Owners Lawrence and Lexie Lambert were former next-door neighbours who kept their eye on the property and were able to purchase it in 1998. They've made some improvements, like new docks for the many boaters who come to stay or eat at the inn, and they've introduced first-rate dining, but happily, they're keeping the rustic, original guest rooms and the leisurely pace of yesteryear.

I arrived in the middle of the night, having dined in Nanaimo, and was shown to one of the original guest rooms facing the marina. I took a welcome hot bath and had a tipple of the sherry that is thoughtfully put out in the bedrooms, and went to sleep to the gentle clink of boats' masts in the bay. Rose, a neighbour and Page Point's morning waitress, served me a continental breakfast in the oceanside Harbour Room, and then I was off to explore the grounds. Just as I headed around to the hot tub, Rose called out, "Lexie has something to show you down on the dock."

That "something" was something else—the 65-foot Australian *Dame Pattie*, which had competed in the 1967 America's Cup. It seems that Lawrence, an avid sailor, had found the boat in bad shape in Victoria and brought it home to Ladysmith to restore. I climbed aboard and swooned at the quality finishings inside and the prospect of returning in the summer for a dinner cruise. This big, beautiful sailboat can be chartered for an afternoon or several days and comes equipped with staff and a chef.

Back on shore later, I was offered the best seat in the house—stoveside in Page Point Inn's kitchen. Chef John Grove, who aims to cook "simple, elegant food from local ingredients," is bringing back some of the classics—original dishes from the Manana Lodge—and I was looking forward to trying a few

examples. From ribs to a dessert trolley to escargots ("as soon as I find a good source outside of France," he tells me), the cuisine is beginning to reflect its beautifully preserved setting. "The more I find out about the history of this place, the more changes I'll make to the menu," says John.

He's certainly got my attention as he whisks a classic brandy-horseradish cocktail sauce for a prawn cocktail. In just the right glass bowl with sloping sides, he places crushed ice, then shredded lettuce. He next hangs six large, succulent-looking prawns around the rim, then takes out his reamer to gut a lemon half. Into the lemon goes a good measure of cocktail sauce. John presents the starter with a slice each of lemon and lime. My culinary memory goes back to Victoria's The Princess Mary Restaurant in the early 1960s, when shrimp cocktails and banana cream pie ruled—a happy place for me.

John's next presentation is grilled and sliced duck breast with a grapefruit reduction and seven (count them!) vegetables, served with a phyllo pastry beggar's purse filled with potatoes that have been mashed with roasted garlic and truffle oil. This fine dinner is followed by a simple yet rich chocolate mousse ("a recipe I've made for 10 years") using John's favourite Belcolade Belgian chocolate and cream. It's served close to room temperature with a sprig of pineapple mint and a delicate chocolate cigar that he's tipped with 24k gold leaf. For me, it's a dinner that's hard to beat in a setting that is both nostalgic and freshly attractive.

John apprenticed at The Aerie Resort and was the pastry chef at The Wickaninnish Inn for three and a half years before coming to Page Point Inn as chef de cuisine. His interest in food began at Esquimalt High School in Victoria, where he took the cook's training program along with Jason Hoskins, now sous-chef at The Wickaninnish. They've worked together many times, been roommates and gone fishing. This is John's first crack at all-out cheffing, and he is enthusiastically yet respectfully embracing the role.

He enjoys the inn's proximity to local ingredients. Andrew Dryden drops off indigenous oysters daily from the family-run Evening Cove Oysters, which is just down the road. John buys produce from Russell's Farm near Chemainus, cheese from Hilary's Cheese Company, herbs from Hazelwood Herb Farm. He makes a point of visiting the herb farm personally when he has a wedding cake to design, to hand-pick edible flowers to decorate it. I saw his portfolio of cakes and was impressed with their diversity, from a tree-shaped chocolate buttercream one with varigated bark made of chocolate to tiny vegan cupcakes no larger than pears that are decorated with intricate fondant icing patterns. Alderlea, Venturi Schulze, Blue Grouse and Saturna Island vineyards figure on the wine list here, although I was, as usual, not able to sample as I was back on the road straight after dinner.

I've interviewed surfing chefs, show-jumping chefs and chefs who aspire to tap dancing. John Grove is a sailing chef who lives "out there" aboard the 30-foot yellow-and-cream sloop *Maria Mhaoi*, which he named for his great-great-grandmother. She and her husband came from Hawaii for the fur trade and lived for many years on Russell Island. It seems Maria was quite a sailor and John has always had sailing in his blood. I ask if he feels he's too close to work. "Not at all," he tells me, "and besides, I can sail away and drop anchor whenever I want to." One day he hopes to get a bigger boat and sail around the world, but for now he's very happy cooking the classics from quality local ingredients and taking the time to greet diners after dinner often taking dessert orders and enjoying the repartee with fellow sailors.

NANAIMO

Carrot on the Run and 24 Carrot Catering

Nanaimo's Island Natural Markets acquired a new neighbour when Carrot on the Run took over from Green Jeans Deli. Cynthia Cooper and I dropped in one cold winter morning and were rewarded with hot coffee and freshly baked chocolate-mint cookies. We loved the giant papier mâché carrot over the display

case that was created for the deli when it participated in Bite of Nanaimo (the city's annual culinary event in September) by Richard Berlingette, husband of co-owner Alexandra.

"Nanaimo is overrun with fast-food restaurants on every corner," says Melissa Hamilton, the deli's other owner, when we sit down to chat, "so we find that locals and travellers appreciate being able to pop in for a quick and healthy lunch, or for takeaways." She and Alex are best friends and have worked together for many years in the food industry. She sees the deli as a natural meshing of their compatibility and talents.

Melissa is Nanaimo-born and -raised. She originally worked as a waitress, and credits Alex with teaching her how to cook. Alex is from Sussex, England, and received her chef's papers through Vancouver Community College. When I caught up with her a few weeks later, she told me she took those papers and headed out to the bush, working for many years in camps and fishing lodges near Bella Bella, BC.

Returning to Nanaimo, she ran the kitchen at Filthy McNasty's, which was where she and Melissa connected. Alex said that whenever she was in town, she was "always hankering to get back to the bush, but as I got older and the work got harder on the body, I started to think about nesting." So, eight years ago, she settled down in Nanaimo and launched 24 Carrot Catering from a commercial kitchen in her house.

When the deli came available, it seemed like "a natural progression for me and it has become a great creative outlet." The day we spoke, she'd created quinoa salad with corn, fresh greens and a light lemon vinaigrette; a vegan cashew-nut pâté; and a yummy vegetable-ricotta cheesecake with breaded tomatoes on top. Alex also makes time to teach a hospitality management course at the Culinary Institute of Vancouver Island. "I teach the restaurant part of it, and the students actually open a temporary restaurant at the college that serves 100 covers a night."

The deli and Island Natural Markets share customers, and Alex and Melissa say they're enjoying the challenge of catering to people with allergies or on special diets. Their "treasure of a baker," Ian, even creates a wonderful range of healthy cookies from things like spelt, soy and potato to satisfy sweet teeth that shouldn't have sugar.

Island Natural Markets

I suppose I've always been under the impression that it takes a large population to support large, full-service organic grocery stores. I am now happy to admit that's wrong. In the middle of sprawling mall country just north of Nanaimo, Urban Beet and Island Natural Markets are doing booming business.

Island Naturals has a very open, almost tropical feel to it (although there are four walls and a ceiling). Shelves are lined with all things organic and there's a bustling deli serving veggie and fruit juices (wheat grass is optional), fruit smoothies (with or without protein powder), yummy energy balls made by Trish Vet of Hornby Island and homemade gourmet pizzas served by the slice.

I enjoy my first Creekmore's BuzzRight coffee of the day and watch the locals shop.

McLean's Specialty Foods

I can never decide what brings me back to McLean's more—the food or the humour. But, of course, it's both. Nowhere outside of England have I found the range of foods near and dear to my homeland except here, where Baxter's soups, Bird's custard powder and Rose's lime marmalade share shelves with pickled fish, remoulade, fried onions and lingonberry jam from Scandinavia and passion-fruit pulp, rooibos and beef biltong from South Africa.

There are also over a hundred cheeses and smoked meats. In the fall, owner Eric McLean holds convivial wine- and cheese-tasting evenings. As early as July, people like me start ordering whisky and cherry brandy Christmas cakes and deluxe puddings that are brought in specially from the Old Country. Says Eric, "Our customers tell us they eagerly await the phone call to

McLean's Specialty Foods is a cheese lover's paradise.

tell them, 'Your cake is ready!'" The selection of German stollen, English chocolates, jams and chutneys is remarkable. As I "ooh" and "ahh" my way around the store with Eric one December afternoon, he keeps darting to the back room to replenish things that he can't keep on the shelves.

My road trips are never quite complete without a stop at McLean's for a cup of tea and an excellent, house-made "bap," a white English roll that's slightly crunchy on the outside and soft inside, filled with cheese, salad cream, lettuce and tomato. There are also delicious made-from-scratch soups and popular sandwiches like the prosciutto with Camembert and sweet chutney, and salads such as bocconcini with tomatoes, fresh basil and quality balsamic vinegar and olive oil. The teapots have handknit cosies and the china has roses on it. For fleeting moments, I'm back in Britain as I chat with Eric ("The Big Cheese") and Sandy McLean, the seriously fun owners.

The couple had lived previously in Maple Ridge on the mainland, where Eric was an account representative for Cadbury-Schweppes and Sandy was an office manager for the provincial government. Fifteen years ago, their Nanaimo friends invited them across the strait for a look around. "They took us to the pub, and we liked the feel of the town—less anonymity." They were fed up with big-city living and wanted to be near the ocean, so they made their crossing permanent.

Eric worked for a food distributor for a while, but became frustrated: "That was when you couldn't get grocers to stock extra-virgin olive oil, good-quality Italian pasta, Parmigiano-Reggiano or balsamic vinegar." From years of doing business with grocers, he realized, "Few people actually knew what they were selling." His frustration led to the opening of McLean's Specialty Foods, a cornucopia of food and sociability. The shop's much anticipated wine- and cheese-tasting evenings are regularly sold out.

Eric was raised in a little Scottish town. His family didn't have much money, but he remembers things like the fishmonger apologizing to his mother if there were still bones in the fish. He appreciated the interest that people took in what they were eating. He believes people need to be educated about their food, and he and Sandy love helping their customers find more interesting alternatives. He doesn't sell mozzarella, which "you can buy everywhere," but recommends trying something new for pizza: Fontina, Asiago or Pecorino. And customers keep coming back.

McLean's picnic hampers are still a bit of a secret, but those in the know rely on Eric and Sandy's creativity and quality foods whenever they want to venture forth into nature or need provisions for the ferry ride back to the mainland or a long-haul flight. How do the McLeans know what to put in a hamper? "We ask a lot of probing questions," says Eric, "Are they wanting food of a particular ethnicity? Is this a special occasion? Are they serious foodies?" Ah, serious foodies. You're home.

Mon Petit Choux

Linda Allen laments, "When I moved to Nanaimo, there wasn't a place I could go for *petit déjeuner*. I was looking for good croissants, coffee...." But now, thanks to Linda, there is a place for her and for those of us who also seek a Continental start to our day. And every day, she has customers telling her, "I'm so glad you're here."

It's no wonder that Linda created her own bakery-café. Her husband, Gaetan, runs the excellent Wesley Street Café nearby and her sister owns Bonjour Brioche in Toronto, which *Zagat* says has "the best croissant west of Paris."

But it was a long wait for the location that Gaetan had spotted years ago, all boarded up. It is smack in the middle of Nanaimo's downtown, a pie-shaped building with vast windows onto the action on Commercial Street. It was eventually purchased by "a sailor from Santa Fe" and Linda quickly secured the lease, opening in June 2007.

Pastry chef Sarah Walbank, who formerly worked under North Vancouver chocolatier Thomas Haas, is producing some very fine breads and sweet and savoury pastries. It's uplifting to see

Cappuccinos and a chocolate-orange-pistachio marzipan slice at Mon Petit Choux.

the classic *épis de blé*, rolls shaped like shafts of wheat; *miche* loaves made with organic Red Fife whole wheat; *fougasses* with olives, garlic and rosemary; and challah on Fridays. The breads are incorporated into a range of sandwiches on offer at lunchtime, such as the yummy roasted chicken breast with house-made rosemary aïoli and cranberry compote on Red Fife *miche*.

Petit déjeuner, naturally, is a big attraction here. There are very good coffees made with Drum Roaster organic coffee to go with a croissant, a baguette with preserves or full breakfasts such as *Croque Madame* or Canadian bacon and eggs.

I'm smitten with an immaculate chocolate-orange-pistachio marzipan slice served with a pitch-perfect cappuccino. These treats, enjoyed in the enthusiastic company of Linda Allen, have taken Nanaimo to a whole new level of hospitality.

The Wesley Street Café

Gaetan Brousseau studied political science at university, but decided he didn't want to be a starving student, so he learned how to cook. He took his chef's training in Lausanne, Switzerland, and his sommelier training in Bordeaux. He and his wife, Linda Allen, worked in the wine-distribution business, then in a restaurant in Arizona. Keen sailors, they ended up in Vancouver where they ran the successful Granite Café, which was awarded best restaurant status in Vancouver two years running. From their sailing jaunts, they learned of an opportunity at Silva Bay on Gabriola Island and ran their restaurant Latitude there for five years.

"And then," says Gaetan, "we decided we were ready to take the boat to Mexico." What changed that plan was another opportunity to take over a restaurant, this time in Nanaimo. The Wesley Street Café quickly established itself as the place to dine well on the mid-island, for both lunch and dinner.

I arrive early for dinner, in order to spend time with Gaetan and his charming chef, Josh Massey. Josh is "Nanaimo born and bred" and did his chef's training at Malaspina University-College. He "cooked all over Nanaimo," then spent two years in the kitchens of Sooke Harbour House, where he was made pastry chef. He is delighted to be at The Wesley Street, a restaurant that he feels "enriches the mid-island's culinary scene."

My first question, as always, is about ingredients. What are they sourcing locally? The answer puts The Wesley Street Café on the same page as restaurants run by the chefs belonging to the Island Chefs Collaborative, who "emphasize locally grown, organic, seasonal and minimally processed ingredients."

The menu features pork from nearby Errington, chicken from Cowichan Bay Farm and venison from Qualicum Farms. Greens are supplied by Nanoose Edibles, and the cheese course showcases Courtenay's Natural Pastures cheeses. Gaetan has put his sommelier training to good use on the wine list, which is garnering a lot of favourable attention. I'm pleased to see featured selections from Alderlea, Glenterra, Blue Grouse and Saturna Island vineyards.

Gaetan pours me the Blue Grouse Vineyard's Pinot Gris, and presents the house-made warmed egg bread as I consult the evening's menu. There is a good variety, pleasingly French-leaning, with some personal favourites of mine like bouillabaisse and grilled rack of lamb. I start with delicate slices of venison carpaccio served with mustard aïoli, Nanoose Edibles' mesclun and toast points and then two large ravioli filled with peas and mascarpone and served with small, sweet scallops and seared prawns, finished with basil and chili oils. Both appetizers are first-class.

Gaetan and I have a lively discussion about eating wild versus farmed fish (he favours wild, and serves wild salmon). Hearing he has a good supply of sockeye from Barkley Sound, I decide to go for the salmon baked on a cedar plank, and served this evening with a warm citrus chutney, a nice slice of eggplant, zucchini and onion tart, carrots and perfect rice. I realize I have eaten everything on my plate and can't even contemplate dessert or cheese. That momentary catastrophe is soon remedied; I will just have to come back, and soon.

As Gaetan attends to other diners, I reflect on my excellent meal and think how fortunate Nanaimo is that he and Linda postponed their journey to Mexico.

GABRIOLA ISLAND

Gabriola Agricultural Association Farmers' Market

Tannie Meyer, one of the founders of the Gabriola Agricultural Association Farmers' Market, is showing me around her farm. We're meeting here because it's January and the market is closed for the season, not least to give the busy vendors a break.

The Gabriola market is one of the area's largest, with 85 regular and up to 20 "casual" stalls. Tannie says the casual vendors are those who take their chances on market day, bringing whatever is abundant in their gardens that week. "After winter," Tannie says, "the market is a big social event. It's like coming home again."

Vendors include Ken Stefanson and Llie Brotherton of Gabriola Gourmet Garlic with their wonderful garlic products and Llie's beautiful baskets; Ike MacKay of Berry Point Fruit and Honey, who brings apples, pears, cherries and honey; Jocelyne Boulanger and Michael Bean of Auld Alliance Farm, who are well known for their herbs and attractively bottled vinegars; Helen Cox and Dale Ferguson of Early Dawn Farm with cucumbers, flowers, peppers, strawberries and more; and Jacinthe and Peter Eastick of Freedom Farm, who come with eggs, greens, chickens and pheasants. There is also a full-service kitchen for snacks and lunch.

Tannie's own 6 Meyer Farm is well represented at the market. Tannie, her husband, Jeff, and her three young children have a regular stall where they sell potatoes and their popular Meyer corn. The whole family is up before the sun on market day to harvest the produce and then have a big breakfast before heading down to the Aggie Hall. Tannie tells me they have always grown organically because "we want the kids to be able to pick food directly from the garden and eat it without any concerns."

Gabriola Gourmet Garlic

Anyone who plays continuous classical music to his chickens is all right with me. As Ken Stefanson gives me a tour of his tranquil Gabriola property, I am particularly taken with his animals: those sophisticated Araucana chickens, a dear miniature horse named Peter and two Angora goats who vie with each other to have their photo taken. Then there are the prize-winning schnauzers. I lose count of how many there are as they frolic around me. Ken's wife, Llie Brotherton, is a professional dog groomer, and the couple has always raised show dogs.

It was Llie who found their Gabriola property. The couple had been living in Vancouver when she paid a visit to the island with a girlfriend. Says Ken, "She came home and reminded me that I'd once said I could live on an island." They are now happily settled in their island home. Llie has a prolific vegetable garden and makes beautiful baskets. Ken, who had previously sold computers, furniture and real estate, and bought and sold 18 restaurants, has found a new profession in garlic and chocolate.

The garlic was his doctor's suggestion. After Ken had suffered four strokes, she told him to get his blood pressure down by eating more garlic. That led Ken to grow garlic, which led to his growing a lot of garlic—more than 6,000 pounds a year. He grows it mainly on the southern, warmer part of the island and has a barn over on Vancouver Island for drying it. Ken tells me he'd always enjoyed garlic, but "I didn't know how much I liked it until I started growing it." Also on Vancouver Island is the chocolate factory where he and his business partner, Ille Jocelyn, produce their amazing array of chocolate bars and truffles.

The chocolate was Ken's own idea. He'd been experimenting with garlic dipped in chocolate. He met Ille, a chocolatier, and they launched The Original Gabriola Bar made of dark chocolate and garlic. The range of Gabriola Gourmet chocolate bars now includes The Exquisit Gabriola Bar (ginger and garlic), Red Hot Chili Bar, Gabriola Island Orange, Gabriola Island Mint and Gabriola Island Espresso. I arrive just as the mint and coffee bars are being launched, and add my praise to the mix between

orgasmic bites of each flavour. Speaking of orgasmic, Ken's new maca bars are infused with the recommended daily dose of Peruvian maca, which he tells me is known for its energy-producing and aphrodisiac qualities. There are also divine truffles.

Other products are the hugely popular garlic chutney, a pure minced garlic (the garlic is preserved in apple cider vinegar) and minced garlic with paprika; pickled- and hot-pickled garlic; three- and four-year-aged garlic; and garlic salad dressing and marinade. Ken also sells fresh and dried garlic, seed, greens and braids. You'll find this charming gentleman and his garlic products all over the island,

Mr. Gabriola Gourmet Garlic, Ken Stefanson.

including at the Nanaimo and Duncan farmers' markets. In season, you can always find him at the Gabriola "Aggie Hall" Farmers' Market on Saturdays and the Silva Bay market on Sundays, and at the Saltspring Island Garlic Festival in August. Ken and Llie have opened a gelato store on Willow Street in Chemainus that offers 180 different flavours on a rotating basis as well as homemade cookies and "all our great garlic products." If you have the chance, go directly to the source; Llie's gardens and the irresistible chocolate studio are open year-round. And don't forget to pay your respects to the animals.

When I catch up with Ken this year, he is incredibly busy. He has been rapidly expanding his distribution, with the goal "to be in all BC supermarkets and delis." Eventually, Ken says, he'll retire and sell his going concern to the next generation of garlic and chocolate aficionados, but for now, he's not slowing down. "If people are nice, I let them sell my chocolate," he laughs.

Heavenly Flowers and the Good Earth Market Garden

There was a good rain the night before I went to visit Rosheen Holland. "Bring your gumboots," she advised me. I parked on the road and tramped down a muddy path into the woods. Her home appeared in a clearing, smoke wafting from the chimney. Rosheen was at the door, inviting me in for freshly brewed green tea.

I'd heard great things about the vegetables and flowers grown by Rosheen and her husband, Bob Shields. They worked in the landscape-maintenance business in Vancouver for 12 years, then thought it would be better to have their own land and grow for themselves. The original idea was to grow ornamentals and trees, but they found their land was best suited to annuals. Actually, they have two pieces of land on Gabriola. Their small parcel at the island's warm, south end is ideal for "starting a lot of our babies." The plants are then moved to the couple's mid-island property, which sits on a flood plain. There, they flourish in the rich soil.

Rosheen and Bob began selling their wares from the Gabriola farmers' market when it started eight years ago. Their produce and flowers were instant successes, but as the market grew from a handful of stalls to over a hundred, they found it more difficult to serve their loyal local customers. Rosheen says that the huge crowds at the market

Rosheen Holland of Gabriola's Heavenly Flowers and the Good Earth Market Garden shows off a bouquet of her famous flowers at the Gabriola Agricultural Association Farmers' Market.

meant "people were struggling to find us, and then actually get to us." So they decided to operate exclusively from their farmgate and by special order.

The special orders are often for Rosheen's extraordinary floral arrangements. She's popular with brides, who visit her flower gardens ("a riot of colour in summer") a week before their weddings, usually with their mothers, to choose the blooms for their big day. Rosheen displays her arrangements at the farmgate, each thoughtfully wrapped in water-filled bubblepacks. Rosheen tells me her flowers are so hardy that they can last up to two weeks.

Rosheen and Bob grow an impressive range of vegetables, many larger than life, like the giant onions Rosheen pulls out of her cold storage to show me. She attributes their quality to the fact that they are organically grown. The couple is always feeding the soil with good things like seaweed, which they get from the east side of the island. "Our soil is 80 per cent humus, which acts like a giant bag of peat moss on the plants and makes things grow big and healthy." Rosheen feels they have a responsibility to produce high-quality produce. "After all," she tells me, "our customers are our neighbours."

Before I leave, we have a wonderful conversation about cooking for oneself versus eating in restaurants. Rosheen loves cooking from the bounty in her garden. She believes "a meal doesn't go anywhere without the best ingredients, and organic ingredients make a meal exceptional." Taught by her mother to understand "what good food is and what it tastes like," she, like me, finds it a challenge to eat out unless the food quality is exceptional.

I leave Rosheen's cosy cottage in the woods and run into Bob cutting firewood. Even though Rosheen has impressed on me that farming "is not as romantic as people think," for the moment I am enchanted by the appearance of their rural idyll.

"Organic ingredients make a meal exceptional."

— Rosheen Holland

LANTZVILLE/
NANOOSE BAY

Black Dog Café

There are certain cafés one simply must know about, the ones that serve the kind of food Oscar Wilde might say "causes happiness." For a peripatetic foodie like me, there is nothing more gratifying than knowing where to find wholesome, delicious and creative food just off the beaten track. The Black Dog Café (formerly the Book Worm Café) is such a spot, and I am indebted to Barbara Ebell of Nanoose Edibles for pointing me in its direction.

The café is owned by sisters Vicky Adamson and Chris Thomas, who grew up in Nanaimo. Vicky is an art teacher who helps out in the café when she can; Chris is the chef. Chris spent 15 years in Prince Rupert, where she also cooked in a café. Moving to Nanoose five years ago, she began looking for a place of her own.

Originally the café had sold used books and served food, but only from a hot plate. Chris and Vicky put in a new kitchen and introduced the neighbourhood to some very good cooking—what Chris calls "casual, West Coast contemporary." She makes everything from scratch except the bagels.

She relies on local suppliers and enjoys changing her menu with the seasons, running with what's available. Nanoose Edibles is the vegetable and fruit source. They provided such lovely strawberries last summer that the café served strawberry shortcake every day. A farmer supplies the eggs, another the chicken and turkey, and local fishers bring in sockeye salmon and shrimp. Chris serves organic, fair-trade Karma Coffee from nearby Errington.

Morning coffee is incredibly popular at the Black Dog Café, and Chris' customers have her trained to make them a different type of muffin every day. One group of retired gentlemen meets here every morning at 10 o'clock, and Chris says the conversation is fascinating. I'm reminded of my father's

Kaffeeklatsch, which also meets at 10 o'clock precisely, behind Oak Bay's tweed curtain, to discuss their portfolios and other weighty matters.

Chris exhibits local artists' work. As with the food suppliers, she is committed to providing a venue for locals. And in recent years, the café has become known for its live music, and its commitment to showcasing local talent.

I dropped in on a June afternoon and enjoyed the cafe's Thai Noodle Salad with Nanoose Edibles' greens and asparagus, then left with the only portable piece of pie I've encountered. The café's pie-shaped O'Henry Bar is a sinfully solid creation of chocolate, peanut butter and Rice Krispies that's perfect for road trippers like myself. Next time, I'm looking forward to trying Chris' famous lemon meringue pie.

Harvest Bounty Festival

Like September's Feast of Fields at the south end of Vancouver Island, the Harvest Bounty Festival is well worth the price of admission. It's coordinated by the Harvest Bounty Festival Society and held at Nanoose Edibles in late August. Also like Feast of Fields, it's a good idea to call well ahead for tickets for this fabulous celebration of local agriculture, food, drink and the culinary arts. Actually, the first year I attended it, the festival was held at Dave and Marnie Evans' 350-acre farm in Qualicum Beach, and I was first through the gate.

Getting there early proved to be beneficial that Sunday, because many of the churches were still in session, and I beat the crowds. It gave me the opportunity I most enjoy: meeting one-on-one with the growers and chefs, and enjoying their exquisite food offerings in a relaxed way.

I found myself grazing first for food and wine, then gravitating to a bench or picnic table where I could enjoy not only the food, but also the other people. I managed to eat and drink my way around the whole exhibition! The Harvest Bounty Festival has a homey, small-community feel even though the exhibitors come from all over the island.

I met up with Mary Ann Hyndman Smith and Edgar Smith of Natural Pastures Cheese and Christie Eng of Shady Creek Ice Cream, who called me over to "try this tuile with roasted banana ice cream" as it was "just right" to eat—

and it was delicious. Sandy and Eric McLean of McLean's Specialty Foods joined me for a sample of 2001 Pinot Gris from Ruth Luxton at the Glenterra Vineyards table.

Barbara Ebell of Nanoose Edibles reports that "as part of our strategy to have this event inform and educate the public about the availability and high quality of locally produced food, future festivals will include students and instructors from the culinary programs in some of the regional high schools."

Nanoose Edibles

It's 9:00 a.m. on a clear Monday morning in Nanoose Bay. I ferried across earlier this morning from Vesuvius on Saltspring Island, excited to see Barbara and Lorne Ebell's popular Nanoose Edibles farm. Such is the quality of their produce that some chefs actually have orders couriered to them.

I've been asked to join a culinary arts class from Malaspina University-College that is touring the farm with instructor Gordon Cower (formerly of Sooke Harbour House). They're a lively bunch of twenty-somethings whose enthusiasm for the whole growing process is infectious.

Our hostess, the indomitable Barbara Ebell, is a former manager of women's programs for the BC Ministry of Agriculture. Lorne holds a Ph.D. in agriculture and has worked for both the provincial and federal governments. The couple retired a few years ago, realized longevity ran on both sides of their family and worked out what they were going to do for the next 40 years. They turned to their 23-acre property in Nanoose, thought they would plant a few apple trees and some raspberries. They are now going full-tilt with a variety of herbs, 20 kinds of nutritional greens and other veggies, flowers and fruit, a box program and a large farmstand.

Located as they are, in a non-farming community, Barbara says it hasn't always been easy, but they are determined to make a go of organic farming. It's the lowest-lying property in the area, located on an old estuary, with some clay and some gravel base. When they took over the land, the soil was seriously degraded. They've spent a lot of time raising its nutritional level through

cover-crop plantings that just get tilled in, and reverse rototilling. They have their own water supply, with a drip-irrigation system operating from six zones on the property. The drip system is used when the wind blows to ensure that water goes where it should and is not wasted.

Nanoose Edibles was certified organic in 1997. When Barbara is asked to explain the road to organic certification to the Malaspina students, she cites a lowly onion. The certification body (in her case, the British Columbia Association for Regenerative Agriculture) requires detailed records on when it was seeded, transplanted and harvested. The way the food is grown and handled must be recorded every step of the way. It's a process that is both laborious and costly, but ultimately gives the consumers complete confidence in what they're buying.

Barbara learned her growing techniques through her association with the Pacific Northwest branch of the North American Direct Farm Marketing Association. At one of their meetings in Portland, Oregon, she happened to be sitting next to the owner of Nicky's Greens, a California business focussed on growing nutritional greens. Nicky befriended Barbara and took the time to explain how her business worked. It was a fortuitous meeting.

Barbara says her first taste of "bitter" herbs was at the Herald Street Caffe in Victoria, where she ate a delicious salad of greens with quail eggs. To her, "bitter is one of the great tastes of the culinary arts," but she says most people want their greens devoid of bitterness. It's certainly a taste worth acquiring, as the nutritional values are impressive.

Fresh is important to Barbara, who notes that green vegetables lose their nutritional value at a rate of 10 per cent per day. She says, "Eating only a lettuce salad probably puts you in a negative nutrition mode." And, of course, eating fresh and local is also good for the economy. Local organic chard is ultimately less expensive because there's no waste. So the moral is, the closer you can get to the grower and the sooner you can eat that just-picked produce, the better.

As a member of the BC AgriTourism Alliance, Nanoose Edibles is marketing the farm to Vancouver Island visitors "as a place to stop and enjoy as well as buy local products." The glorious farmstand is open year-round, proffering the farm's own produce as well as that of other food producers in the region and an organic flower boutique for those flower lovers among us with a conscience about toxic sprays.

PARKSVILLE/QUALICUM BEACH/COOMBS

 Creekmore's Coffee and Espresso Bar

I once had the pleasure of sharing a stall at Victoria's Banana Belt Fine Foods' customer appreciation day with two wonderful fellas, Richard Lewin of Golda's Fine Foods and David Creekmore of Creekmore's Coffee. Suffice it to say, I learned a few things about promotion from both of them. And I sure developed a taste for BuzzRight coffee, a dark-roasted, full-bodied blend that is one of Creekmore's most popular.

David and Elaine Creekmore have always been "coffee hounds," but their careers took them in other directions. David was a furniture maker and then a salesman for the largest beverage company in Alaska; Elaine was a children's librarian. Elaine says, "David and I are very different. If you had told me 10 years ago that we'd be working together, I wouldn't have believed you, but we love it."

It turns out their differences have made them a great team. David is very gregarious, so he's responsible for the marketing, promotion and delivery of their coffee. Elaine enjoys the roasting process and has become so expert that she almost never refers to her daily logbook when roasting a batch of green beans.

Together, they are very proud of their Little Red Primo drum roaster, and treat me to an exclusive demonstration. They are rigorous about roasting in small batches to ensure the quality and consistency of the coffee they sell. Elaine turns on the machine and waits for the burners to reach a certain temperature. She is a petite woman, but has no difficulty shouldering 40 pounds of green coffee beans and pouring them into the roaster.

Michael, Elaine and David Creekmore with their original Little Red Primo drum roaster.

Each type of coffee requires a different starting temperature. Today, Elaine is roasting Peruvian beans, and she is able to tell by sight (the colour of the beans as they roast is visible through a glass window) and sound (at around 400°F, the beans start to pop like popcorn). There is also a "tryer," a small spout that extracts a few beans from the batch as it's roasting. Depending on what she sees in the sample, Elaine may adjust the temperature up or down.

After the beans are roasted, Elaine releases them into the cooling tray where a continuous agitator with steel brushes kicks off the chaff. The chaff goes directly into a collecting vessel and is then put on the Creekmores' compost pile. It takes at least seven minutes to cool the beans, and then they are weighed. What started out at 40 pounds has been reduced to 33.5, as beans lose between 12 and 25 per cent moisture in the roasting process.

Elaine records every batch in her logbook, taking note of how the different coffee beans from different countries react. David points to their many sources of organic coffee: bags of beans from Peru, Indonesia, Sumatra and Colombia are stacked around the room. Their decaffeinated coffee is made from beans from the well-known Mexican Isman co-operative. David says that with coffee, "freshness is everything," and that's why he does his own distribution. More recently, the couple have moved their roaster and opened an espresso bar at the Coombs/Alberni junction. This lively spot sells coffee by the pound as well as espresso drinks and baked goods. I'm always happy to see it on the horizon when I head to Tofino because I know there is a dearth of good coffee shops along that route.

The Final Approach

Lawrence is the Louisiana-born chef. Richard is from Cochrane, Alberta, and works part-time with survivors of violence. Two years ago, the life partners happened to be dining at the airport restaurant in Qualicum Beach when, says Richard, "It became very apparent that the owners wanted out of both the business and their own relationship."

The sweet potato pie that's worth the drive to the Qualicum Beach airport!

So Lawrence and Richard took a life-altering turn and bought the place. Their transformation of the bistro is definitely worth a trip to the airport, whether you're planning to fly or not. I was immediately drawn to the strings of pearls hanging from the ceiling, the red walls and the theatrical touches like year-round Christmas lights. And I loved the comic timing of the waitress serving customers at the next table. She asks the man, "Fries or salad?" and when he doesn't reply as quickly as she'd wanted, "You're getting the salad."

The Final Approach isn't about where the food comes from or who is dropping off indigenous ingredients at the kitchen door. It's about good, plain cooking, like the restaurant's Heavenly Veggie Clubhouse with a side of roasted squash soup, Wild Richard's Buffalo Burger with bacon, cheese and mushrooms or Louisiana Style Ribs with homemade barbecue sauce and coleslaw.

The restaurant has a loyal local customer base, with many of its elderly clientele clearly having dressed to dine—at lunchtime, no less, at the airport in Qualicum Beach. I loved the place and the warm personalities of its owners.

And I particularly loved the mile-high sweet potato pie, whose reputation preceded an enormous slice to my table. Wow! And ditto for the sticky toffee pudding. At The Final Approach, I really wouldn't hesitate to order anything the waitress told me I was getting!

Fore & Aft Foods

Years ago, I used to enjoy breakfasts at a little café on the dock at Brentwood Bay, just north of Victoria. In addition to serving meals, the café sold wonderful jams and condiments.

Wandering around the What's Cooking? cookshop in Qualicum Beach, I came across jars of divine Fore & Aft antipasto—a taste from my past. The labels showed that the company was now in Qualicum Beach.

With no address or phone number to follow up, I had to do a bit of serious foodie sleuthing before I knocked on a door that was opened by Beverley Child, co-owner of the company. "When we left Brentwood Bay, we ran the teahouse at Filberg Lodge in Comox for five years, then started our own catering company." She and her husband, and business partner, Patrick Brownrigg, had never stopped making their condiments. Wine jellies, jams, vinegars, chutneys and that great antipasto are all available from their commercial kitchen, at Muffet & Louisa and Slater's First Class Meats in Victoria and at What's Cooking? in Qualicum Beach. A very popular new product is balsamic jelly, which is good with sharp cheese, baked Brie or cold meats, as well as with roast lamb and oysters. The couple sources a lot of their ingredients locally, and most of the fruit is organic. Trained at Dubrulle in Vancouver, Beverley says she is delighted to be doing what she does and seems pleased to be have been rediscovered by one of her old customers.

La Boulange Organic Breads

If you expect to find an elderly French gentleman behind La Boulange breads, you would at least be half right. Roger Floch had been a baker in Bordeaux before bringing the spirit of levain breads to Cumberland, British Columbia.

John Taraynor was a carpenter who happened to be working on a building project in Qualicum Beach with a fellow who knew Roger. At that time, Roger had his house on the market and was looking to sell his bakery and return to France. John was reminiscing about the epiphany brought on by a

The staff of life, fresh from the oven at La Boulange Organic Breads.

sourdough bun in Zurich (when he ate that bun, he realized he'd never eaten good bread before). There was no doubt that John, looking for a change of careers, was in the right place at the right time. He and his wife, Jean Wilson, bought the business from Roger, who stayed nearly two years to train them. When their mentor returned to France, the couple hired two locals, Ron Postl and Jamie Barter, neither of whom were bakers, and their success has pleasantly delighted them all. Ron formerly owned a local gift shop specializing in environmentally friendly products, and Jamie is a musician.

Jamie says they're passionate about what they do, that "the weird thing is, it's about the bread. I'd be bored if I was making donuts, but this is a fascinating journey through 48 hours." They all seem to have inherited a certain fanaticism from Roger, who was obsessed with the microbiotic requirements of making the bread, and they turn out very impressive loaves: seven-grain flax, seven-grain raisin and nut, kamut/spelt multi-grain (my husband's favourite), 100 per cent rye, rye with whole wheat flours, kamut, spelt, French and a new rice bread. There also are organic raisin squares that practically make a full meal.

The bakery is now located on John and Jean's six-acre property in Qualicum Beach, in what was once the horse barn. Jean's parents formerly owned the property; when they wanted a smaller place in town, the two couples agreed to exchange houses!

I arrive just as their baking shift is over, and Jean and the boys are having a cup of tea. We sit around in the bakery, surrounded by loaves of bread on the cooling racks, chatting about the importance of levain, the wild culture that's made from the flour itself. Roger used to tell them that, from a nutritional point of view, "Yeast is the enemy," so they are very rigorous about using their secret-recipe levain.

As we chat, local folks drop by to pick up their bread. Ron, a Vermont transplant, goes off with a loaf of multi-grain, telling me, "This is real, artisan bread. I moved here to be closer to La Boulange." A woman who had picked up La Boulange kamut bread in Vancouver sent Jean an email when she got home: "Where's your outlet in Manhattan?"

La Boulange makes about 2,000 loaves of bread a week for outlets in Vancouver and the Lower Mainland, Victoria, Campbell River and on Saltspring, Hornby and Gabriola islands. Their Cinelli gas-fired, rotating-tray oven bakes up to 160 loaves at a time. It really is a 48-hour process to make each loaf, and John says they're taking expansion very slowly. Eventually, he would like to install a wood-fired oven to make some rustic loaves.

Little Qualicum Cheeseworks

My parents join me on a drive through Qualicum Beach to the 68-acre dairy farm where Clarke and Nancy Gourlay tend a small mixed herd of Ayrshire, Holstein, Canadienne and Brown Swiss cows and make wonderful fresh and ripened cheese. We are greeted by Tiger, a lovely ginger cat, and Nancy, who cheerfully shows us around the cheese factory. Nancy says they pride themselves on making cheese from their own "best-quality milk." Their cows are "fed only sweet grass and grains." No pesticides, fermented feeds, growth hormones or antibiotics are used on the farm, and the Gourlays are active supporters of sustainable agricultural practices and the humane treatment of animals.

From their small operation come French-style *fromage frais*, which the Gourlays recommend "served with raspberries for an awesome breakfast treat"; raclette, the raw-milk cheese that transforms boiled potatoes into a melting treat; feta, in its own whey or in a sun-dried tomato, garlic and rosemary marinade; San Pareil, a seasonal soft cheese with a "mixed" rind; and other treats, like my mother's favourite, Caerphilly.

One of their most popular creations is the fresh cheese curds that are produced on Thursdays after 3:00 p.m. (locals have this recorded on their

BlackBerrys!). They are delicious eaten on their own, but are best known as the indispensable ingredient in poutine, the Québécois concoction of French fries topped with fresh cheese curds and gravy. (If you've never tried poutine, go directly to Pirate Chips in Nanaimo, where owner Angela Negrin uses Little Qualicum Cheeseworks' squeaky-fresh curds and a dynamite vegan gravy that makes this rustic dish sing.)

Clarke and Nancy worked for the Humanitarian Aid Organization in Switzerland, Lebanon, Kosovo and Afghanistan before returning to Vancouver Island with their three sons in 1999. They bought the farm that had been owned by dairy farmer Jim Lowry in the late 1800s, and have retained his sweet old cabin on the site. They were inspired by the wonderful cheese they ate in Switzerland "to set out to learn and practise the ancient and noble art of cheesemaking." It seems that their cheesemaking benefits from the "cool, moist climate in the shadow of Mount Arrowsmith," which has proven to be ideal for the ripening of washed-rind cheese.

Qualicum Beach Farmers' Market

One Saturday morning in September, my parents and I visited the Qualicum Beach Farmers' Market with one thing on our minds: apples. In particular, Mother was after Cox's Orange Pippins, and she was soon rewarded at the East Cider Orchard table. East Cider Orchard is actually on Denman Island, but Kris Chand, president of the Qualicum market, tells me they often welcome vendors selling "things we don't have locally in order to widen our offerings."

Kris and his wife, Maria, operate Blue Heron Farm in Parksville, a 12-acre property with five to six acres in certified organic cultivation. Their story is an interesting one, in that Kris was a business consultant to Fortune 500 companies and Maria managed a chocolate shop in Vancouver's tony Kerrisdale neighbourhood when they decided to spring themselves from the rat race. Kris' family had farmed in India. He had spent his summers working in the

Port Alberni mill while attending university, so moving to Vancouver Island to start a farm was "like coming home."

Kris laughs as he describes his former colleagues' reaction when they see him farming ("eyes roll"), but he and Maria have never been happier. He is quick to give Maria "all the credit" for the actual farming side of the operation; he organizes the distribution of their 40 to 45 crops to Granville Island Public Market's Zara Italian Deli, the Heaven on Earth health food store in Qualicum Beach, Cormie's Farm Market on the Island Highway near Parksville and through the Qualicum Beach Farmers' Market (where they sell nearly 75 per cent of their produce).

While garlic is their largest crop, Kris tells me they "can't grow enough of things like fava beans, Tuscan onions, garlic scallions and mixed lettuce—people want variety and the specialty vegetables." This year, the Wickaninnish Inn's chef dropped by the farm, and The Pointe Restaurant is now a customer, receiving the Chands' just-picked squash, garlic, beets and leeks by daily courier.

I first met Kris when he chaired the Harvest Bounty Festival at Nanoose Edibles. He was a founding director of the Qualicum market and served as its vice-president for four years. What he likes about the market is that "it's exclusively a food market. All of our vendors are directly associated with food production."

While Mother focussed on apples and my father chatted to an old colleague from Victoria, I visited with Marilyn Mant and Tami Treit of RainBarrel Farm, Beverley Child of Fore & Aft Foods, Barbara Ebell of Nanoose Edibles and Clarke Gourlay of Little Qualicum Cheeseworks. This is a lively, food-focussed market that gives customers a great taste of the variety and quality of food in the Oceanside area.

"It's exclusively a food market. All of our vendors are directly associated with food production."

– Kris Chand

RainBarrel Farm

Mother and daughter Marilyn Mant and Tami Treit pick dahlias for four or five hours every Friday, in order to have enough bouquets for the Qualicum Farmers' Market on Saturday mornings. Whether they have 70 or 100 bouquets at their stall, they all are quickly bought up.

Also on Fridays, they prepare beautiful baskets of fruits and vegetables from the farm for their brown-box customers. The baskets are so artistic that I was stopped in my tracks when I saw them at the Harvest Bounty Festival. They also supply the local Thrifty Foods and Quality Foods with their lettuce mix and other veggies.

When I visit Marilyn and her husband, Henry, on their 35-acre farm on the outskirts of Qualicum Beach, I learn that their exquisite produce comes from a long history of hard work. Henry's parents arrived in the Qualicum area from England in 1913 with very little money. Over the years, they slowly bought land, five acres at a time, until they had 150 acres.

Today, the Mants raise miniature horses, Muscovy ducks and hundreds of plants: 300 broccoli, 200 cabbage and 200 cauliflower plus endless corn, beets, tomatoes, English cucumbers, zucchini, peppers, raspberries, strawberries and grapes. There are also 700 dahlia plants, which Marilyn is getting ready to dig out for storage until next season.

The Mants have always farmed organically, but when Thrifty Foods said they'd buy a significant amount of produce if the Mants became officially certified, they went through the process. The soil and their farming practices were so exemplary that the certification process took less than a year. Like many farmers I've met, Marilyn would rather not have the cost and amount of paperwork that certification involves, but she is adamant that her family eat organics. "I've got a grandchild," she tells me, "so I'm not going to grow food with tons of junk on it."

Marilyn and Henry live in a most interesting home—their former hayloft. As we enter the house, Marilyn points to where the cows used to be milked. Local potter Larry Aguilar has recently moved into another house on the property and set up a studio for public visits.

DENMAN ISLAND

Denman Island Chocolate

Ruth and Daniel Terry WWOOFed their way around Europe and the interior of British Columbia, got turned on to organics and finally settled on Denman Island. Like many Gulf Islanders, Daniel worked a variety of jobs, including recycling-depot manager, firefighter and carpenter.

Ruth holds a Master's degree in English from Cambridge University. She started to make vegan truffles (no cream or butter) for the island's annual Christmas craft fair, and people went crazy for them. Having sourced high-quality organic chocolate from Belgium, hazelnuts and raspberries from the Fraser Valley's In Season Farms, fair-traded Nicaraguan coffee and pure orange and mint essences from England, Daniel began to develop the ultimate organic chocolate bar. He is a self-taught chocolatier and marketer, who clearly thrives on the business side of things. As Ruth, who continued to make truffles for special orders until she passed away in 2004, once told me, "He likes selling chocolate and I like giving it away."

I visited the couple when they were making chocolate in a tiny factory in their home. The business has since moved into a larger facility, although it is still not open to the public. But that's okay, because the company's solid little bars are available throughout Canada (with literally hundreds of locations on Vancouver Island) and the States in flavour combinations that could make you as seriously addicted as me: Razzle Dazzle (raspberry), Gingerama and Coco Loco are just a few. Daniel says their latest rosemary bar "has divided people into the majority, who don't like it, and the discerning minority, who love it." I'm a savoury kind of gal, so I'm all over it and happy to be in the minority!

Denman Island Farmers' Market

Anne de Cosson of East Cider Orchard is a big promoter of the Denman Island Farmers' Market. She wrote to tell me that "our tiny market grew in stature this summer and we hope to keep growing." Indeed, after I mentioned it in the second edition of *Journey*, she wrote to say that new customers were showing up at the market with the book in hand. The Denman market is held on Saturday mornings at the Old School Centre to coincide with the on-site recycling depot's hours of operation. It reminds me of Saturdays on Galiano Island, when I would regularly drop off the week's recyclables before visiting their seasonal market in the community centre on Sturdies Bay Road. On the islands, it's important to remember that the markets aren't just about shopping for fruit and veggies; they're also essential social meeting places for islanders, many of whom live in some degree of isolation during the week.

Anne says, "The original Old School was built in the early 1900s and was used continuously until the 1980s when it had the distinction of being one of the oldest two-room schoolhouses still in operation." A new school building replaced it in 1989, and the old one now houses the market, the recycling depot, a women's centre and a meeting room.

At the market, you'll find East Cider Orchard, Windy Marsh Farm and the Denman Island Fruit and Nut Farm represented, and you can expect an "increase in size and variety" every year. Anne says, "We plan on more baked goodies, Denman specialty produce and products, crafts, music and kids' stuff."

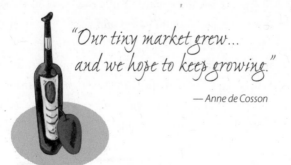

"Our tiny market grew... and we hope to keep growing."

— Anne de Cosson

East Cider Orchard

The sun is just beginning to dip in the sky as Anne de Cosson and I sit on her back patio, watching a promenade of peacocks through the orchard (seriously!) and sipping apple cider from the second pressing of her Gravenstein apples. Anne was happy to take a break from painting an upstairs bedroom to chat with a curious urbanite.

She and her husband, Larry Berg, had worked at Capilano College in Vancouver, travelled through India and then had the chance to house-sit for friends on Denman Island. Anne had been raised on her father's homegrown vegetables, and she was always aware of the marked contrast between garden-fresh and store-bought.

The couple lost no time finding a property on this very peaceful island. They bought their orchard in 1979 when it was nothing but a fallen-down house and 25 apple trees. They got together with two other families and formed a co-operative called Apple Lane Orchards. The co-op seemed like a good idea then, but over time, the families found differences in their growing philosophies, and the de Cosson/Berg contingent struck out on their own with East Cider Orchard.

It was always important to Anne to grow organically, so theirs is a fully certified operation, and all the juice, or soft cider as they call it, is pasteurized.

 Anne says they never know how much money the orchard will generate annually, as organic farming is much more dependent on weather and other forces of nature than conventional farming. They have 1,000 trees from which they make between 300 and 900 gallons of cider per year.

They take the apples by the truckload to Bill LePage, of The Cider Press in Courtenay. Bill presses it into juice that fills two- and four-litre jugs, and then it's sold at Vancouver's Granville Island and East Vancouver markets and at the Courtenay Farmers' Market.

At harvest time, the whole family pitches in, together with eight to 10 WWOOFers. As Anne says, "The world comes to work in our orchard, so it's been a really interesting experience for our family. We've had lots of workers from the Czech Republic when it opened up."

Jacquie's Ices

In 1970, Jacquie Barnett and her then-husband, having built a boat in their Chicago backyard, set out for three and a half years at sea. "We were anti-war protestors," she tells me. They had a friend on Denman Island and sailed on up. Thirty-three years later, Jacquie has a thriving ice cream business on the island.

She started with cattle, but "it gets very hot on my side [the west side] of the island. It's hot until 10 o'clock at night," so she was looking for a cooler occupation. She spotted a 1957 white Dodge truck in Courtenay one day and thought it would make an excellent ice cream truck. Fifty dollars later, the truck was hers. "It overheated all the time, so I would put ice cubes on the carburetor." Jacquie started making ice cream for local fairs, driving it around in the Dodge. Sometimes she had leftover stock on her hands, so Jacquie's Ices at the dock for the ferry to Hornby Island was established 20 years ago. It's a cute trailer with big photos of Einstein enjoying an ice cream cone just like you and me.

Jacquie picks the wild plums and rhubarb on her property and adds them, along with chocolate, vanilla and other gourmet ingredients, to ice cream. She makes her own giant waffle cones, and "people just love them." She says she loves to watch tourists recharge on the island. People buy her ice cream, then sit on a rock and look out to sea. "It's a great form of meditation," she tells me, and I agree as I devour a rhubarb-chocolate double scoop (no worries: I'll work it off writing!).

Windy Marsh Farm

The contrast between the strip malls of any modern city and the back roads of any Gulf Island is startling. The malls offer a parade of predictable fast-food magnets—different city, but same fatty smorgasbord. Rural roads produce erratic offerings—a farmstand around the bend that only sells beans and flowers, and then nothing for 10 kilometres. Ah, but the unpredictability of snacking from back-road farmstands is the whole point. It's an adventure, and every trip is a clean canvas for the intrepid hunter-gatherer.

On one late summer afternoon, my husband and I were touring the back roads of Denman Island, enjoying the scenery, but feeling peckish. Up ahead, we glimpsed a farmstand. Beans and flowers? Well, yes and no. The Windy Marsh farmstand, a labour of love by Bob and Velda Parsons, has a range of produce to convert any hot-blooded, fast-food junkie. We dive right into a basket of sun-warmed raspberries.

The Parsons grow 100 per cent organically, and Velda says they strive for variety: big, cream-coloured vegetable marrows, dillweed at a nickel a stem, shiny fresh snow peas, just-picked red raspberries, parsley, kale, beet thinnings, zucchini, artichokes, peppers, cucumbers, tomatoes, fat shelling peas, potatoes and lettuce. Their chickens produce enough eggs for, as the sign says, "One dozen per family, please."

She and Bob, a boat builder, bought the farm 12 years ago. They had been living in a floathome on Genoa Bay, but says Velda, "It was in danger of sinking from the number of plants we had growing on it—especially tropical plants." A New Zealander, Bob has always grown tropicals and today coaxes along papayas and bananas in his greenhouse.

Velda told me they looked around the Gulf Islands, and settled on the 10-acre Denman Island property because it was located next to a marsh, and "water is essential for growing veg." It's proven time and again to have been a wise choice. They bought the property with "every cent we had," cleared three acres, and have learned to grow what suits the soil.

Velda says they grow organically because it is "morally correct," but, like many local producers who sell to people who know them, they feel no need to certify. They grow primarily for their farmgate, and sell any surplus at the in-season Saturday morning farmers' market held next to the elementary school.

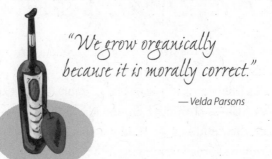

"We grow organically because it is morally correct."

— Velda Parsons

HORNBY ISLAND

Hornby Island Co-op

No visit to Hornby is complete without a stop at the co-op, the island's heart-beat, where shopping for groceries and supplies plays second fiddle to picking up your mail, checking out the bulletin board and meeting up with friends. It's the most social grocery store I know.

Produce manager Sue Horner, a former sign-language interpreter from Vancouver, is unpacking organic veggies, and stops to tell me where they all come from. The store buys a lot through Vancouver's Wildwest and Thrifty Foods' wholesale distributor, but when a resident arrives at the back door with a bag of plums, they're also set out for sale. The result is an impressive range of organic fruit and vegetables and a good selection of dry goods. Bread is baked fresh daily by the island's Cardboard House Bakery.

This is the best place to pick up picnic supplies before heading out for the day to Tribune Bay or Ford Cove.

Hornby Island Farmers' Market

Every market has its own special flavour. To me, the Hornby Island Farmers' Market is a vibrant statement of how things could be if the world didn't encroach. Certainly, it has that latter-day hippie look and feel, but once you've met the vendors and sampled their wares, you will appreciate the quality of food that's grown with great understanding and lovingly prepared. The local musicians and an exotic belly dancer add an air of festivity.

Fifteen years ago, islanders like "flower lady" Anna MacKay started the market "so that people could remember what good food tastes like." Anna tells me she enjoys being in direct contact with the buyers, and thinks "the most positive thing that could happen [in our food-distribution system] would be to cut out the middle man—the transportation." Like so many people I speak to in my

Anna MacKay's smile and colourful posies light up her stall at the Hornby Island Farmers' Market.

travels, she is concerned about food miles and advocates eating only what we grow locally.

Another vendor, "sushi lady" Tania Hale, credits Hornby Island with having "freedom, but still an economy." On market days, she rises early to pick herbs and veggies from her own organic garden, then creates little jewel boxes of exquisite sushi. With a glass of her cool lemonade, this West Coast foodie experience rates very highly on my list.

Savoie Farm

Chatting with Andrea and David at the Savoie farmstand in the market led me to one of the most magical flower and vegetable gardens on the west coast. "You'll find Elaine at the farm today because she's setting up for tonight's art exhibit," says David. I will always remember my journey to the farm at the end of Carmichael Road, and how the sea seemed to rise up and meet me when I stopped the car.

I found Elaine Savoie in her house on the property, cleaning up for the 150 guests who were coming that evening for her annual art exhibition. The house originally had no electricity or running water, and she has only recently installed a phone. Her paintings are a unique style of chicken iconography, which has been well received by the artistic community and, not surprisingly, questioned by the religious sector. She welcomes me like an old friend, and doesn't hesitate to take me out to see the gardens and meet her sister and gardening partner, Mary.

Sisters and growers Elaine and Mary Savoie at Savoie Farm.

We cross a nondescript field before I stop in my tracks at the first sight of their garden. I cannot believe that, just six years ago, this was also a field. Today, there are vast plantings of veggies and herbs: squashes, basil, thyme, blueberries, hot peppers, onions, asparagus, strawberries and more, mostly grown in raised beds to keep the roots out of the water. There are rows upon rows of cutting flowers like dahlias, gladioli, bachelor's button (Mary's favourite) and statice. In one section, local basket-maker Alistair Hesseltine grows willow for his craft. To complete the picture, there are a dozen Hereford cows just nonchalantly wandering about. Mary and I walk over to the property's big pond, from which they run a drip-irrigation system. When the pond gets low, they cut the watering to every second day.

The farm was started in the 1920s by the sisters' grandfather, Leo Savoie, who came from France with his Métis wife, looking for paradise. He certainly found it: 80 waterfront acres on the north side of the island. Elaine and Mary's father continued the tradition of growing his family's food. When he passed away, the land was divided into two 40-acre parcels. The girls, with their brother, Remi, hold title to both sections; their closest neighbour is a cousin who operates a cattle ranch.

Elaine paints and tends the vegetable beds. Mary lives close by. She is the custodian at the local school, but her passion is the flowers. In summer, bunches of her fresh and dried flowers are sold at the market and also from a stand across from the Cardboard House Bakery. In the cooler months, Mary and her mother make dried flower sachets.

Mary tells me she started growing organic because she wanted to buy organic strawberries at a reasonable price. The farm offers fair prices, particularly on bulk orders over five pounds.

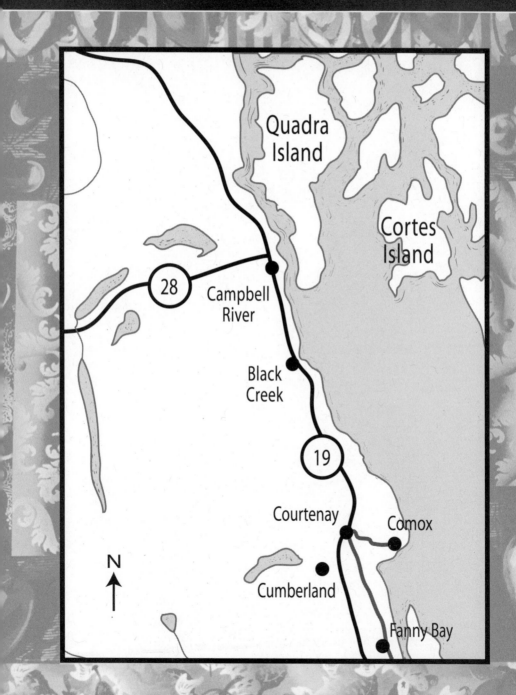

CUMBERLAND

Cumberland Village Bakery

After John Auchterlonie retired, the bakery that bore his family's name for 80 years sat vacant for many months. With no warm, sticky, yeasted doughnuts coming out of the oven in the early mornings, there was no question that depression and sugar withdrawal settled over this quaint little town. Then along came David Murray and Megan Sommers, two townsfolk who worked as tree planters but had Dubrulle's baking program behind them. They realized they were "taking over a business with a large reputation," but have proven themselves up to the task.

Happily, David and Megan inherited the original doughnut recipe from John but the new Cumberland Village Bakery is about a lot more than doughnuts. "We want this place to have a real community feel," says David, as we chat on a whimsical twig bench produced by local furniture-maker Michael Chesters. And a community feel it has. Local residents stream in for the 10 types of bread from artisan sourdough rye to roasted garlic and feta; for the raspberry and blueberry

Co-owner David Murray of Cumberland Village Bakery.

cream cheese Danishes (it's a good thing that I have to drive three hours to buy these or I'd be eating them every day!); the almond croissants with ground almond filling; the green onion and cheddar, and black olive and feta, bread rolls; and of course those quintessential doughnuts.

I arrived one drizzly morning just as the latest batch of doughnuts was proofing. It had been two years since I'd eaten one and I couldn't wait!

David says the secret is hard to define. Sure, they're handmade in small batches (just 15 at a time) and they're hand-dipped in sugar, but "it's a pretty standard recipe." It used to be that folks queued to buy them, because when they were gone—usually by 9:00 a.m.—they were gone. Today, David and Megan make sure that doughnuts are coming out of the oven all-day long to keep the sugar hounds happy.

David tells me that he and Megan have "lots of ideas and inspiration," and they have gradually introduced more artisan breads and pastries. They satisfy the local market with classics like the sandwich loaves and buttery dinner rolls, but have also introduced organic grains and vegan specialties to tantalize taste buds. Also on offer are their house-made soups, meat pies, bagels, sausage rolls, local cheeses and a full evening pizza menu—great news for those of us whose edible journeys take us to this sweet little town.

The Great Escape

Many people had recommended The Great Escape in Cumberland, and I was excited to hear that a good restaurant had opened across from the newly con-structed Village Square in this quaint little former mining town. Oddly, no one had mentioned (and the name hardly indicated it) that the place was East Indian, so that came as another delightful revelation.

Before I arrived, I learned that The Great Escape was an evolution for its owners, who had previously offered popular "Indian food nights" at another location in Cumberland. When the present building came up for sale, they jumped at the opportunity to have their home and a 40-seat restaurant located in one place.

The dining room is decorated in modern Indian Bohemian with a statue of Ganesh, the Hindu elephant god, prominently displayed. There is a relaxed and inviting vibe, even before one is greeted by the affable Jean-François Larche and offered a cup of chai. Jean-François is the barman and host; his wife, Nicola Cunha, is the chef.

The chai, though utterly delicious and warming on this cold November night, is probably the most pedestrian drink on offer. Jean-François has created a

Owners Jean-François Larche and Nicola Cunha with their prized statue of Ganesh.

unique menu of cocktails, all designed to complement Nicola's cuisine. There are many palate-elevating options here, from the Boozy Mango Lassi, which incorporates Havana Club rum into a fresh mango lassi, and the Mumbai Caesar, which is rimmed with spicy homemade "gunpowder" to the classic Bombay Sapphire gin and tonic. The Raj Premium Lager is a favourite as are local options such as Middle Mountain Mead from Hornby Island and Hermann's Bavarian Dark Lager from Victoria. After dinner, an Americano coffee with Mangalore—cardamon, cinnamon and chili liqueur—sets one right for the walk home.

The food created by Nicola has been variously described as "urban, street, and modern Indian" in the heralded style of Vij's in Vancouver, yet Nicola clearly brings her own originality and command of spicing to the kitchen. "My mother is my comparison," she tells me. "Her food is light and flavourful." And certainly Nicola's devotion to organics and her insistence on sourcing ingredients locally ("I didn't want to get everything from Sysco") has kept the food fresh and meaningful.

I sampled small plates from the Tiffin menu, including the Wild Salmon Wontons flavoured with Goan spice and served with Nicola's mother's tomato chutney; Masala Wadas, lentil patties served with pumpkin chutney; Papadom Cigars, cigar-shaped vegetable-filled pastries that I dipped first in tamarind chutney; and, what to me was the *pièce de résistance*, the very simple seasonal Salad Pomegranate with its mango-cumin vinaigrette.

Nicola's earlier career as a film caterer gave her great opportunities to experiment with her native cuisine. Through this work, she mastered the ability to awaken the senses of what can often be a cynical clientele, and she has brought the truly delicious results to Cumberland. Nicola laughs when I ask about the layers of flavour in her dishes, "Look, I'm not comfortable with explaining. I roast my own spices. I didn't eat cheese until high school. I simply want people to enjoy my food."

Hazelmere Farms

When Lijen and Sherlene Hua emigrated from Taiwan, they took their time finding the perfect farm and the perfect crop. They had never farmed before—he was a civil engineer and she worked for a consumer co-op back home—but they knew they "wanted to be close to nature and do something we really believe in."

They finally came upon 63 acres near Cumberland, where they are creating a certified organic, self-sustaining farm. They raise chickens, ducks and sheep and are growing Oriental vegetables such as burdock and cucumbers, as well as garlic. Their number-one crop is wasabi, which I first sampled at the Harvest Bounty Festival in September. Sherlene encourages me to visit in the spring when her acre of wasabi "looks its most lovely." It is a mass of little white flowers, which are edible, along with the rest of the plant. The leaves and flowers are slightly spicy and make lively additions to salad.

Wasabi takes at least two years to harvest, but the couple now has a steady crop. They sell their wasabi to several local restaurants and the Edible Island

Owners Sherlene and Lijen Hua of Hazelmere Farms selling their produce at the farmers' market in Courtenay.

grocery in Courtenay and will be expanding their distribution to other locations on the island.

This year, I ran into the Huas at the farmers' market in Courtenay, and returned to Victoria munching their apples and pears.

Seeds Natural Food Market

"No problem can be solved by the same consciousness that created it."
—*Albert Einstein*

So says a prominent sign on the wall of a cosy little grocery store in Cumberland, population 2,800. As I stroll around looking at the carefully selected foodstuffs and produce, I discover more signage that makes good sense to me. A "Food Travel Glossary" marks each produce item in accordance with the distance it travelled to Seeds.

A plane indicates the item came from "beyond Mexico or more than 2,000 km;" a truck symbolizes it travelled between 150 and 2,000 km, which includes the West Coast, Mexico and most of North America; and a bicycle (the best symbol!) tells customers that the item travelled less than 150 km, which includes Campbell River, Nanaimo, the Sunshine Coast and "everywhere in between."

Guided by a commitment to proffer "good, clean whole food" locally as much as possible, owner Christina ("everyone calls me Tina") Willard-Stepan buys from neighbouring farms including Pattison Farm and Nature's Way Farm.

Although Seeds had only been open a few months when I visited, I could see that the shelves were already lined with good food and an equally good measure of sense and sensibility. And what a pleasure to find a plastic-bag-free grocery shop!

Owner Christina Willard-Stepan holds a sugar pumpkin in Seeds Natural Food Market.

COURTENAY

Atlas Café and Bar

I settle into a window seat for breakfast at Atlas, the legendary café in downtown Courtenay that's won oodles of "best of" awards and justly so, and ask to speak to the owner if she's available. "She's making your breve," I'm told. "She's a barista?" I inquire. "She does it all!" is the cheerful reply.

And when I've devoured a big plateful of huevos rancheros (Mexican-style eggs on a blue corn tortilla with roasted sweet chili yams, black beans, smoked Asiago cheese, salsa, sour cream and guacamole) and downed the breve, I am joined by an elegant woman in a perfect little black dress, who I feel couldn't possibly be the owner that "does it all." But of course this is Sandra Viney, the pretty girl from Australia's Byron Bay who met Trent McIntyre, a snowboarding vegan chef, in the Comox Valley; together, they launched its most popular restaurant on October 7, 1995.

Co-owner Sandra Viney in front of the Atlas Café's busy open kitchen.

Sandra is warm and approachable, and it's not surprising that she loves the restaurant for "all its human connections. It's a meeting place on many levels." And it's easy to see those connections all around me: the elderly couple having their regular Sunday breakfast, the family gathering, the former staff member bringing her baby by to greet Sandra.

The restaurant is painted appetite-stimulating rusty red with red tiles around the open kitchen and red oilcloths on the tables. It's rustic and homey and the food is "meant to nourish body and spirit." Sandra credits Trent, now

A couple of regulars enjoy their Sunday breakfast at Atlas Café and Bar.

her husband, for the creativity in the kitchen and I must say it's evident even in the details. The fruit garnish on my breakfast plate is a beautiful stack of watermelon, red grapes, kiwi, banana and a Cape gooseberry.

The human connections extend to the restaurant's suppliers. "We're in the land of plenty here," says Sandra, "and we have always bought our ingredients locally. The 100-Mile Diet is here to stay!"

Besides breakfast, Atlas also serves lunch and dinner, and has extensive takeout and catering menus. Recently, Sandra and Trent opened Avenue in Comox, which I only had time to glimpse on this edible journey. However, it looks very chic, modern and promising—another spot designed for breakfast, lunch and dinner. With breakfast on my mind, I look forward to starting another day at Avenue with buttered eggs, fried bread and tomato.

CakeBread Artisan Bakery

Since I last visited, Hot Chocolates (see page 220) has moved to a much larger location in order to accommodate its new artisan bakery—a place, I discovered, where my swooning could happily continue.

I ran into Susie Moscovich in line at the bakery counter. She's a Campbell River foodie and bed and breakfast owner who tells me that when she and her husband moved to the area from West Vancouver, "We couldn't get good bread—until now." She now drives to Courtenay weekly for CakeBread's bread. (Susie also gave me an indispensable insider's tip while I was waiting to chat with the shop's co-owner, Jorden Marshall, "Don't miss Thyme on the Ocean in Comox.")

Before touring the bakery and sampling some of its delicious creations, I took note of the words of Sherry Marshall-Bruce (wife of Jorden, and the other owner) painted over the door, "Look through the window and you will see into the heart and soul of our bakery." Indeed, the window opens onto a truly high-tech, entirely stainless steel heart that beats along with the gentle

Co-owner Jorden Marshall with the delectable Loo-Loo Lemon cake at CakeBread Artisan Bakery.

rhythms of kneading, shaping, baking and decorating. The soul is the great people who work here, beginning with Sherry herself, whom her husband calls "the creative genius" of the operation.

It was Sherry who wanted to add a bakery to the chocolate shop, who attended bread-baking courses at the San Francisco Baking Institute, and then learned the ropes of running a bakery under Chris Brown at Ecco il Pane in Vancouver. Jorden, who administers both sides of the shop and fills in for staff when they take their breaks, calls himself "the background," but it is evident to me that he and his wife are a dynamic team.

Says Jorden, "We can only take in so many calories, so why not take in the best?" There are so many "best calories" to choose from in this new bakery, from the square, deadly delicious carrot cake (it was so good that I took some home to Victoria) to the stunning Loo-Loo Lemon cake, which contains fresh lemon mousse and lemon curd and is decorated with large multi-coloured icing polka dots, to the perfect accompaniment for my afternoon coffee, orange spice pound cake.

The breads are baked with organic flour and "all the best ingredients. We feel we've really elevated the game," says Jorden. And there are many choices: Courtenay sourdough, farmers multigrain, fig and roasted walnut, artisan rye and Moroccan flatbread.

What I like about the all-new chocolate shop and bakery is the relaxed seating, which means you can stop for a coffee and cake, or a gelato, and really feel part of a lively, urban foodie scene in the heart and soul of the Comox Valley.

Edible Island
Whole Foods Market

Another inviting organic grocery store is Edible Island, a shop that makes me want to become a resident of Courtenay. Opened more than 25 years ago by three entrepreneurial local women, Sue Tupper, Sue Clark and Jackie Somerville, it draws appreciative customers from all over the Comox Valley.

It's also the perfect stop for picnic supplies when you're touring in that area. When I visited the store, I picked up some La Boulange bread, Natural Pastures fresh curds and organic cherry tomatoes for a picnic.

The owners came from diverse working backgrounds—the recording industry, graphic arts and private- and public-sector accounting, respectively—but Jackie tells me they share "a passion for healthy, clean food and a concern for the environmental impact of mass production." Their shelves are lined with between 50 and 75 per cent organic foodstuffs, and they "choose organically grown and non-GMO certified products whenever possible."

Hot Chocolates

I had the good fortune to visit Hot Chocolates mere hours before Valentine's Day in 2005, when the store was a press of Cupidean fervour as people happily queued to buy sweets for their sweethearts. Passing through the doorway, I was hit with an explosion of red wrapping paper, chocolates stacked high and intoxicating aromas. Naturally, I swooned. Shop manager Arlene Wallace and long-time employee Ruth Vanderlinden, whose Swiss heritage rightfully makes her "the shop's chocolate critic," were quick to revive me with a steaming mug of their secret-recipe hot chocolate and two bonbons: a classic truffle and an organic Australian orange slice dipped in dark chocolate. A regular customer, entering the shop and eyeing my indulgences, nodded approvingly.

Hot Chocolates is one of those small, family-run establishments whose success we can somehow all feel pleased about (must be the theobromine and phenylethylamine in chocolate that imparts those benevolent feelings). It was started nearly 20 years ago by Deanna Gagnon and her daughter, Sherry Marshall-Bruce, and is now run by Sherry and her husband, Jorden Marshall. The business has grown to 32 employees, but still manages to retain its original philosophy of hand-making small batches of chocolates and truffles using no preservatives.

Once I'd been revived, Arlene gave me a requisite hairnet and invited me to view the "factory," a large and spotlessly clean room next-door to the shop where all the chocolate-making, packaging and shipping takes place. I was reminded of a tour I'd taken earlier that year of the famous Peyrano chocolate factory in Turin, and realized that, even though I now understand "how they get the caramel in the bar," there is still a mysterious aspect to chocolate that will always make these behind-the-scenes tours exciting for me.

My love affair with Hot Chocolates continued a couple of days later when I "coerced" my husband into sampling a few more sweets that I'd brought back from my edible journey: a raspberry heart filled with buttercream and raspberry confit; the Berry Quartet taste explosion, a milk chocolate truffle made with four different berries, coated in dark chocolate and dusted with dried berry powder; a *fleur de sel* caramel that reminded us of French pâtisseries; and the Asian-inspired Ko Chang, a chocolate-dipped truffle of coconut milk, lemongrass and kaffir lime. They all had us wishing we could buy such hedonistic pleasures closer to home. An extensive line of sugar-free chocolates is also available. My diabetic father proclaimed the chocolate-dipped ginger and orange creams "delish."

Sweet indulgences are not limited to *Theobroma cacao* here. In summer, there are 24 house-made gelati flavours to choose from, all made with special Italian equipment and containing "as many fresh local organic fruits, berries and herbs as we can get ahold of." I sampled blood orange, strawberry made with quark and probably the best maple-walnut ice cream ever. Hot Chocolates is also the place to treat yourself to an authentic milkshake, tea, organic El Café Negro coffee or one of those superb hot-chocolate beverages (Arlene did allow that the latter are made with the shop's dark chocolate, but her "recipe" stopped there!).

As I reluctantly went to leave the shop, an American woman, buying chocolates for her Courtenay hosts, anxiously asked, "Do you deliver to the States?" and seemed to relax instantly when told, "All the time." Cupid must be thinking, like Puck, "what fools [for love and chocolate] these mortals be!"

The dining room at Locals is known for locally sourced, exemplary cooking.

Locals

The first things I noticed on entering Locals were the pictures of food producers on the walls. In fact, I have to say that I was blown away by the care that had been taken to photograph and frame information about the local, organic food suppliers used by this restaurant, which is located in a nondescript strip mall in Courtenay. The highlighting of food suppliers and the lovely little pots of parsley that had been placed on each table signalled promise. And it was a promise more than fulfilled.

In fact, the care and detailing of chef Ronald St. Pierre and his wife, Tricia, are still on my mind as I reflect on the meal I ate at Locals.

Ronald comes to his restaurant's concept honestly. He began his career in Quebec City at Relais & Châteaux restaurant Le Trois Tillieul then went to Vancouver, where he worked at the Hotel Vancouver, at Jean-Pierre in the Bentall Centre and at the Delta Hotel. He met Tricia in 1986 and the two travelled to the Comox Valley. They had always loved the idea of living near the mountains and ocean, and wanted to settle in a coastal town where Tricia could work as a nurse (she later became a nursing instructor with North Island College) and Ronald could cook.

Ronald began his Comox Valley career as sous-chef, then chef, at the legendary The Old House Restaurant (now Tomato, Tomato) in Courtenay. He tells me, "To see all of the local food that was available in the valley—that was incredible. Fishermen would come to the back door [of the restaurant], their shellfish still clapping."

In those days, to obtain the best produce for the restaurant, Ronald worked closely with Lang Price of On Line Farm (in an earlier edition of this book, I interviewed Lang and his wife, Marjan de Jong, who have since retired from the farm and moved to a house in town). Says Ronald, "For me,

Owners Tricia and Ronald St. Pierre offer warm hospitality at Locals.

it has always been about—if you have great ingredients, the cooking is easy." He went on to work at The Kingfisher Oceanside Resort, where he continued to build relationships with local food producers.

Then, sometime in the middle of what Tricia describes as "one of our hot tub summits," they decided to open their own restaurant. They had help from friends, and, says Tricia, "From the moment we opened, we had a vibe." Yet Ronald gives the greatest credit to his suppliers, "They are the source of what I'm doing and without the producers, I wouldn't be able to do it."

So just who provides those stellar ingredients that make the food here sing? Pattison Farms is the main supplier, putting in specialty crops for the restaurant and over-wintering vegetables in a root cellar. Sarah and Wally Walsh learned to make pasta in Italy and keep the kitchen stocked with their Prontissima Pasta. Other "food from the heart of the island" reads like a "who's who" of local producers: Lo Lanning of Seaview Game Farms, Larry and Angelina Watrin of Watrin Orchard, Bruce Devereux of the MV *Estevan*, Delton and Karen Henrich of Island Bison, Edgar and Mary Ann Smith of Natural Pastures Cheese, Michael and France Sanderson of Sea Monster Fishing and Rose Pena Garnica, who makes amazing salsas and tamales (and many of them can be found on Saturdays, in season, at the Comox Valley Farmers' market in Courtenay).

I stopped in for a memorable lunch of Chanterelle and Pumpkin Pasta. The pumpkin tripolini from Prontissima Pasta were tossed to rich perfection with sautéed wild chanterelle mushrooms, cranberries and sage butter. I sampled my companions' Albacore Tuna Salad Melt made with MV *Estevan*'s tuna loin and the Comox Valley Grilled Salmon Salad that presented Sea Monster Fishing's catch atop seasonal greens from Pattison Farms and Eatmore Sprouts. Everything was fresh, local and treated with the respect and detailing of a top chef.

Locals has become so busy that Tricia has left her nursing position to work full-time as the restaurant's gracious hostess, and the St. Pierres' son and daughter fill in as servers after school. Eating at Locals makes me want to be a local in this region, where the bar has been set high for both the quality of local ingredients and the craftsmanship in the kitchen.

Natural Pastures Cheese Company

Third-generation Comox Valley dairy farmer Edgar Smith is the former president of the local co-operative creamery, the oldest association of its kind in British Columbia. When the co-op was sold to a conglomerate, he was concerned. He wanted to ensure that the industry continued to be viable in his community and, most importantly, that it employed local people. So he decided to make cheese.

With help from his wife, Mary Ann Hyndman Smith, and their partner, Rick Adams, Edgar founded the Natural Pastures Cheese Company just a year ago. They brought in a Swiss-trained cheese master, Paul Sutter, whose artisan cheeses have since gained national acclaim. Natural Pastures' Comox Camembert, Boerenkaas and Cumin Seed Verdelait were have all been awarded gold medals at the prestigious Canadian Cheese Grand Prix.

I visited Edgar and Mary Ann, wanting to know the secret behind their seemingly overnight success. It was no surprise to discover that the secret was passion for their product, good planning and plain old hard work. They are also devoted to their local market. Edgar says demand for their cheeses far

Cheesemaker Paul Sutter and an assistant fill moulds at Natural Pastures Cheese Company.

outweighs supply at the moment, but they are committed to filling local orders first. Mary Ann, who takes their cheese to the Courtenay Farmers' Market, says she is touched by people with tears in their eyes who thank her for bringing them "a taste of their childhood."

No product is more likely to generate those tears than their fresh cheese curds, which fly off the grocers' shelves. Handmade curds are noshed straight from the packet, but many people use them to make a popular Québécois dish. For poutine, the curds are sprinkled over a plate of piping-hot french fries (organic potatoes, please!), then smothered with hot gravy.

Mary Ann was a caterer in Vancouver before marrying Edgar and moving to the valley. She brings a discriminating palate to the company, telling me she is inspired by different ingredients and how they come together to create West Coast "fusion" flavours. She works with Paul to develop the company's original cheese recipes. Case in point is their Wasabi Banzai. As I taste it with Mary Ann, she explains why I'm enjoying it so much: "First, you are hit by the wasabi, then the fresh garlic, and finally the rounded, curvaceous flavour of the ginger." Whatever the design, the outcome is addictive, and I'm not surprised that this is another cheese she can't keep on the shelves.

Once I'm appropriately attired in a white "spacesuit" and gumboots, Edgar takes me on a fascinating tour of the cheese factory. The simple story is that milk from the Smiths' 1930s-era heritage dairy farm in Comox is delivered directly to the back door. It is immediately pasteurized. One side of the factory

is dedicated to producing semi-hard cheese; the other to soft cheese.

We first enter the semi-hard production area, where the pasteurized milk is placed in a 4,000-litre vat. The curds are separated from the whey, pressed into moulds and placed in a brine solution for two days. They are then cured in the aging room, at an average temperature of 11°C, for a period of time appropriate to their type (from 6 to 8 weeks, or up to 10 months). After the aging process, some of the cheeses are also dipped in wax.

Across the way, the soft cheeses are made in smaller batches. They take less time to make and age, but need more attention. These cheeses are formed, left to drain, then turned over and drained again. When dry enough, they are placed in a brine bath for just 30 minutes before being set out to age for up to two weeks at a temperature of 15° to 16°C. It is at this stage that the trademark white moulds develop on the outside of the cheeses. In the final stage, the Bries and Camemberts cure at 6°C. Natural Pastures buys a special type of paper from France for wrapping the soft cheeses. Edgar says the paper quality is critical: one layer has microscopic holes that allow the cheese to breathe and the other provides hygienic protection.

Edgar is committed to mastering his craft. He tells me how deeply satisfying it is to see the milk come directly from his cows, "a still-living biological system that produces the wonderful taste of the cheese." For him, the cheesemaking "completes the whole cycle of the farmer in touch with the craftsman and the consumer."

Before I leave, he proffers a sample of Sky Blue Cheddar, another successful example of contrasting flavours created by Mary Ann and made by Edgar and Paul. I savour the combined creaminess of the blue Stilton and the solidness of the white cheddar, and realize how much the couple's commitment to making the highest quality handcrafted cheese is reflected in their products. When, several weeks later, I serve only Natural Pastures cheeses on my cheese tray, friends think I've travelled around the world to please their palates.

Tita's Mexican Restaurant

I ran into Martin Metz in Portuguese Joe's where he was buying fish for his wife Lisa's 40th birthday dinner, which he was preparing at home that evening. While I was sorry they wouldn't be on the line that night at their downtown Courtenay restaurant, Tita's, I was pleased to at least have a reservation at this popular spot that Lisa calls her "giant art project."

Named for Tita, the exuberant heroine in the novel *Like Water for Chocolate*, who "is born and raised in the kitchen and finds an outlet through cooking to express her powerful emotions," this deep yellow hacienda exudes South American *alegría de vivir*. Even before stepping into the cosy dining rooms (there are two), I linger in the remarkable organic gardens that surround them. An article about Tita's gardens in the June 2002 issue of *Gardens West* magazine shows the proliferation that I can only imagine during my January visit. Food crops such as squash, purple cabbages, quince, fig, everbearing strawberries, calendulas, thyme, filigree-leaf fennel, jalapeno and Anaheim peppers, sunflowers, red amaranth and quinoa were carefully planted by Lisa so that she and her cooks "wouldn't need to reach more than two feet in any direction" to access their ingredients. This garden embodies the palette of South American artwork, with hues that speak to hot climates and long, warm nights drinking tequila and dancing to mariachi bands. But perhaps I digress.

What's for supper? Heather Standish, the restaurant's manager, has "worked and eaten here almost every day for the past five years," and is exceptionally knowledgeable about Mexican food and its flavours (which in Mexican cuisine go deep, way deep, and tend to surprise one's palate from beginning to end).

She settles me at the bar and suggests a starter of ceviche tostada made with snapper that has been cold-"cooked" in fresh-squeezed lime juice and tossed with the house *pico de gallo* salsa. It reminds me of those killer tacos made by Lisa Ahier at SoBo in Tofino and really awakens my taste buds, which have been focussed on North American cuisine for several days.

Another taco is topped with black beans (cooked without oil), pasilla chilis and a mixture of local wild mushrooms seasoned with roasted garlic, feta cheese, red onions and cilantro. The combination is earthy and satisfying. I order guacamole and more taco chips and sample some of the sauces that are all made from scratch here. Heather and I compare notes. Her favourite is the Olvera, created by Lisa in honour of Olvera Street in Los Angeles where "every second establishment serves it." It is a smooth and spicy sauce of avocados, tomatillos and roasted jalapenos, which comes on cool and then packs a fiery punch. My favourite is the *mole de chabacano* made of apricots, onions and mulato and pasilla chilies that usually envelops broiled wild boar chops from Twin Peaks Farm but which I enjoy with chicken. Another couple of noteworthy sauces are the *mole rojo*, a classic *mole* with plantains and tomato, and the *mole con pollo*, made from chilies, onions, spices, nuts and chocolate, in which chicken thighs from Tanadice Farm pasture-raised birds are gently simmered.

Other Courtenay suppliers contributing to Tita's menu include Natural Pastures, which custom-makes its Queso Fresco cheese, Eatmore Sprouts ("Greg's a chef turned gardener and I'm a gardener turned chef," says Lisa, "so we have a great relationship"), and Glen Elwin Farm, which supplies lamb.

Tita's beverage selection acknowledges the North American love affair with Corona beer, sangria, margaritas, et al., but also recommends pairing a good wine with the "rich and lively flavours" of the various entrées—a Pinot Grigio from Cowichan Bay's Vigneti Zanatta, perhaps, or one of the menu's organic offerings, Côtes du Ventoux Syrah or the Colli Euganei Merlot, which I enjoyed straight through to *postres*. And speaking of dessert, leave room for the signature ancho chocolate ganache that's enlivened with the tastes of raisins and chili, or the classic Mexican flan, which Lisa decorates in summer with strawberries from her garden.

The journey of Martin and Lisa began 20 years ago in Vancouver and took them to the Yukon (where Lisa had a bakery/café) and to Berlin before they decided they "wanted to live somewhere in the Canadian wilderness." They settled for 12 years on Maurelle Island, a fairly large but sparsely populated island (says Lisa, "When we left, the population fell to 15") near Quadra Island. It was there that Lisa "really honed my gardening and cooking skills." By growing their own food and raising their own meat, they were largely self-sufficient. The Metzes raised their family on Maurelle and found the quality of life there so good that their move to Courtenay and shopping in grocery stores again was challenging. "At first," says Lisa, "we didn't know what to eat."

COMOX

Benino

I first met Ruth Vanderlinden when she was working at Hot Chocolates in Courtenay and was delighted to find her now minding her own shop, a distinctly modern Euro ice cream parlour called Benino (meaning, appropriately, "good" in Italian) in beautiful downtown Comox. Although she tells me that "not in a million years did I think I would do this," she is clearly enjoying her new venture.

When her son-in-law's parents visited three years ago, the entire family was strolling along Comox's main road. "You need a gelateria here!" professed the father, and, says Ruth, "That sparked the whole thing."

While I tuck into a cup of silky hazelnut ice cream, Ruth single-handedly serves a long lineup of loyal customers. Since she and her daughter Aline and son-in-law Tomi opened the shop in May 2006, those customers have spanned "a whole palette of ages."

I see that whole palette before me now, ordering preservative-free sorbets and ice creams and special coffee drinks. And I laugh to myself at the accuracy of Ruth's description, "The children don't walk into my shop—they fly in!"

Ice cream on a hot day always generates happiness, but Benino's ice creams—made in-house with the best-quality imported ingredients such as Belgian chocolate—and sorbets—rendered from fresh, local fruit in season—seem to have an even greater power. Says Ruth, "Having an ice cream is such a high," and who could disagree? The flavours and silky consistency are ethereal.

With 24 flavours offered in the high season, it's difficult to settle on a favourite. The bilberry (a wild blueberry the store gets from Newfoundland) and raspberry sorbets taste as fresh as the fruit on the vine; the rich and chocolatey chocolate ice cream is made with 74 per cent cocoa content chocolate; and the pannacotta, made from cooked cream and caramel, brings a true taste of Italy to Comox. There are also milkshakes and floats, and gorgeous sundaes, including a traditional Coupe Denmark of vanilla ice cream topped with hot chocolate sauce and freshly whipped cream and the Snowbird, pannacotta ice cream topped with hot raspberry sauce and whipped cream.

Of the special coffees on offer, the most popular is the Café Benino, which is a two-shot Americano topped with a scoop of vanilla ice cream (or any flavour of choice) and whipped cream. When Ruth mentions that she will be applying for a liquor licence, I can see the attraction of being able to sit on the patio with a coffee and grappa, and I encourage her in that pursuit.

Portuguese Joe's Fish Market

The late José Domingues Veloso of Portugal courted his wife, Nilda, by swimming across the River Mino to see her in northern Spain. After she married him, he came on his own to Canada to see if they could spend their lives here. He first went to Nova Scotia, then to Kitimat, British Columbia, where he worked building bunkhouses for miners. Eventually, he made his way to Vancouver Island, where he found that the Comox Valley reminded him of home. He put down roots and sent for Nilda.

José worked for Crown Zellerbach in the valley and soon bought a 20-acre farm. But he always fished, and it was that passion that led him to open the now-legendary Portuguese Joe's. Before he died, José and Nilda and their children lived above the shop on Comox Road, which I visited with great expectations.

It was exactly the no-fuss, no-muss place I'd imagined, with a beautiful array of fresh and frozen wild seafood and a well-worn counter with a box of plastic bags, twist ties and a massive stack of newspaper sheets. Brothers Eddy and Cecil were serving customers hand-over-hand. A long queue of customers raised their eyebrows and smiled in unison as Eddy measured out two pounds of prawns by sight, then threw them on scales that confirmed his measure to the ounce. Having been raised in the business, these guys know their fish.

Cecil is bagging peeled shrimp that his other brother, Lito, had caught that day. "Lito," he tells me, "is the spitting image of our father." He and Eddy debate whether Lito was actually born in the taxi right in front of the shop or in the taxi heading to the hospital. With Nilda away for the weekend, this debate can't be resolved, but suffice it to say that "Lito is the serious fisher," the Veloso most closely tied to the product they sell.

This has been a family operation since the early 1960s (the exact date becoming another point of debate between Eddy and Cecil). There are two other employees, a Vietnamese couple whom the Velosos helped out when they first arrived in Comox, that have assisted with the cutting and filleting for 15 years.

Cecil stops for a chat over the counter, and tells me about the early days, and the shop's huge support of the military personnel based in Comox. He shows me a wall of military crests and a photo of his father that hangs above an old adding machine. He decries the fast society that "doesn't stop like you and I are doing now, to have a chat, to shop locally. It's cultural; it's about having a relationship." I agree about the loss and realize that this is one man I don't have to preach to about the Slow Food philosophy, the way I tend to do in the city.

The gentleman standing beside me, a customer for 25 years, orders up some shrimp and herring and Cecil is back in action. I nibble away on a piece of house-candied salmon and think of his father's invigorating, life-changing (even Byronesque!) swim across the River Mino.

Thyme on the Ocean

I believe the secret to Comox's best-kept secret is love. Love in the kitchen of Thyme on the Ocean translates into love on the plate every time.

Two foodies had pointed me in the restaurant's direction: Marcus Fedoruk, an excellent Victoria home cook, and Susie Moscovich, a Campbell River bed and breakfast owner and long-time friend and patron of Umberto Menghi's Vancouver restaurants and his Villa Delia in Tuscany. I can't be accused of not listening to my sources.

It was a miserable, rainy evening at the end of a long leg of my edible journey when my husband insisted we try to get a reservation at Thyme on the Ocean. Co-owner Emil Shelborn was most accommodating, given the impossibly short notice, and, in fact, found us a lovely table by the window. And there was something soothing about the place —the grey neutrality of its decor induced relaxation and anticipation of the best sort. Suddenly, I was looking forward to my meal.

Co-owners and chefs Emil Shelborn and Nah Yoon Kim put great love into their food at Thyme on the Ocean.

An *amuse bouche* of a pasta chip with fresh salsa set the tone for simple elegance (I am always nervous when the *amuse bouche* is overly complex; simplicity, on the other hand, shows the chef's confidence). It was followed by a lively salad of local mixed greens with Okanagan goat's milk cheese and slow-roasted tomatoes. The pasta course was divine: handmade cheese tortellini with peas in a lemon-basil sauce. And then roasted sablefish with baby carrots, gnocchi and chanterelles—the fish plump and perfectly flaking. When it seemed no course could exceed these ones in flavour, a plate of thin-as-air chicken scallopini with truffled mashed potatoes and chanterelle mushroom sauce stopped conversation.

As we lingered over coffee and oozingly delicious hot chocolate torte with Chantilly cream, vanilla-bean pannacotta with huckleberry sauce and caramelized lemon torte, I realized I could be in any top restaurant in New York, London or

Paris, but here I was in Comox on Vancouver Island enjoying fine, respectful preparations of the best local ingredients. It is no wonder that one food writer has compared Emil to Jamie Oliver: he has a young man's passion for his craft and is not afraid to err on the side of homestyle cooking over grand preparations.

Emil and Nah Yoon Kim met in Calgary, where both worked at Il Sogno. Their love for each other and for Italian cooking brought them to the Comox Valley, where they are now serving what I am afraid to advertise for fear that reservations may soon need to be made months in advance!

CORTES ISLAND

Cortes Café

If you're lucky enough to be visiting Cortes Island on market day, or indeed, on any postal delivery day, then you'll want to eat at the Cortes Café. Established in a cosy back room of Manson's Hall, full of local art and artsy people, the café dishes up delicious fare.

I stopped shopping in the market to enjoy the last piece of their home-made carrot cake and a good cup of coffee, and to soak up some of the local colour and chat around me. It was a warm haven on that cold winter's day, and I loved listening in on the market-related conversations, "I bought some lovely Ribston Pippins from Bill Wheeler," "Does L.J. have her Brie *en croute* today?" and, "What do you say we grab an ice cream before we go?"

"What do you say we grab an ice cream before we go?"

– Cortes Café customer

Cortes Island Farmers' Market

The Cortes market runs year-round. Its offerings change with the seasons, with a little island eclecticism thrown in. In summer, there's lots of fresh produce, and don't be surprised that there's still a lineup for the organic ice cream in winter.

John Gordon is a photographer whose lovely images of island flora and fauna sell from his gallery at Smelt Bay. He and his wife, Ruby, decided they should offer something in addition to the photographs and settled on ice cream. It's proven to be a big hit, especially the organic berry flavours (made from their homegrown strawberries, raspberries, loganberries, blackberries and even tayberries).

Lisa Jo Osland caught my eye with her mane of red hair and celadon silk jacket. Her stall was laden with goodies and she was surrounded by children—four of whom turned out to be her own. Her story put the whole island lifestyle into perspective for me. A caterer in the film industry, she and her family were living the urban life in North Vancouver before they moved to

Cortes for one reason: Linnaea School, the famed environment-oriented private school for children that operates from a 350-acre farm. "L.J." caters the school's organic hot lunch program, in addition to her private catering and weekly market offerings. I only wish her lunch program could be instituted at all schools, in place of the unhealthy "pizza or hotdog days."

I meet a customer of hers, Bud, who says L.J. has "really made a job for herself" on the island. In addition to her catering, she will begin teaching an Asian fusion cuisine workshop at Hollyhock in the fall.

L.J. presents her goodies as "more fooling around from L.J.'s kitchen," and on the day I visit, the selection is awesome: Giant Raviolis (for poaching and napping with a favourite sauce); pastry-covered Salacious Brie ("for when your sweetie's coming over"); Garlic Cream (a "pasta positive" sauce that's also delicious on garlic bread); homemade fettuccini and bocconcini. As I'm on the road, I buy the bocconcini to nibble on. This generous helping of tiny mozzarellas marinating in fresh herbs and olive oil is sealed in an airtight bag and lasts me four road-trip days without refrigeration.

Brigid Weiler proffers a range of botanical body products. She is a cook who has worked in the island's tree-planting camps and also at Hollyhock. I buy a copy of the wonderful book she co-wrote with Jill Milton, *Recipes from Garden, Sea and Bush* (Rasmussen Company), which is full of instructions for great back-to-the-land fare. Brigid leads mushroom-foraging walks on Saturday mornings in season.

Also on offer the day I visit the market are a huge selection of apples from Bill Wheeler and Mary Clare Preston's Inner Coast Nursery, incredible baking, such as baguettes and cookies, and Wild Harvest smoked salmon from Andrea and Gary Block. The craft stalls are equally impressive with reasonably priced hand-knit sweaters, slippers made from hand-spun sheep's wool and jewellery fashioned from elk antlers and feathers.

Hollyhock

The first time I visited Hollyhock and stood on its beach, looking out to sea, I felt I was standing on the edge of Planet Earth. The property has a special, indescribable quality that one has to experience to understand. And, of course, that quality and the array of New Age, experiential learning programs have kept people coming here from all over the world for 20 years.

The second time I visited was to interview then-head chef Debra Fontaine. It was in late November, when Hollyhock is essentially closed. There was a small group of writers using the lodge for a retreat; it was otherwise quiet, but

Relaxation, healing and good food are on the menu at Hollyhock, where the gardens produce veggies and herbs for the kitchen.

Hollyhock is perched idyllically between the wilderness and the ocean.

still magical. Debra invited me to sit by the fire with her, and we talked about her responsibility of feeding up to 140 people every day, many of whom are on special diets or suffer from food allergies.

The week before, she had cooked the last dinner of the season for workshop participants: local salmon, sautéed local prawns with pesto made from Hollyhock basil, mushroom risotto with Asiago, baked squash and chocolate mousse. She spent five hours stirring the huge pot of risotto, and loved every minute of it. "I choose what I am the most passionate about, what gives me the most joy," she tells me.

Working with a brigade of 22 to 25 people, she says each meal "is like doing a big party." She approaches cooking like an artist approaching a canvas, telling her cooks she wants "healthy, fresh food with great taste that also catches the eye. I'm looking for lots of textures—soft and chewy and crunchy—and colours; and a balance of heat." It's important, she says, to think about food both visually and texturally, and to be mindful of "how it is going to sit in the stomach."

Hollyhock subscribed to a vegetarian-food-only kitchen until 11 years ago, when fish was introduced. Debra says she is also open to free-range poultry. She cooked a big turkey dinner at Thanksgiving that was hugely popular. She wondered if the vegetarian model hadn't gone a bit too far when a guest asked, "Did you debone the tofu?"

Still, Debra loves cooking veggies and herbs, which travel only a few feet from Hollyhock's gardens to its kitchen. The growers provide daily lists for the cooks of what will be available from the garden the next morning. All produce is picked before the sun heats the plants. Menu-planning follows what the earth provides, not what has been driven for three days up the I-5 from California.

Head gardener Nori Fletcher has worked the Hollyhock gardens for over 20 years using the biodynamic/French intensive method she learned at the Farallones Institute in California. Her assistant, Myann Reid, is a graduate of Linnaea Farm's ecological gardening program. Their training and passion are reflected in their incomparable kitchen garden.

There are always fascinating culinary workshops on offer at Hollyhock, from specialists like Victoria tea master Daniela Cubelic and food-security expert Carolyn Herriot, as well Moreka Jolar, another former Hollyhock chef and one of the authors of *Hollyhock Cooks* (New Society, 2003).

Reef Point Farm

When Queen Elizabeth II and Prince Philip stayed with their relatives, Markgraf Max von Baden and Markgräfin Valerie von Baden, on the Twin Islands just off Cortes, Ginnie Ellingsen was called over to cook for six weeks. Such is Ginnie's modesty that I wouldn't have known that fact had Hollyhock's Debra Fontaine, on learning I would be spending the night at Reef Point Farm, not sent me off there with a wink and a suggestion: "Ask her about cooking for the Queen."

Not only did Ginnie tell me about that singular experience but she also kindly shared her photographs of the very relaxed sovereign enjoying her holiday. Of course, what was cooked and eaten by Her Majesty could not be revealed, but the story certainly

The bed and breakfast at Reef Point Farm serves scones fit for a queen!

gave me a window into the interesting world of Ginnie and her husband, Bruce.

Bruce's great-grandfather was the first white settler on Cortes—Michael Manson, for whom Manson's Landing is named. The property where he and Ginnie live, a 96-acre west-facing waterfront paradise, has been in the family since 1938. I had a stimulating morning walk with the couple through their apple, cherry, filbert and walnut orchard and vegetable gardens, and down to the beach. Ginnie planned to harvest seaweed for the gardens later that day, and wanted to check on the tide.

While their rambunctious dog swam out to annoy the seals, we stood at Sacred Point on their property and looked across to Mitlenatch Island, which the Manson family owned prior to its becoming a provincial park. Bruce tells me that Michael Manson and his brother, John, used to row their sheep out to graze on Mitlenatch for the summer. "John's wife, Margaret, used to love staying out there. The lack of trees and its openness reminded her of the Shetland Islands where they came from. During the tough times of the Dirty Thirties, they stopped grazing the sheep there because of the poaching that went on."

We walked to the beach on one of the remaining horse-logging roads. Horses were used to drag logs to the water to be floated off to buyers in the late 1880s when Japanese settlers logged the island. Bruce has worked in the forest industry, and now runs his own sawmill on the island with one of his four sons.

As a board member of the Cortes Eco-forestry Society, Bruce is committed to selective logging and logging in situ, meaning that he takes his own Mobile Dimension sawmill into the woods "on a light-duty road system, to cut logs from roadside piles or bunks." He built his own house from timber taken from the property. Bruce is also helping with the divestiture of some 4,000 acres of Weyerhauser-owned lands on Cortes.

I loved my cosy room at Reef Point Farm, and was honoured to have dinner *en famille* with the Ellingsens. Ginnie's interest in serving only locally produced foods (much from her own garden) shone through in her cooking, and I enjoyed a lovely beef daube (made with beef from the island's Linnaea Farm), mashed potatoes, Ginnie's French beans and pickled beets. There was a local birthday girl at the table that night so Ginnie had made a first-rate and not overly sweet chocolate cake, which she served with her own canned peaches. As it stormed outside, the rain sheeting down on the kitchen's tin roof, we were a very content and convivial party inside.

Reef Point Farm has connections to the famed Rebar restaurant in Victoria: son David was a prominent fixture there before pursuing his photography career full-time in Vancouver, and Lizzie, the restaurant's longest-serving waitress, is a good friend of the Ellingsen family.

The morning I reluctantly left, I opted for the lighter version of breakfast: a fresh fruit salad, Ginnie's currant scones and steaming coffee. Everything was presented on good English china and everything was scrumptious. Reef Point Farm is a place to immerse oneself in peace and tranquillity as well as to eat and sleep like a queen.

CAMPBELL RIVER

Anglers Dining Room at The Dolphins Resort

Not everything works out as planned on one's edible journeys, but sometimes it's enough to know that a discovery has been made and a door has been opened.

Having heard from several sources that the Anglers Dining Room at The Dolphins Resort, which overlooks Discovery Passage, had started opening to the public in addition to resort guests, I attempted to secure a table. That simply wasn't possible as a convention had taken over the resort and its tiny, 26-seat dining room, but I was able to slip in before service to chat with the chef and sous-chef and watch some of the dinner preparations—oh, and also sample the best-ever whole wheat focaccia with olive oil and rock salt as it was pulled out of the oven!

It was a lovely surprise to find that Jessica Willott was at the stove. I had previously known Jessica when she worked at the brilliant but short-lived

Chef Jessica Willott in her enviable waterfront kitchen at Anglers Dining Room.

Earthshake Café in Parksville. She had gone on to work at Sooke Harbour House and at Café Brio, and then lived in Rome for half a year, working in cafés and becoming immersed in the culture of "fresh and seasonal and not rushing things—putting the love in it, because the food was the main event of the day."

When Anglers started opening to the public, Jessica was asked to cook classic meals to suit the charming ambiance of the place. She has responded with daily menus that follow the seasons. The afternoon I visited, she had a big copper pot of seafood chowder bubbling on the stove, and was carefully preparing a saffron-and-tomato cream sauce for the Pan Seared Snapper Tagliatelle. Other entrées that would be offered that evening were Pan-Roasted Filet Mignon and Rosemary Roast Pork Tenderloin.

Jessica may have the best kitchen on Vancouver Island. It's small but very workable and it has a front-row view across to Quadra Island that is breathtaking at any time of day. No wonder that she is happy here, "doing what I love to do"—a sentiment passionately reflected in her excellent cooking.

Cheddar & Co. Specialty Foods

Michelle Yasinski has really set a new culinary tone in Campbell River. Her *fromagerie* and bakery, named for her late black Labrador, is a foodie's dream. The shelves are lined with "must-haves," from Spanish and French olive oils to vinegars (including the Cowichan Valley's Venturi Schulze vinegar), chutneys and preserves to dried pasta, "frog-friendly" wild coffee and an exciting range of salts.

On the Saturday morning that I visited, Michelle was expecting her Michel Cluizel chocolate rep and her wild-coffee rep, both of whom would be offering tastings of their products throughout the day. For me, it was still too early for chocolate, but I was thrilled with a mug of coffee brewed from *Altura rustica* beans that grow wild in the forests near Oaxaca, Mexico, and a just-baked banana muffin. I sat at the counter enjoying the bustle and requests of customers.

One lady wanted to make a carrot cake but was lactose intolerant. Michelle recommended making the icing with Saltspring Cheese Company's

Owner Michelle Yasinski and baker Madonna Hall of Cheddar & Co. Specialty Foods.

plain chèvre, and the customer was delighted. Another was looking for a takeaway for lunch and Michelle suggested the new cheddar pasta with caramelized onions. Other fabulous offerings in her deli case were open-faced sandwiches of wild smoked salmon with lemon-dill cream cheese on rye, Moroccan galettes made of lamb and zucchini and a salad of roasted yams, dried cranberries, toasted pecans and blue cheese. On the bakery side, Madonna Hall was pulling tray after tray of muffins, breads and scones out of the ovens.

The night before, Cheddar & Co. had organized a beer and cheese pairing soirée, one of several fabulous culinary events held each season. I would love to have stayed for "Rome in a Day (or Night)," "Middle Eastern/North African" and "Cheese with Wine," but Michelle assured me that all will be repeated. She also partners with Lisa Ron of Campbell River's The Tasting Room for informative wine and cheese tastings.

When Michelle is able to take a break, I ask what had inspired her to get into the business. She is originally from Campbell River, but left to pursue her chef's ticket at Camosun College in Victoria, apprenticing at April Point Lodge in Campbell River and then working at The Ranch in Calgary. She met her husband at a fishing camp in Tweedsmuir Provincial Park where he was a guide and she was the chef.

"I had always wanted to create a shop like Meinhardt in Vancouver and McLean's Fine Foods in Nanaimo," she tells me. The timing was right to return to her hometown with her family. "With the Food Network encouraging cooking at home and people building new homes that they want to show off," opening a gourmet food shop in Campbell River finally made sense. Michelle has many customers from the nearby Northern Gulf Islands and "chefs are always dropping in off the yachts that come into port here."

Michelle has always had a passion for cheese—"one of my favourite foods"—so the shop's real attraction is its range of 40 to 50 cheeses, including some local Vancouver Island favourites from Hilary's Cheese, Saltspring Cheese Company and Moonstruck Organic Cheese. Her cheddars are among the world's best, brought in from Neils Yard, Keens and Montgomery, and when a big wheel of Avonlea raw mild Cheddar arrives from Ontario, there is such demand from customers that "it barely lasts the day."

With the merry season approaching, Michelle shares some of her finds with me. Customers can look forward to chili threads from the Côte d'Azur, marzipan pigs from Germany, Scottish shortbread, caramels coated with chocolate and dipped in *fleur de sel* and a product she is very excited about: a chunk of pink Himalayan salt that comes with its own grinder.

Haig-Brown House

In Campbell River, I stayed at a favourite bed and breakfast right on the eponymous river: the old home of former magistrate, author and conservationist Roderick Haig-Brown and his family. It is an unassuming 1937 heritage-designated house with an inviting living/breakfast room on the ground floor and three bedrooms with shared bathrooms upstairs. There's a simple conservatory off the dining room where a Concord grape vine grows, having pushed its way through the wall from the garden where Ann Haig-Brown planted it in 1944. I ate some of those delicious grapes for breakfast, seeds and all.

The real attraction here is the Haig-Browns' extensive library of 4,000 volumes, which the brochure aptly describes as "a true symbolic representation of

Haig-Brown House bed and breakfast owner Dory Montague in her greenhouse.

the life and love of Roderick and Ann." Their wide interests are reflected in the collection of books on art, English literature, nature, fishing and law, and there are also copies of the 30 volumes that Roderick Haig-Brown penned during his lifetime.

Having arrived exhausted one night, I was grateful for a good mattress and an open screened window, through which the murmur of the river lulled me to sleep. In the morning, I found site manager and bed and breakfast host Dory Montague in the living room where we chatted before breakfast.

Dory first came to Haig-Brown House to assist Marcy Prior, who has tended the gardens for 24 years (she was originally hired by Ann Haig-Brown). Dory had worked in "the high-powered financial world" most of her life, a career she is "proud of but it wasn't meaningful." She found meaning and satisfaction in the garden of Haig-Brown House, and happily accepted the position of site manager.

Dory has added her infectious love of life and a great deal of intelligent conversation to the property, along with a new greenhouse that she arranged to have built on-site by the students from nearby Discovery College. From the greenhouse and vegetable garden comes the delicious organic produce proffered at breakfast. Her garden is so bountiful that she "couldn't keep up with putting up the produce" so she regularly donates vegetables to the Ann Elmor Transition House (Elmor was Ann Haig-Brown's maiden name). She is currently petitioning the heritage powers-that-be to allow her to raise chickens on the property, just as the Haig-Browns did.

I begin my day with a big glass of apple cider made from Cox's Orange Pippin apples from Marcy Prior's own garden, then feast on a parfait of yogurt, Dory's Green Granola and chopped apples (and then begged for the granola recipe); a dense kale frittata served with freshly baked challah (which Dory had so kindly made on the Friday night that I arrived); and very good direct-trade Three Frogs coffee, which is available at Cheddar & Co. in town.

Looking after the property and running the bed and breakfast somehow also gives Dory time to write, something she "had always wanted to do since I was a little girl." She is currently working on her first novel, about her many adventures at Haig-Brown House. Of course, I was careful to behave myself during my visit there so as not to be considered an "adventure!"

WEST COAST

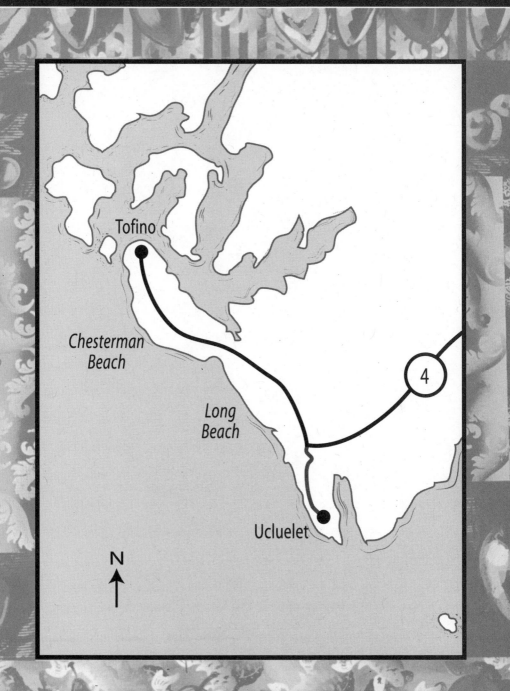

Tofino

Chesterman
Beach

Long
Beach

4

Ucluelet

N

Chocolate Tofino

I'm always impressed when people follow their passion. Gordon Austin graduated as a Red Seal chef from Malaspina University-College in 1996 and went to work at Chateau Whistler. He completed his journeyman papers in the pastry department of The Wickaninnish Inn under the tutelage of Matthias Conradi, and eventually took over the department when Matthias left.

Gordon began to notice a big demand from guests "for all things chocolate." When Bernard Callebaut gave a workshop at The Wickaninnish, Gordon "really picked his brains about the specialization and the entrepreneurial side of chocolate-making." With help in the costing and bookkeeping department from his wife, Leah, Gordon soon opened his own chocolate shop near The Beaches grocery.

The quaint entrance to Chocolate Tofino.

Lavender truffles tempt at Chocolate Tofino.

Stepping inside, one is immediately oohing and ahhing at the aroma from a big pot of bittersweet chocolate that is bubbling away. This is the fabulous Chocolate Elixir, simply the best way to stave off the winter cold. The display cases hold many promises of ecstasy, so choosing is difficult. I sample the popular Clayoquot-blackberry-and-white-chocolate bonbon. Gordon often picks the berries himself and makes them into a compound that he "freezes to ensure a supply of flavour year-round." The marzipan truffle is a wicked combination of marzipan with a layer of honey ganache dipped in bittersweet chocolate and the lavender truffles, understandably, have a huge following.

Gelato is very big here in summer, either on its own in a cone or in decadent sundaes. The product is made as close to the Italian version as possible, with "concentrated flavours of fruit, chocolate or vanilla." The shop always tries to have a non-dairy option on hand: the tofu latte flavour is a big hit. Chocolate Tofino also produces elaborate wedding and birthday cakes, often wrapping the whole in chocolate couverture. Gordon says, "Making people happy through the use of classical and fresh ingredients is my thing."

When I dropped in recently, Ray and Verna Austin, Gordon's parents, were over from Abbotsford minding the store while Gordon and Leah experienced the chocolate harvest in Costa Rica. While Ray kept an eye on the Chocolate Elixir, Verna showed me the famous Chocolate Tofino Bear. "It's become our mascot," she tells me, unwrapping a bear and revealing a collection of tiny turtles and salmon in its tummy. Though inspired by edible Russian bears that she and Ray had seen in their travels, the Tofino Bear tells its own story of the threatened species living in Clayoquot Sound.

Festival of Oysters and the Sea

Like the south island's Feast of Fields and the mid-island's Harvest Bounty Festival, Tofino's oyster festival is a benchmark local event that I highly recommend. It's a celebration of the fruits of the local oyster fishers, and literally thousands of oysters are consumed (one year, I understand, 4,000 oysters were slurped in 4 hours at the Oyster Gala!).

Held in mid-November, the festival offers boat tours to the oyster fields (see my private tour with Oyster Jim Martin); seminars with marine biologists on "where oysters live, what they eat and, perhaps most interestingly, the legends of what they can do for you when you eat them"; an oyster brunch and a stupendous oyster gala, where oysters are presented every which way by all the prominent local chefs.

Tofino, and particularly Lemmens Inlet in Clayoquot Sound, where most of the deep-water oyster tenures are situated, produces around 50,000 gallons of bivalves annually. The District of Tofino has marked the industry's significance by declaring November "Oyster Month in Tofino." Many of the luxury hotels offer special rates for the festival weekend, but getting tickets to the oyster festival can be challenging. It's best to book everything ahead if your edible journey will be taking you to Tofino in November.

I'm a bit shy around bivalves, so I asked around at the oyster gala before selecting three fine specimens to sample. Artie and Lisa Ahier of SoBo had sandwiched a locally smoked oyster, wasabi cheese from Natural Pastures

Cheese Company, Thai-style green papaya sauce and pea shoots between two homemade organic potato chips, which packed a powerful punch. Long Beach Lodge's Rob Wheaton had smoked oysters in chai tea, then served them on the half-shell with a Champagne ginger vinaigrette and wasabi tobiko on a pea-shoot salad. The recipient of the 2004 juried award, and my personal fave, was the Asian oyster baked in spinach, onion and miso broth by Tough City Sushi's chef Jojo Villaresis.

In Tin Wis Resort's "Oyster Palace," decorated in blue paper jellyfish and filled to capacity with an eager foodie crowd, the chefs performed admirably. When everyone was finally sated with oysters and a great deal of local wine had been consumed, the dance floor was opened and The Continentals, a local jazz ensemble, sparked hours of dancing.

Another reason to take a west coast edible journey in November is the colourful parade of pumpkins that runs for several kilometres starting at Cathedral Grove. For Hallowe'en, locals traditionally line the side of the highway with hundreds of carved pumpkins. It's one of those unique organic events, which somehow reminds us that there is a place in all our lives for whimsy, especially on a grey fall day. En route to the oyster festival I drove my husband crazy for at least half an hour with frequent outbursts of "Oh look, there's another stand of pumpkins."

The Goat Lady

Years ago, The Wickaninnish Inn's Nanoose Organic Greens and Ucluelet Goats' Cheese Salad with Sun-dried Blueberry and Sesame Vinaigrette led me to Jane Hunt. It was another once-in-a-lifetime foodie adventure, and I'll never forget her. Former Wickaninnish chef Jim Garraway had given me Jane's phone number with the instruction that, as I would be calling a radiophone, I would need to say "over." Piece of cake. Jane and I had many successful conversations before I headed into the wild hills behind Ucluelet to meet her at Westerly Wynds Farm.

A goat named Puddle Jumper at Westerly Wynds Farm.

Jane graduated from the first veterinary class at the University of Guelph in 1964, and set up a clinic in Victoria's Vic West neighbourhood. Her husband, Don, says it got a bit crazy some nights when animals were being brought in from accidents. Twenty years later, seeking a more peaceful life, they bought 15 acres in the hills outside Ucluelet from a logging syndicate, and embarked on a journey towards self-sufficiency.

My trip to the farm is both breathtaking and poignant. Much of the area has been logged, and when I spot a black bear cub foraging for food in the middle of a clearcut, my heart stops. Jane's instructions are very specific, and once I've made two rights, a left and a very sharp right, the farm and a frisky welcoming committee of 27 goats are before me.

The goats are Saanen, brought from Alberta. The youngest, Summer, is six weeks old the day I visit. The eldest, Clinton, is a fearless buck who has a little smooch through the fence with every doe that passes by. Poor Clinton doesn't know yet that a new buck has arrived on the farm. Jane and Don drove to Abbotsford "in a raging snowstorm" to bring back Puddle

The Goat Lady, Jane Hunt, with a few of her 27 goats at Westerly Wynds Farm.

Jumper, who is settling in nicely in his own pen. There are many other residents: peacocks, ducks, guinea fowl, pheasants, turkeys, chickens, French Angora rabbits, Great Pyrenees dogs, Shetland sheep, alpacas and 13 cats.

One can only marvel at the extraordinary *tableau vivant* created by the many creatures, organic gardens, the house and a dozen outbuildings ranging from a barn to a water tower. And even though everything seems to be in motion, there is a peace and stillness to the place that makes me see why the Hunts chose to settle here. There is also a stunning view of Barkley Sound from the top of the cliffs. Jane says every kid has taken a plunge over the cliffs, and she's managed to coax each one up with a rope.

Jane started making goat's milk cheese nine years ago and "selling it to hippie friends." It was soon coveted by locals, including the trail-blazing Rodney Butters, The Wickaninnish Inn's chef at the time. Rodney often visited Jane with his cat, and the sublime chèvre started to appear on the inn's dinner menu.

Out of a very small *fromagerie* in the back of her house, Jane pasteurizes 50 to 60 litres of goat's milk and produces 35 pounds of cheese a week. She always has chèvre and feta on hand for her regular customers, and, in the summertime, also makes butter and ice cream—which the local children love—from the leftover milk.

Hungry Bear Naturals

After Salals grocery store closed, along came Hungry Bear Naturals with the same healthy mix of dry goods, condiments, fresh produce, meats, cheeses and dairy. Friends Dwane Bell and Doug Wright own a gym downstairs in the building and, when the upstairs space became available, they felt the combination of the two businesses would be a natural fit.

"We're about promoting health and wellness through exercising and eating right," Doug tells me. Certainly the proximity of the gym is a good reminder to food shoppers that it does take both activities to achieve those ends.

And who are the hungry bears? "We were looking for a name that makes people smile," says Doug, "and also has some association with the area." When I stopped in, there were several "hungry bears" stocking up on organic produce, not to mention on the Virani chocolate that had just come in. Good health never tasted so good.

Long Beach Lodge

Long Beach Lodge's great room is like a magnetic force for me. While the lodge has high-quality accommodation, friendly staff and instant beach access, it is its great room that draws me in. It's not unlike The Bengal Lounge at Victoria's Fairmont Empress Hotel: large, with high ceilings, comfortable groupings of couches, chairs and tables and a central fireplace. While the Empress has views across to the Inner Harbour, Long Beach Lodge's great room is like sitting in a fishbowl at the ocean's edge. The views across Cox Bay are spectacular, particularly during the famed "storm season," and the food prepared by executive chef Josh Anker ensures that all senses are equally thrilled.

It wasn't so long ago that Lisa Ahier (now of SoBo) and then Rob Wheaton (now of Shelter) were cooking at Long Beach Lodge. I mention this because, while there is a fair amount of movement among chefs, Tofino chefs tend to stay in the area. That's a good thing because their collective sensibility about cooking with fresh, organic island ingredients is never lost wherever they happen to be working.

Sublime fish presentations from Long Beach Lodge's executive chef, Josh Anker, and a few wild huckleberries picked from the property.

Josh certainly brought that good sense with him when he took over the kitchen here in October 2007. He sits with me before dinner to discuss his approach to the menu. "I want to bring really good food to Long Beach Lodge," he tells me.

Josh points to the plethora of high-quality ingredients at his doorstep: Jeff Mikus' fresh scallops; Outlandish Seafood's "clams right out of the water"; greens from Nanoose Edibles that owner Barbara Ebell "grows to order for us"; cheeses from some of the region's best *fromageries*, including Little Qualicum Cheeseworks, Saltspring Island Cheese Company and Courtenay's Natural Pastures; Cowichan Bay Farm's pastured chicken; venison from Seaview Farm at Black Creek; and macro-kelp from Bamfield.

Having embraced classic French cooking in his background (he was schooled at Camosun College and the Culinary Institute of Vancouver Island, and worked previously at Sonora Resort in Campbell River and The Landing and Tigh-Na-Mara resorts in Parksville), he is now like an artist who has perfected his technique and is showing the confidence of his own style. That style is somewhat reverential in that it is "based on letting the food speak for itself," but it also shows wit (such as his use of agar agar, gels, foams, oils and powders to create surprise elements on the plate). An example was the butternut squash soup with roasted apple compote starter that was pure and true to the produce being represented, and neither overpowered by nor competing with a brush-stroke of chorizo froth. There is a real art to his cooking.

Executive chef Josh Anker of Long Beach Lodge.

Immaculate greens from Nanoose Edibles followed, the hearty and delicate leaves lightly coated with a wildflower-honey vinaigrette; then a Frenched lamb chop crusted with pistachio nuts and parsley; a Cowichan Bay duck breast, served with a chocolate jus, baby beets and herb gnocchi; wild salmon with a fresh watercress sauce, orange pearls (alchemy in the kitchen!); and, finally, a lovely nutty-tasting red quinoa and prawn risotto. These were the tenderest renderings of meats, the flakiest treatments of fish—the work of a very competent chef.

Richly satisfying desserts followed, including the warm almond cake with cinnamon ice cream, candied pecans and vanilla poached plums, but I think I will most remember Josh for his enthusiasm about huckleberries. They grow fairly profusely in the area, and he made sure I sampled some of the ones that grow wild at the front door of Long Beach Lodge. Black as the ocean had become outside the dining room, with a tart and clean taste, they symbolized for me the affinity for nature and passion for indigenous foods that exists among the bright young chefs of Tofino.

 *Oyster Jim*

It's 7:00 a.m. on a clear spring morning as Jim Martin slips his skiff into the still water of Grice Bay. We're heading for his famed oyster beds, scattered throughout the islands of Clayoquot Sound.

To understand these oysters, one first needs to understand their shepherd. Oyster Jim is a seriously rugged guy, a former boilermaker who emigrated from Colorado to the sleepy little fishing village of Ucluelet in 1985. He is a gentle giant, a man with great capacity for invention and work study, who is as eloquent in describing his patented holistic exercise program as he is in expressing his delight at the little acts of kindness from the boys in his Scout troop. It's no overstatement to call him a legend in these parts. Whenever I mention his name, folks praise his local accomplishments and unwavering community spirit.

He recently brought a great dream to fruition when he and a battery of volunteers blazed and marked out the 2.5-km Wild Pacific Trail. Skirting the coastline around Ucluelet, it provides hikers with stunning vantage points of the ocean and islands below. I think of Jim each time I hike that trail, grateful for his determination to preserve the area's unique rugged beauty.

I'd heard about Oyster Jim long before our breakfast cruise. His large, succulent oysters are featured on the menu at The Wickaninnish Inn, where my fellow diners always rave about their meatiness and sublime flavour.

The West Coast doesn't get much better than this: breakfast served by Oyster Jim Martin.

One of the chef's recent takes on these amazing oysters was: Three Oyster Jim's Clayoquot Sound Roasting Oysters with Basil Goat's Cheese Crust, Garlic and Pancetta, and Horseradish Root Ketchup.

But I was determined to try my first Oyster Jim oyster with the man himself. Charles McDiarmid told me some of the best meals he's ever had were sitting on a log with Jim—a pile of oysters, a shucker and a few squeezes of lemon juice. It sounded like a hunter-gatherer's dream date.

Charles had explained to me, "A lot of places grow oysters on inflated drums that go up and down with the tide, but Jim grows his on the shore. The tide goes in and out. They take longer, but they turn out plumper, juicier, larger." As my past experiences with oysters had more often than not been chewy, I was ready for something sensational.

Jim tells me to put away my notebook and pen just before he lets out the throttle, and we are skimming the water through Fortune Passage en route to Kershaw and Wood islands. This is indeed a fortunate passage, for we are not long out when a school of porpoises crosses the bow. Jim says they're used to his boat now, so our presence doesn't disturb their herring feast. Within seconds, Jim has spotted a black bear searching the shore for rock crabs, and he shuts off the motor so we can take a closer look. He has been keeping an eye on the bear for two years, and thinks it was orphaned early on in life.

Before my tour of the oyster beds, we head over to Wood Island, where Jim lights a small fire on the beach in preparation for, and fuelling my anticipation of, the feast to come. We scramble back over barnacled rocks, and I gladly accept a piggyback ride through shallow water to the skiff.

The cultivation process is simple. Jim starts the oysters at home from larvae and small barnacle chips. They next go into nursery trays that are laid out on the beach. The temperature in these waters is perfect for growing shellfish. As the oysters grow, Jim spreads them along the beach, separating out the single units from the clusters. At this stage, the oysters are susceptible to attack by rock crabs, so Jim has devised a special collapsing crab fence. It does a good job of keeping the crabs at bay, but collapses as necessary to allow spawning salmon through.

Once the oysters reach three inches in length, they are transported to trays that get stacked underwater. There are up to 95 stacks at any given time, each containing 1,200 oysters. We cruise over the stacks, en route to the oysters' final resting beach, and Jim harvests a dozen specimens. He delights in the beautiful shell formations, and promises me a delicious breakfast.

Back on Wood Island, with the fire smouldering nicely, Jim roasts his prize oysters. He grows them specifically to be cooked in the shell, and within 10 minutes, they're ready to shuck. Jim hands me what proves to be the biggest, juiciest, most flavourful oyster I have ever eaten. He shows me where to start, and how to spoon the flesh out. I'm sitting on a log with the oyster guru of Clayoquot Sound, enjoying the unsurpassed calm of early morning and thinking life can't get much better than this. Pass the seafood sauce, eh?

Raincoast Café

With memories of some extraordinary rice cakes served with a roasted cashew and ginger sauce, I arrive back at the Raincoast Café to chat with owners Lisa Henderson and Larry Nicolay. It's mid-afternoon, one of the rare quiet times in their day. The restaurant is only open for dinner, so the prep work is mostly done and the flowers are arranged. Larry is taking time to check the evening's reservations, and Lisa draws me over to a corner table.

The couple first came to Tofino from Vancouver 13 years ago. They'd spent a summer looking around, and then found themselves managing the Alleyway Cafe, a charming little place tucked in behind shops in the centre of town. Their time at the Alleyway was enjoyable, but, as Lisa says, "It didn't feel like ours."

When the opportunity to be part of a brand-new building came up, they jumped at it. Larry's brother, who had previously designed restaurants in Vancouver like Global and Crush, was their designer, and other family members pitched in, too. The result is a small but functional prep room, and an open kitchen along one wall of the cleanly executed dining room. There are interesting flower arrangements, but generally the design is understated—a perfect foil for the food.

Lisa was a secretary who moonlighted in the front of house of various Vancouver restaurants. She is a self-trained chef, with no preconceived notions

Chef Lisa Henderson and Larry Nicolay are the delightful owners of the Raincoast Café.

about what she should or should not be cooking. She and Larry agree that their goal is always "to challenge ourselves and other people."

They are inclined towards Asian flavours, and allow me to label their style as "modern, with Asian influences," but really, anything goes. Lisa's Thai fish bowl includes local and exotic fish and shellfish, rice noodles, passion fruit, cilantro and jalapenos with coconut cream. Fresh Sooke trout is stuffed with Dungeness crab and cilantro lime cream cheese and served with yam mash. Cowichan Bay Farm's chicken is matched with shiitake mushrooms, balsamic shallot cream and herb-roasted new potatoes. Lisa was excited about a dish served the previous night where she had wrapped halibut in skunk-cabbage leaves.

She says she is inspired by what comes in the door from her local suppliers: Clayoquot Organics, Trilogy Fish Company and the neighbouring fishers, shellfish growers and mushroom, fiddlehead and edible-flower pickers.

Wines are mostly from British Columbia, with several organic choices; the coffee is Nicaraguan organic, and the teas are Tazo. As members of the Endangered Fish Alliance (a coalition of concerned chefs searching for sustainable options), Lisa says they "are diligent about serving only non-endangered, local and sustainable fish and shellfish."

Dinner is served seven nights a week. Reservations are highly recommended, but people have been known to straggle in close to closing time, and Lisa makes sure they're fed. The restaurant seats 24, plus there are two high stools right in front of the kitchen (great for nosy foodies like me), and it regularly turns over three or four times a night. With recommendations from *USA Today*, *Travel + Leisure*, *Frommer's* and *Best Places in the Northwest* and, recently, a recipe in *Bon Appétit*, Raincoast Café is indelibly inked on the culinary map.

Shelter Restaurant

Gimme shelter from any storm or any heat wave at Shelter Restaurant. This is the dining room to eat well in, the bar to be seen at and the patio, which glows in the summertime with big heat lamps and flares, where you can snuggle into a blanket and sip Vancouver Island reds until the stars come out over Clayoquot Sound.

Since I was last at Shelter, owner Jay Gildenhuys has undertaken a major renovation that's etched the place even more firmly into the Tofino lifestyle and made it the go-to restaurant for visitors.

Jay had been a fixture on the Victoria restaurant scene since 1995, when he opened the charming Cho Cho's in Oak Bay, a small coffee shop that I frequented with my father and niece. He later launched Suze, a funky fusion place, and then the non-stop Lucky Bar.

He told me he had been coming to Tofino for years, always admiring the building that housed The Crab Bar, a restaurant started by John Fraser (formerly of Trilogy Fish and now the mayor of Tofino). One night, Jay was "working the floor at Suze" and suddenly decided to call the owner of that building to see if it was for sale. Coincidentally (or not, if you believe that there are no coincidences in life) "the guy was coming to Victoria the next day and suggested

Owner Jay Gildenhuys, manager Shawna Gardham and chef Rob Wheaton of Shelter Restaurant.

a meeting." In short order, Jay sold Suze, bought the building of his dreams in Tofino and established the warm and cosy Shelter. And, as a necessary adjunct to any professional life in the food industry in Tofino, he learned to surf.

Today, I'm sitting around the restaurant's fireplace with Jay, his affable manager Shawna Gardham and chef Rob Wheaton, learning a lot more about what makes this place tick. While ultimately it's about fun and good food, Shelter has a huge commitment to sourcing locally, operating sustainably and giving back to the community—but this isn't necessarily evident at first glance.

Since these are the things that interest me, I wanted to dig deeper. So I asked about the waterless urinals in the men's washrooms (I have my sources), and got a tour of the on-site grey-water catchment system out back. Shawna told me about the major beach clean-ups that the restaurant helps with through the international Surf Riders organization. And I noticed that all male employees were sporting facial hair—something atypical for staff in the food industry—and discovered they'd done it on purpose as part of a Vancouver Island-wide campaign to raise money for testicular cancer.

Rob filled me in on some of his suppliers, most notably Medicine Farm in the hills behind Ucluelet ("the best greens we've ever had"). Last year, Shelter was able to finance a new irrigation system for the farm. I first met Rob at the 2004 Tofino Festival of Oysters and the Sea, when he was the chef at Long Beach Lodge. He'd previously cooked at Brentwood Bay Lodge and at Bishop's in Vancouver.

Rob is a highly competent chef who has always had a sure hand with fish, so I was delighted to sample some of his specialties. The Alaskan weathervane scallops, served with a green apple and Dungeness crab salad and lemongrass coconut cream, were fresh and zingy; the sesame-crusted local albacore tuna was radiant with daikon, orange segments, scallion and a sesame-lime ponzu; and finally, Rob's pan-seared wild coho salmon, served with sautéed spot prawn risotto and an apple-honey *beurre blanc*, gave me yet another reason to be thankful for living on the West Coast.

On the beverage side, the wine list put together by Jayelle Malleck is "rotated and kept fun." Says Jay, "We always want to be presenting customers with good finds." There is also a short, well-chosen list of artisan draught beers—several brewed on Vancouver Island—and original cocktails. The organic coffee comes from Vancouver's 49th Parallel.

There's local original art on the walls, movie nights, surf videos playing in the bathrooms and great magazines. Think ultra-modern living/dining room stocked with the best food and wine and friends; who wouldn't want to take shelter here?

600 Degrees Bakery

Trust Lisa and Artie Ahier of SoBo to have Tofino's best local bread on their menu. As someone who thrives on connecting the dots, I naturally wanted to meet the baker and hear her story.

When I found Julie Lomenda and her purpose-built wood oven tucked into a cul-de-sac just outside town, I met a young woman with an old soul's passion for her craft. She credits her interest in baking bread to her maternal grandmother, Mildred, a woman who "makes everything herself—doesn't waste anything."

When Julie worked in the kitchen at a kids' summer camp in North Vancouver, she found herself "a free wheel, able to do what I wanted." This was her chance to experiment with baking yeasted breads, and "I got a good reaction."

She later baked for Tofino's Long Beach Lodge when Lisa Ahier was the executive chef, and "played around with natural leavened breads" There, someone gave her a book about leavened breads and brick ovens, and the rest is a happy history focussed on the staff of life.

Julie has more than served her apprenticeship in the specialized world of wood-fired oven building. She became an assistant to oven-building guru Alan Scott, who has designed and built brick ovens all over the world. She also took a course in oven-building at a Tibetan monastery in Trinity Alps, California, and then went on to build several ovens with Alan. Although he has since relocated to Tasmania, Lomenda has kept in touch with him and others in the oven-building guild over the years.

Julie Lomenda pulls loaves from the oven she built for her 600 Degrees Bakery.

When it came time to build her own oven and baking kitchen, she solicited the help of her life partner, a builder, and her brother, a stainless steel fabricator. She also had help from Cliff Leir of Victoria, whose Fol Epi bakery has the newest wood-fired oven on Vancouver Island, and "great support from Lisa Ahier." But essentially she built her own oven and now uses it to bake her own bread.

Even though she isn't baking the day I visit, it's not difficult to imagine the physical demands of her profession. Julie describes the process, "The day before the bake, I chop the wood [to fuel the oven] and fire the oven to 1,200°F. The next day, I rake out the white ash and then clean out the oven with a mop. When the temperature hits 600 to 650°F—usually around 2:00 p.m. on the second day—the bread goes in." Lomenda bakes 20 to 30 loaves at a time and a total of 120 loaves per bake.

Her breads are as organic as possible, made with Anita's flour, water and sea salt. Julie uses her own whole-grain spelt and wheat starters, and is known for making a couple of plain loaves in addition to sun-dried tomato and rosemary, ancient grain, white country, walnut, olive and chocolate versions. They are available in many places in Tofino.

SoBo (a.k.a., Sophisticated Bohemian)

The more things change at SoBo, the more—happily—they remain the same. While Artie and Lisa Ahier's legendary restaurant has made a significant move since I wrote about them in the 2005 edition of this book (and they've become parents again), the food on their tables has only become more delectable and the couple's *joie de vivre* has become even more infectious.

I dropped in to wish them well at their new location, and found them just as warm and upbeat about good food, and living and raising their family in Tofino. They've transitioned smoothly from the original "purple people eater," a steel, former film-industry catering truck painted royal purple that was once parked in Tofino's Botanical Gardens and served thousands of foodies, surfers and top chefs from the area's other restaurants (always a good sign that a restaurant's food is first rate) to their current 3,300 square feet on the second floor of the "downtown" Conradi Building.

The new room includes a large bakery and retail area, an open kitchen (which Lisa proudly points out is fully "manned" by women!), a bar and a casual dining area. There is lots of room between tables but one still feels that old conviviality as though we were back in the lineup at the catering truck and chatting with the locals. The truck was always a "happening," and the new restaurant has that same friendly buzz. Lisa tells me that they were very much inspired by Vancouver's Meinhardt food shop and also Vikram Vij's Vancouver restaurants, Vij's and Rangoli, with their open kitchens and the opportunity

The ultimate sophisticated Bohemians, owners Lisa and Artie Ahier of SoBo.

to purchase housemade meals and condiments to enjoy at home (not to mention the comparison with their all-women kitchens!).

The addition of a bakery, under former Long Beach Lodge pastry chef Jen Scott, means that locals can pick up bread, cookies, meringues, very good housemade granola, Key lime pies and slices of (or whole) Flourless Chocolate Bombs—the signature chocolate cake covered with chocolate mousse and chocolate ganache nobody can resist.

The menu remains true to Lisa's original concept of fresh, healthy "sophisticated street food," and I was delighted to find my old favourite still available: Killer Fish Tacos. These blue corn tortillas filled with wild local fish and topped with fresh fruit salsa take some beating. The night I dined at SoBo, there were blueberries in the salsa and a tangy citrus vinaigrette on the local Medicine Farm organic greens. The crispy albacore tuna spring roll with its peanut sauce and winter vegetable slaw was a winning combination, and I went nuts—walnuts, to be precise—for the Natural Pastures Brie *en croûte* with walnuts, Lisa's apple-pear chutney (please start bottling this stuff!) and the first-rate toasted walnut bread from 600 Degrees Bakery.

It is more than possible to make a meal of appetizers, but for those wanting mains, there are handmade ravioli served with local spot prawns, herb-roasted chicken and a bouillabaisse-style Vancouver Island Seafood Stew brimming with scallops, ling cod, clams, mussels, crab and spot prawns in a saffron-tomato-fennel broth with red-pepper aïoli. Also of note are the new wood-stone-oven pizzas with healthy, succulent toppings like house-made duck confit, caramelized onions and Gorgonzola.

Artie's recent celiac disease diagnosis has contributed to the kitchen's even greater interest in providing uncompromised options for those with food intolerances, and many menu items are noted as being "wheat-free."

Killer Fish Tacos rock at SoBo.

The Ahiers continue to be hugely supportive of local food producers and the output from their new, larger kitchen means they are able to buy greater volumes. Fish comes straight from the local fishers including Jeff Mikus; Nanoose Edibles and Medicine Farm grow the restaurant's produce and most of the nettles and local berries come from Carl Martin and his daughter Giselle, local First Nations people.

Most telling of the Ahiers' dedication to good eating is their kids' menu, which caters to "little Bohemians" and offers all the goodness of the "big Bohemian menu" in smaller portions. Lisa has said this before but it bears repeating, "I am so inspired by the little ones, the children who are really digging good food, and I'm pleased to be firing up the next generation to get into what our grandparents had—pure foods—quality ingredients grown close to home." And I continue to say to her, "You go, girl!"

A breathtaking view of The Wickaninnish Inn.

The Pointe Restaurant at The Wickaninnish Inn

When I returned from dining at The Pointe Restaurant for this edition, I compared notes with a prominent food-magazine publisher, who told me, "The food at The Wick is its best ever." And I agreed, even though perfection is a hard thing to improve upon.

Chef Nicholas Nutting and his brigade are the young shining stars behind the "best ever" menu in The Pointe Restaurant. I think one reason for their success is, in fact, their relative youth (Nick later told me the age range in his kitchen is 19 to 29). Though the restaurant and resort now proudly flies the Relais & Châteaux banner, this is not a brigade that is intimidated by that. They have confidence in their own creativity and ability, and, as Nick says, "We feed off the pressure of those high expectations."

I brought my own high expectations with me. Having been married 10 years ago at The Wick, and a not-infrequent guest thereafter, I know this is a restaurant that can be world-class, so I looked forward to my dinner.

Service at The Pointe is unobtrusive theatre: there is always an element of performance but it is particularly well choreographed, as are the intermissions. A sense of anticipation has been created, and one can't help but look forward to each course, each pour. So, in that respect, I must acknowledge the dining room captain, Ali El-Khalafawi, who comes to gracious service honestly—his father runs a hotel school on the island—and my very knowledgeable and sweet server, Rachel, who illuminated each dish as though she had made it herself.

Food as delicious as it is artistic at The Pointe Restaurant.

The dining room itself is semicircular, with seating set around a blazing fireplace on one side and against the windows that practically hang over Chesterman Beach on the other. The carpet has a rippled effect like the sea it seems to meet. Deep orange sconces on the walls become more noticeable as the sun sets. Eventually, the room is lit only by the sconces and candles set into rocks on the old-growth fir tables, and is it my imagination, or has someone opened a window? Actually, a magic wand has been waved behind the scenes: microphones strategically placed outside enable the crashing waves to be heard beneath the classical music inside. Such a brilliant score.

My first taste of Nick's cuisine is the *amuse bouche*, customized for me because of my "no-pork" request. I enjoy a slice of seared Ahi tuna with tamarind-and-ginger glaze with Asian pear, all atop a little mound of micro-greens from Medicine Farm in Ucluelet. These are the fresh, natural flavours that signal good things to come.

Next is Alaskan sablefish with a mustard glaze, squash purée, an apple-and-squash coleslaw on braised winter greens, with diced grenadine apple on top. Then there is some last-of-the-season halibut crusted with thinly sliced potato that had been baked in Pinot Noir with cardamon; the plate finished

Chef Nicholas Nutting of The Pointe Restaurant.

with parsnip purée and toasted parsnip chips. And, finally, there is sockeye salmon poached in olive oil atop fine herbes and crème fraîche risotto, with parsley purée and braised fennel, served with a fresh salad of fennel, grapefruit and orange.

From fish, I move on to succulent duck breast served over shredded Brussels sprouts with seared Quebec foie gras and melted Blossom's Blue cheese from Saltspring Island's Moonstruck Organic Cheese. The Alberta AAA medium-rare sirloin that follows is perfectly complemented by sautéed wild pine and hedgehog mushrooms from the local area, house-made agnolotti stuffed with puréed pumpkin, roasted chestnuts and chestnut purée, with a side of cedar jelly (made from peeled cedar branches that have been steeped in a tea with added apple pectin).

Rachel matched a couple of 2003 reds (an Austrian Pinot Noir and a French Pommard Clos des Ursulines) and a British Columbia white—the always-rewarding Quail's Gate 2006 Steward Family Reserve Chardonnay—to my food, all of which worked well.

And somewhere between my main courses and dessert, I have the opportunity to chat with Nick Nutting. He's had a lot of attention, but he's modest about it. "That comes from having practised, practised, practised" along the way. Nick graduated from the South Alberta Culinary Institute, worked at

"We feed off the pressure of those high expectations."

– Chef Nicholas Nutting

A private dining room at The Wickaninnish Inn.

Catch with Michael Noble in Calgary, did a stint at Daniel in New York and then went to Montreal. "But I missed the West Coast and Tofino," he tells me, and he's delighted to have landed the job of Pointe Restaurant chef.

It's surely true that a happy cook produces good food, and Nick appears to be a happy guy. He's living the Tofino lifestyle to its full potential: hiking, surfing and jogging along Chesterman beach five mornings a week. "It's a great culture of food and friends here in Tofino," he tells me. "I love being able to gather mushrooms in the forest, going home and making up some squash soup and gnocchi to eat with them." He's particularly excited that it's pine mushroom season now—"the jewels of this area," he says.

The Pointe Restaurant has always been a big supporter of island food suppliers, "We get our fish from Jeff Mikus of Wildside Grill (sockeye salmon, shrimp, prawns) and from Trilogy Fish Store in town; other shellfish comes from the Outlandish Shellfish Guild in Qualicum. Greens are specially grown for us by the Barbara Ebell of Nanoose Edibles and by Douglas and Lisa Broker at Medicine Farm in Ucluelet."

I know these are long-time suppliers of The Wick. These good relationships with suppliers ensure that high-quality ingredients can be sourced from an area that's not exactly known as a "farming community." It's ironic that there aren't farms up here. One has only to look around at the amazing old-growth trees (yes, there is still old growth, most notably on Meares Island) and wonder that other "crops" can't grow. It has something to do with the salt from the sea, apparently, but at least there is always the prospect of mushroom and berry foraging and the anticipation of waiting at the docks for the fishboats to pull in.

The dessert of seasonal apples done three ways might just be the best conclusion to a meal *ever*: grenadine apples from Saltspring Island have been thinly sliced and baked until soft, resulting in a meltingly sublime *pavé*; a sorbet of Granny Smith apples is clean and refreshing; and Ambrosia apple cream between dried apple slices is pure genius.

Driftwood Lounge

The Wickaninnish Inn now offers two styles of accommodation: the original building (a.k.a., Wickaninnish at the Pointe), and the newly built Wickaninnish on the Beach. I made a point of staying in the latter, which has the same "rustic elegance" as the Wick at the Pointe, but with a more casual feel. Amenities include an exercise room for rainy days; a library and Internet lounge, where there's a nice selection of books and magazines and big comfy chairs to flop into; and the beach-level Driftwood Lounge, where coffee and sweet treats are available all day long.

Charles McDiarmid, The Wickaninnish Inn's managing director.

The lounge has a unique coffee bar fashioned from the trunk (with its roots still intact) of a yellow cedar that toppled over in a storm. The trunk has been levelled off on one side to create a countertop. When I dropped in after an invigorating walk on Chesterman Beach, server Michael had just put on a fresh pot of coffee and taken delivery of a pear and frangipane tart from the inn's pastry chef. With a copy of *The Globe and Mail* in hand, I was all set to curl up by the fire and enjoy some tranquillity.

Michael told me the lounge is "a great place to watch the sun rise over the trees on the beach." It's also the place to buy souvenirs for your friends back home—house-made "aphrodisiac chocolates" anyone?

Wildside Grill

I've always regarded Tofino and environs as the "wild side" of the island; the Wildside Grill fits right in. The concept came naturally to Jeff Mikus and Jesse Blake who are both fishers.

"We've both fished out of here for years," Jeff tells me, "and I've always wanted my own fish and chip shack where I could sell my catch—from the boat to the plate." Jeff runs a freezer boat—"a typical 40-foot West Coast gillnet boat"—and catches the fabulous salmon, shrimp and prawns for which the area is so justly famous. He gets ling cod from another fisher and has also added pulled pork, chicken and bison to the burger menu.

Guests of The Wickaninnish Inn (wearing the inn's telltale rain jackets) order up some great fish at Wildside Grill.

Fish, chips and burgers al fresco *at Wildside Grill.*

I first met Jesse, who is the son of Victoria *Times Colonist* reporter Joseph Blake, when he was cooking at Shelter. He has since gone back to fishing but Jeff credits him with "putting together an awesome menu" for the Wildside Grill.

I dropped in for a great panko-crusted piece of ling cod, some fine hand-cut chips and a taste of the best last-of-the-season halibut burger. Jeff had returned late the night before from deep-sea fishing, but he was happy to chat about his shop and the fishing scene in the area.

PHOTO CREDITS

Andrei Fedorov 59, 63, 64, 65

Blue Grouse 146 (left)

Brasserie L'École 4

Clive Levinson 10, 15, 24, 26, 49, 70, 97, 123, 140, 151, 153, 155, 179, 194, 211, 212, 213, 215, 216, 217, 221, 222, 223, 230, 232, 240, 241, 243, 247, 248, 250, 251, 253, 254, 255, 258, 260, 262, 264, 265, 268, 271

Creekmore's Coffee 193

Elizabeth Levinson 8, 36, 47, 51, 81, 94, 105, 108, 131, 137, 139, 147, 149, 159, 160, 163, 166, 196, 206, 207, 218, 225, 255

Fairburn Farm 138

Gabriola Gourmet Garlic 182

Gary Hynes 20

Hastings House 73, 74, 75, 76

Hollyhock 236

House Piccolo 78

istockphoto.com xiv

Monsoon Coast Exotic World Spices 82

Natural Pastures Cheese Company 226

Reef Point Farm 237

Reeta Moorman 6, 17, 22, 28, 34

Rosheen Holland 185

Shari MacDonald 84

Steeples 126

TouchWood Editions 146 (right), 170

Travel With Taste Tours 32

Wickaninnish Inn 266, 267, 269

CONTACTS

SOUTH ISLAND AND THE GULF ISLANDS

VICTORIA

Brasserie L'École
1715 Government Street
Victoria V8W 1Z4
Tel: 250-475-6260
www.lecole.ca
eat@lecole.ca
Sean Brennan, chef/owner
Marc Morrison, sommelier/owner

Café Brio
944 Fort Street
Victoria V8V 3K2
Tel: 250-383-0009
www.cafe-brio.com
reservations@cafe-brio.com
Silvia Marcolini and Greg Hays, owners
Laurie Munn, chef

Choux Choux Charcuterie
830 Fort Street
Victoria V8W H8H
Tel: 250-382-7572
www.chouxchoux.ca
info@chouxchoux.ca
Luke Young and Paige Symonds,
chefs/owners

Fol Epi
#101–398 Harbour Road
Victoria V9A 0B7
(Dockside Green)
Tel: 250-477-8882
midnightbreads@yahoo.ca
Cliff Leir, baker/owner

FoodRoots Co-op Pocket Markets and Sustainable Feasts
Unit 2/3–625 Hillside Avenue
Victoria V8T 1Z1
Tel: 250-385-7974
www.foodroots.ca
leefuge@pacificcoast.net
Lee Fuge, Susan Tychie and
Brian Hughes, partners

Habit Coffee and Culture
552 Pandora Avenue
Victoria V8W 1N7
Tel: 250-704-8304
www.habitcoffee.com
habitcoffee@gmail.com
Shane Devereaux, barista/owner

Hernande'z on Yates
#130 – 737 Yates Street
Victoria V8W 1L6
(no telephone)
Hernande'z on Bay
1600 Bay Street
Victoria V8R 2B6
(no telephone)
www.hernandezrestaurant.com
Tamara Hernandez (hostess) and
Jerson Hernandez (chef), owners

Mirjana
Loft 10
532-1/2 Fisgard Street
Victoria V8W 1R4
Tel: 250-360-1348
Mirjana, chef/owner

Moss Street Market
corner of Moss Street and Fairfield
Road (Sir James Douglas School)
www.mossstreetmarket.com
Tel: 250-361-1747
Marnie Smith

Ottavio's Italian Bakery and Delicatessen
2278 Oak Bay Avenue
Victoria V8R 1G7
Tel: 250-592-4080
www.ottaviovictoria.com
Monica Pozzolo and Andrew Moyer,
owners

Planet Organic
3995 Quadra Street
Victoria V8X 1J8
Tel: 250-727-9888
www.planetorganic.ca
Diane Shaskin and Mark Craft,
owners

Plenty Epicurean Pantry
1034 Fort Street
Victoria V8V 3K4
Tel: 250-380-7654
www.epicureanpantry.ca
trevor@epicureanpantry.ca
Trevor Walker and Erica Sangster, owners

Red Fish, Blue Fish
1006 Wharf Street
(at the foot of Broughton Street on the pier below Wharf Street)
Victoria V8W 1T4
Tel: 250-298-6877
One Fish, Two Fish
Market Square, 560 Johnson Street
(no telephone)
www.redfish-bluefish.com
Kunal Ghose and Simon Sobolewski, chefs/owners

Share Organics
Tel: 250-595-6729
www.shareorganics.bc.ca
susan@shareorganics.bc.ca
Susan Tychie, owner

Stage
1307 Gladstone Avenue
Victoria V8R 1R9
Tel: 250-388-4222
www.stagewinebar.com
info@stagewinebar.com
Linda and George Szasz, owners

Travel with Taste Tours
Tel: 250-385-1527
www.travelwithtaste.com
info@travelwithtaste.com
Kathy McAree, owner

Zambri's
#110–911 Yates Street
Victoria V8V 4X3
Tel: 250- 360-1171
www.zambris.com
zambris@shaw.ca
Jo Zambri (hostess) and
Peter Zambri (chef), owners

SAANICH/ BRENTWOOD BAY

Dragonfly Hill Vineyard
Tel: 250-652-3782
www.dragonhillfarmvineyard.com
Carol Wallace, owner/ vintner

Fruit Trees & More
724 Wain Road
Sidney V8L 5N8
Tel: 250-656-4269
www.fruittreesandmore.com
bvduncan@fruittreesandmore.com
Bob and Verna Duncan, owners

Marley Farm Winery
1831D Mount Newton X Road
Saanichton V8M 1L1
Tel: 250- 652-8667
www.marleyfarm.ca
info@marleyfarm.ca
Beverly Marley, vintner/owner

Mount Newton Cottage
7969 West Saanich Road
Saanichton V8M 1S4
Tel: 250-544-1780
www.mountnewtoncottage.ca
David Crone and Jenny Cameron, owners

SeaGrille at Brentwood Bay Lodge
849 Verdier Avenue
Brentwood Bay V8M 1C5
Tel: 250-544-2079
Dining reservations: 250-544-5100
www.brentwoodbaylodge.com
Dan Bethune, general manager
Peter Whatmough, executive chef

Victoria Spirits
6170 Old West Saanich Road
Victoria V9E 2G8
Tel: 250-544-8217
www.victoriagin.com
Brian Murray, owner
Peter Hunt, distiller

METCHOSIN

The Broken Paddle
4480C Happy Valley Road
Metchosin V9C 3Z3
Tel: 250-474-2999
Shannon Meeker, chef/owner

Happy Valley Lavender and Herb Farm
3505 Happy Valley Road
Victoria V9C 2Y2
Tel: 250-474-5767
www.happyvalleylavender.com
lynda@happyvalleylavender.com
Lynda Dowling, owner

Metchosin Farmers' Market
Municipal Grounds, Happy Valley Road
Metchosin
Tel: 250-474-3156
Bob Mitchell, coordinator

SOOKE

Cooper's Cove Guesthouse and Angelo's Cooking School
5301 Sooke Road
Sooke V0S 1N0
Tel: 250-642-5727
www.cooperscove.com
info@cooperscove.com
Angelo Prosperi-Porta (chef) and
Ina Haegemann (hostess), owners

Little Vienna Bakery
#6–6726 West Coast Road
Sooke V0S 1N0
Tel: 250-642-6833
www.littlevienna.com
Andreas Ruttkiewicz and
Michelle Ruttkiewicz (baker), owners

Markus' Wharfside Restaurant
1831 Maple Avenue
Sooke V0S 1N0
Tel: 250-642-3596
www.markuswharfsiderestaurant.com
markuswharfside@hotmail.com
Markus Wieland (chef) and Tatum
Wieland (sommelier/hostess), owners

Outer Coast Seaweeds
(a.k.a., The Seaweed Lady)
2018 Penang Road
Sooke V0S 1N0
Tel: 250- 642-5328
www.outercoastseaweeds.com
outercoastseaweeds@shaw.ca
Diane Bernard, owner

Ragley Farm
5717 East Sooke Road
Sooke V0S 1N0
Tel: 250- 642-7349
ragley@telus.net
Josephine Hill, owner

Sooke Harbour House
1528 Whiffen Spit Road
Sooke V0S 1N0
Tel: 250-642-3421
www.sookeharbourhouse.com
info@sookeharbourhouse.com
Sinclair and Frédérique Philip, owners
Edward Tuson, executive chef

Tugwell Creek Honey Farm
8750 West Coast Road
Sooke V0S 1N0
Tel: 250- 642-1956
www.tugwellcreekfarm.com
dana-l@shaw.ca
Robert Liptrot and Dana Le Comte,
owners

SALTSPRING ISLAND

Bright Farm
176 Tripp Road
Saltspring Island V8K 1K5
Tel: 250- 537-4319
ceagle@saltspring.com
Charlie Eagle, Judy Horvath and Bree
Eagle, farmers/owners

**Foxglove Farm and The Centre for
Art, Ecology and Agriculture**
1200 Mount Maxwell Road
Saltspring Island V8K 2H7
Tel: 250-537-1989
www.foxglovefarmretreat.com
info@foxglovefarmretreat.com
Michael and Jeanne-Marie Ableman,
farmers/owners

Hastings House
160 Upper Ganges Road
Saltspring Island V8K 2S2
Tel: 250-537-2362
1-800-661-9255 Canada and USA
www.hastingshouse.com
info@hastingshouse.com
Shirley McLaughlin, manager
Marcel Kauer, executive chef

House Piccolo
108 Hereford Avenue
Saltspring Island V8K 2V9
Tel: 250- 537-1844
www.housepiccolo.com
piccolo@saltspring.com
Piccolo Lyytikainen, owner/chef

Jana's Bake Shop
324 Lower Ganges Road
Ganges, Saltspring Island
V8K 2V3
Tel: 250-537-0029
islandtoisland@canada.com
Jana Roerick (baker) and
Marcus Dowrich, owners

Market-in-the-Park
Centennial Park, downtown Ganges,
Saltspring Island
Tel: 250-537-4448
www.saltspringmarket.com
CRD Parks and Recreation

Monsoon Coast Exotic World Spices
Tel: 250-537-9447
www.monsooncoast.com
Satva and Chintan Hall, owners

Moonstruck Organic Cheese
Tel/fax: 250-537-4987
www.moonstruckcheese.com
grace@saltspring.com
Julia and Susan Grace, owners

**Morningside Organic Bakery
and Café**
108 Morningside Road
Saltspring Island V8K 1X1
Tel: 250-653-4414
Alan Golding and Manon Darrette,
owners

Salt Spring Flour Mill
169 Dogwood Lane
Saltspring Island V8K 1A4
Tel: 250-537-4282
dogwoodlane@saltspring.com
Pat Reichert, miller/owner

**Salt Spring Island Bread Company
(a.k.a., The Bread Lady)**
Tel: 250-653-4809
pvanhorn@saltspring.com
Heather Campbell, baker/owner

Saltspring Island Cheese Company
285 Reynolds Road
Saltspring Island V8K 1Y2
Tel: 250-653-2304
David and Nancy Wood,
cheesemakers/owners

Saltspring Island Garlic Festival
Farmers' Institute Grounds
351 Rainbow Road
Saltspring Island
Tel:250-537-1219

Salt Spring Vineyards
151 Lee Road
Saltspring Island V8K 2A5
Tel: 250-653-9463
www.saltspringvineyards.com
vineyards@saltspring.com
Devlin and Joanne McIntyre, owners

Soya Nova Tofu
1200 Beddis Road
Saltspring Island V8K 2C8
Tel: 250-537-9651
www.soyanova.ca
soyanova@saltspring.com
Deborah Lauzon, owner

Wave Hill Farm
Tel: 250-653-4121
Mark Whitear and Rosalie Beach,
farmers/owners

PENDER ISLANDS

Aurora at Poets Cove Resort
9801 Spalding Road
South Pender Island V0N 2M3
Tel: 1-888-512-7638
www.poetscove.com
Walter Kohli, general manager
Steven Boudreau, executive chef

Iona Farm
Tel: 250-629-6700
iona@cablean.net
Rob and Ellen Willingham,
farmers/owners

Jane's Herb Garden
3719 Rum Road
South Pender Island V0N 2M2
Tel: 250-629-6670
janesherbgarden@cablelan.net
Jane Gregory, grower/baker/owner

Morning Bay Vineyard and Estate Winery
6621 Harbour Hill Drive
North Pender Island V0N 2M1
Tel: 250-629-8350
www.morningbay.ca
info@morningbay.ca
Keith Watt and Barbara Reid,
vintners/owners

Pender Island Bakery Café
Driftwood Centre
North Pender Island V0N 2M1
Tel: 250-629-6453
www.penderislandbakery.com
info@penderislandbakery.com
Dorothy Murdoch, owner

Pistou Grill
Driftwood Centre
North Pender Island V0N 2M.1
Tel: 250-629-3131
www.pistougrill.ca
pistougrill@cablelan.net
Pierre Delacôte, chef/owner

SATURNA ISLAND

Haggis Farm Bakery
Tel: 250-539-2591
Jon Guy (baker) and Priscilla Ewbank,
owners

Saturna General Store and Café
101 Narvaez Bay Road
Saturna Island V0N 2Y0
Tel: 250-539-2936
Fax: 250-539-5136
Jon Guy, Priscilla Ewbank and
Hubertus Surm, owners

Saturna Herbs
Breezy Bay Farm
131 Payne Road
Saturna Island V0N 2Y0
Tel: 250-539-5200
www.saturnaherbs.com
saturnaherbs@canada.com
Flora House, owner

Saturna Island Vineyards
8 Quarry Trail
Saturna Island V0N 2Y0
Tel: 250-539-5139
www.saturnavineyards.com
wine@saturnavineyards.com
Rebecca Page, general manager

MAYNE ISLAND

Deacon Vale Farm
Tel/Fax: 250-539-5456
www.deaconvalefarm.com
dvf@gulfislands.com
Don and Shanti McDougall,
farmers/owners

Mayne Island Farmers' Market
Agricultural Hall Grounds
Miners Bay, Mayne Island
Tel: 250-539-5456
Shanti McDougall

Oceanwood Country Inn
630 Dinner Bay Road
Mayne Island V0N 2J0
Tel: 250-539-5074
www.oceanwood.com
oceanwood@gulfislands.com
Jonathan Chilvers, owner
David Kruse, chef de cuisine

GALIANO ISLAND

Daystar Market and Market Café
96 Georgeson Bay Road
Galiano V0N 1P0
Tel: 250-539-2505
Lony Rockafella, owner

Max & Moritz
Spicy Island Food House
at the ferry dock in summer
Tel: 250-539-5888
Christian and Lucy Banski, owners

MID-ISLAND

SHAWNIGAN LAKE

Amusé
1753 Shawnigan-Mill Bay Road
Shawnigan Lake V0R 2W0
Tel: 250-743-3667
www.amusebistro.com
amusebistro@shaw.ca
Bradford Boisvert (chef) and
Leah Bellerive (hostess), owners

Elford Farm Bakery
2769 Shawnigan Lake Road
Shawnigan Lake V0R 2W0
Tel: 250-743-9226
elfordfarmpastries@shaw.ca
Gerald Billings, baker/owner

Steeples
2744 East Shawnigan Lake Road
Shawnigan Lake V0R 2W0
Tel: 250-743-1887
www.steeplesrestaurant.ca
darren@steeplesrestaurant.ca
Darren Cole, chef/owner

MAPLE BAY

Grapevine on the Bay
6701 Beaumont Avenue
Maple Bay V9L 5X8
Tel: 250-746-0797
Daniel and Ruth van den Wildenberg,
owners

GLENORA/DUNCAN

Alderlea Vineyards
1751 Stamps Road
Duncan V9L 5W2
Tel: 250-746-7122
Roger (vintner) and Nancy Dosman,
owners

Black Coffee and Other Delights
4705 E. Trans-Canada Highway
Whippletree Junction,
Duncan V9L 6E1
Tel: 250-746-9973
cleveland@cvnet.net
Corrine Wilson (bookkeeper),
Andrew Simonson (baker) and
Morris Cleveland (barista), owners

**The Community Farm Store and
Corfield's Coffee Shop**
330 Duncan Street
Duncan V9L 3W4
Tel: 250-715-1383
Susan Minette, owner and baker

Deerholme Farm and Cottage
4830 Stelfox Road
Duncan V9L 6S9
Tel: 250-748-7450
www.magnorth.bc.ca
bill@magnorth.bc.ca
Bill (chef) and Lynn Jones (farmer),
owners

**Fairburn Farm and Culinary
Retreat Guesthouse**
3310 Jackson Road
Duncan V9L 6N7
Tel: 250-746-4637
www.fairburnfarm.bc.ca
info@fairburnfarm.bc.ca
Darrel and Anthea Archer,
farmers/owners
Mara Jernigan, farmer/chef/
Fairburn Farm Culinary Retreat owner

Feast of Fields
Tel: 250-746-4637
Mara Jernigan, founder

Godfrey-Brownell Vineyards
4911 Marshall Road
Duncan V9L 6T1
Tel: 250-715-0504
www.gbvineyards.com
gbvineyards@gmail.com
David Godfrey (vintner) and
Ellen Godfrey, owners

Providence Farm
1843 Tzouhalem Road
Duncan V9L 5L6
Tel: 250-746-4204
www.providence.bc.ca
kori@providence.bc.ca
Kori Kelloway, kitchen manager

Vigneti Zanatta
5039 Marshall Road
Duncan V9L 6S3
Tel: vineyard: 250-748-2338
Tel: restaurant: 250-709-2279
www.zanatta.ca
Loretta Zanatta and Jim Moody
and family, owners

COBBLE HILL/ COWICHAN BAY

The Asparagus Farm
1550 Robson Lane
Cobble Hill
Tel: 250-743-5073
www.islandnet.com/~cford/
Charles and Carole Ford,
farmers/owners

Blue Grouse Vineyards
4365 Blue Grouse Road
Cobble Hill V9L 6M3
Tel: 250-743-3834
www.bluegrousevineyards.com
skiltz@islandnet.com
Dr. Hans Kiltz and Evangeline Kiltz,
vintners/owners

Broken Briar Fallow Deer Farm
2692 Mt. Sicker Road
Chemainus V0R 1K0
Tel: 250-246-9749
tdgroves@island.net
David Groves, farmer/owner

Cowichan Bay Farm
1560 Cowichan Bay Road, RR #1
Cowichan Bay V0R 1N0
Tel: 250-746-7884
farmer@cowichanbayfarm.com
www.cowichanbayfarm.com
Lyle and Fiona Young,
farmers/owners

Drum Roaster Coffee
#24-1400 Cowichan Bay Road
Cobble Hill V0R 1L0
Tel: 250-743-5200
www.drumroaster.com
geir@shaw.ca
Geir and Patricia Øglend, owners

Glenterra Vineyards and Thistles Café
3897 Cobble Hill Road
Cobble Hill V0R 1L0
Tel: 250-743-2330
www.glenterravineyards.com
wine@glenterravineyards.com
John Kelly (vintner) and
Ruth Luxton (chef), owners

Hilary's Cheese Company
1737 Cowichan Bay Road
Cowichan Bay V0R 1N0
Store tel: 250-748-5992
Farm tel: 250-715-0563
(tours for groups of 10 or more
by appointment only)
hilary@hilaryscheese.com
Hilary and Patty Abbott, owners

Merridale Ciderworks
1230 Merridale Road
Cobble Hill V0R 1L0
Tel: 250-743-4293
www.merridalecider.com
Rick Pipes and Janet Docherty,
owners

Saskatoon Berry Farm
1245 Fisher Road
Cobble Hill V0R 1L0
Tel: 250-743-1189
toonfarm@yahoo.com
Alwin and Connie Dyrland, owners

Venturi Schulze Vineyards
4235 Trans Canada Highway
Cobble Hill V0R 1L0
Tel: 250-743-5630
www.venturischulze.com
info@venturischulze.com
Giordano Venturi and Marilyn Schulze,
vintners/owners

CEDAR/
YELLOW POINT

Cedar Farmers' Market
Crow and Gate Pub, off Cedar Road
Tel: 250-722-3526
George Benson, coordinator

The Crow and Gate Pub
2313 Yellow Point Road
Yellow Point V9X 1W5
Tel: 250-722-3731
Bryce and Linda Olson, publicans

Mahle House Restaurant
2104 Hemer Road
Nanaimo V9X 1L8
Tel: 250-722-3621
www.mahlehouse.com
info@mahlehouse.com
Maureen Loucks, chef/owner
Delbert Horrocks, sommelier/owner

Yellow Point Cranberries
4532 Yellow Point Road
Ladysmith V9G 1G5
Tel: 250-245-5283
www.yellowpointcranberries.com
Grant and Justine Keefer

LADYSMITH

Hazelwood Herb Farm
13576 Adshead Road
Ladysmith V9G 1H6
Tel: 250-245-8007
www.herbfarm.com
info@hazelwoodherbfarm.com
Richard Wright and Jacynthe Dugas

Kiwi Cove Lodge
5130 Brenton Page Road
Ladysmith V9G 1L6
Tel: 250-245-8051
www.kiwicovelodge.com
kiwicove@shaw.ca
Peggy and Doug Kolosoff

Page Point Inn
4760 Brenton-Page Road
Ladysmith V9G 1L7
Tel: 250-245-2312
www.pagepointinn.com
info@pagepointinn.com
Lawrence and Lexie Lambert, owners
John Grove, chef

NANAIMO

**Carrot on the Run and
24 Carrot Catering**
6560 Metral Drive
Nanaimo V9T 2L9
Tel: 250-390-0008
www.24carrotcatering.bc.ca
carrot@direct.ca
Alexandra Berlingette and Melissa
Hamilton, owners

Island Natural Markets
6560 Metral Drive
Nanaimo V9T 2L9
Tel: 250-390-1955
islandnatural@shaw.ca
Rhonda Lambert and Casey Mitchell,
owners

McLean's Specialty Foods
426 Fitzwilliam Street
Nanaimo V9R 3B1
Tel: 250-754-0100
www.mcleansfoods.com
mcleans@nisa.net
Eric and Sandy McLean, owners

Mon Petit Choux
#10 –120 Commercial Street
Nanaimo V9R 5J6
Tel: 250-753-6002
Linda Allen, owner

The Wesley Street Café
#1–321 Wesley Street
Nanaimo V9R 2T5
Tel: 250-753-6057
Gaetan Brousseau and
Linda Allen, owners
Josh Massey, chef

GABRIOLA ISLAND

**Gabriola Agricultural Association
Farmers' Market**
Agi Hall
465 South Road
(top of the hill from the ferry)
Gabriola Island
Tel: 250-247-8216
ebus87@island.net
Tannie Meyer, coordinator

Gabriola Gourmet Garlic
1025 Horseshoe Road
Gabriola Island V0R 1X0
Tel: 250-247-0132
www.gabriolagourmetgarlic.com
gabriolagourmetgarlic@shaw.ca
Ken Stefanson and Llie Brotherton,
owners

**Heavenly Flowers and the Good
Earth Market Garden**
600 South Road
Gabriola Island V0R 1X0
Tel: 250-668-0670
Rosheen Holland and Bob Shields,
farmers/owners

LANTZVILLE/ NANOOSE BAY

Black Dog Café
7221 Lantzville Road
Lantzville V0R 2H0
Tel: 250-390-4541
Chris Thomas and Vicky Adamson, owners

Harvest Bounty Festival
Tel: 250- 248-8207
Debbie Schug, coordinator

Nanoose Edibles
1960A Stewart Road
Nanoose Bay V9P 9E7
Tel: 250-468-2332
Barbara and Lorne Ebell, farmers/owners

PARKSVILLE/ QUALICUM BEACH/COOMBS

Creekmore's Coffee and Espresso Bar
2701 Alberni Highway
Coombs
Tel: (250) 752-0158
www.creekmorescoffee.com
coffeecreek@shaw.ca
David and Elaine Creekmore, owners

The Final Approach
1000 Ravensbourne Lane
Qualicum Beach V9K 1P9
Tel: 250-752-8966
Richard (host) and Lawrence (chef), owners

Fore & Aft Foods
5390 Island Highway
Qualicum Beach V9K 2E8
Tel: 250-757-8682
Beverley Child and Patrick Brownrigg, owners

La Boulange Organic Breads
692 Bennett Road
Qualicum Beach V9K 1N1
Tel: 250-752-0077
laboulange@home.com
John Taraynor and Jean Wilson, bakers/owners

Little Qualicum Cheeseworks
403 Lowry's Road
Parksville V9P 2B5
Tel: 250-954-3931
cheese@island.net
Clarke and Nancy Gourlay, owners

Qualicum Beach Farmers' Market
Fir Street at Memorial Avenue
Qualicum Beach
Tel: 250-752-2857

RainBarrel Farm
599 Garden Road East
Qualicum Beach V9K 1M5
Tel: 250-752-0424
lmant@shaw.ca
Marilyn Mant and Tami Treit, farmers/owners

DENMAN ISLAND

Denman Island Chocolate
Tel: 250-335-2418
www.denmanislandchocolate.com
info@denmanislandchocolate.com
Daniel Terry, chocolatier/owner

Denman Island Farmers' Market
Old School Centre
5277 Denman Central Road
Denman Island
Tel: 250-335-2294
Anne de Cosson, coordinator

East Cider Orchard
2831 East Road
Denman Island V0R 1T0
Tel: 250-335-2294
decosson@mars.ark.com
Anne de Cosson and Larry Berg, farmers/owners

Jacquie's Ices
Gravelly Bay
Denman Island
Tel: 250-335-2199
Jacquie Barnett, owner

Windy Marsh Farm
8700 Owl Crescent
Denman Island V0R 1T0
Tel: 250-335-1252
Bob and Velda Parsons, farmers/owners

HORNBY ISLAND

Hornby Island Co-op
Central Road
Hornby Island V0R 1Z0
Tel: 250-335-1121
Phoebe Long, manager

Hornby Island Farmers' Market
behind the Community Hall
Hornby Island

Savoie Farm
Tel: 250-335-0276
Elaine and Mary Savoie, farmers/owners

NORTH ISLAND

CUMBERLAND

Cumberland Village Bakery
2747 Dunsmuir Avenue
Cumberland V0R 1S0
Tel: 250-336-2411
David Murray and Megan Sommers,
bakers/owners

The Great Escape
2744 Dunsmuir Avenue
Cumberland V0R 1S0
Tel: 250-336-8831
www.greatescape-cumberland.com
great-escape@shaw.ca
Jean-François Larche (host) and
Nicola Cunha (chef), owners

Hazelmere Farms
3222 Grant Road
Cumberland V0R 1S0
Tel: 250-336-2308
huawongs@telus.net
Lijen and Sherlene Hua,
farmers/owners

Seeds Natural Food Market
2733A Dunsmuir Avenue
Cumberland V0R 1S0
Tel: 250-336-0129
www.seedsfoodmarket.ca
Christina Willard-Stepan, owner

COURTENAY

Atlas Café and Bar
250 Sixth Street
Courtenay V9N 1M1
Tel: 250-338-9838
www.comoxvalleyrestaurants.ca/atlas
atlascafe@shaw.ca
Trent McIntyre (chef) and
Sandra Viney (hostess), owners

Edible Island Whole Foods Market
477 6th Street
Courtenay V9N 1M4
Tel: 250-334-3116
edible@island.net
Sue Tupper, Sue Clark and
Jackie Somerville, owners

**Hot Chocolates and
CakeBread Artisan Bakery**
368 Fifth Street
Courtenay V9N 1K1
Tel: 250-338-8211
www.hotchocolates.ca
comments@hotchocolates.ca
Jorden Marshall and
Sherry Marshall-Bruce, owners

Locals
Unit C – 368 8th Street
Courtenay V9N 1N3
Tel: 250-338-6493
www.localscomoxvalley.com
chef@localscomoxvalley.com
Ronald St. Pierre (chef) and
Tricia St. Pierre (hostess), owners

Natural Pastures Cheese Company
635 McPhee Avenue
Courtenay V9N 2Z7
Tel: 250-334-4422
www.naturalpastures.com
naturalpasturescheese@telus.net
Mary Ann Hyndman Smith,
Edgar Smith and Rick Adams, owners

Tita's Mexican Restaurant
536 Sixth Street
Courtenay V9N 1M6
Tel: 250-334-8033
www.titas.ca
Martin and Lisa Metz, owners

COMOX

Benino
1700 Comox Avenue
Comox V9M 4H4
Tel: 250-339-3494
www.beninogelato.com
thescoop@beninogelato.com
Ruth Vanderlinden, owner

Portuguese Joe's Fish Market
3025 Comox Road
Courtenay V9N 3P7
Tel: 250-339-2119
Nilda, Eddy, Cecil and Lito Veloso,
owners

Thyme on the Ocean
1832 Comox Avenue
Comox V9M 3M7
Tel: 250-339-5570
www.thymeontheocean.com
Emil Shelborn and Nah Yoon Kim,
chefs/owners

CORTES ISLAND

Cortes Café
Manson's Hall
corner of Sutil Point Road and
Beasley Road

Cortes Island Farmers' Market
Manson's Hall
corner of Sutil Point Road and
Beasley Road

Hollyhock
end of Highfield Road
Cortes Island V0P 1K0
www.hollyhock.ca
Tel: 1-800-933-6339

Reef Point Farm
end of Sutil Point Road
Cortes Island, V0P 1K0
Tel: 250-935-6797
Ginnie and Bruce Ellingsen, owners

CAMPBELL RIVER

**Anglers Dining Room at
The Dolphins Resort**
4125 Discovery Drive
Campbell River V9W 4X6
Tel: 250-287-3066
www.dolphinsresort.com
fish@dolphinsresort.com
Clint and Linda Cameron, owners
Jessica Willott, chef

Cheddar & Co. Specialty Foods
1090 Shoppers Row
Campbell River V9W 2C6
Tel: 250-830-0244
info@cheddarandco.com
www.cheddarandco.com
Michelle Yasinski, chef/owner

Haig-Brown House
2250 Campbell River Road
Campbell River V9W 4N7
Tel: 250-286-6646
www.haig-brown.bc.ca
haig.brown@crmuseum.ca
Dory Montague, host/manager

TOFINO

Chocolate Tofino
1180-A Pacific Rim Highway
Tofino V0R 2Z0
Tel: 250-725-2526
www.chocolatetofino.com
chocolate_tofino@alberni.net
Gordon and Leah Austin, chocolatiers/owners

Festival of Oysters and the Sea
Tel: 250- 725-4222
www.oystergala.com

The Goat Lady
Tel: 250-726-2682
Jane Hunt, cheesemaker

Hungry Bear Naturals
150 Fourth Street
Tofino V0R 2Z0
Tel: 250-725-8008
Dwane Bell and Doug Wright, owners

Long Beach Lodge Resort
1441 Pacific Rim Highway
Tofino V0R 2Z0
Tel: 250-725-2442
www.longbeachlodgeresort.com
Joshua Anker, executive chef

Oyster Jim
2480 Pacific Rim Highway
Ucluelet V0R 3A0
Tel: 250-726-7350
Jim Martin, oyster fisher/owner

Raincoast Café
101-120 Fourth Street
Tofino V0R 2Z0
Tel: 250-725-2215
www.raincoastcafe.com
raincafe@island.net
Lisa Henderson (chef) and
Larry Nicolay (host), owners

Shelter Restaurant
601 Campbell Street
Tofino V0R 2Z0
Tel: 250-725-3353
www.shelterrestaurant.com
Jay Gildenhuys, owner
Rob Wheaton, chef

600 Degrees Bakery
600degrees@gmail.com
Julie Lomenda, baker/owner

SoBo
311 Neill Street
Tofino V0R 2Z0
Tel: 250-725-2341
www.sobo.ca
eat@sobo.ca
Artie (host) and Lisa (chef) Ahier, owners

The Pointe Restaurant and the Driftwood Lounge at The Wickaninnish Inn
Osprey Lane at Chesterman Beach
Tofino V0R 2Z0
Tel: 250-725-3100
www.wickinn.com
info@wickinn.com
Charles McDiarmid, manager
Nick Nutting, executive chef

Wildside Grill
1080 Pacific Rim Highway
Tofino V0R 2Z0
Tel: 250-725-WILD (9453)
Jeff Mikus, fisher/owner